D0327647

G. William Domhoff is a professor of psychology and sociology at the University of California, Santa Cruz. The noted author of *Who Rules America?* (Prentice-Hall/Spectrum Books, 1967), Mr. Domhoff has written numerous books and articles on the subject of political and social power.

Prentice-Hall International, Inc., *London*
Prentice-Hall of Australia Pty. Limited, *Sydney*
Prentice-Hall Canada Inc., *Toronto*
Prentice-Hall of India Private Limited, *New Delhi*
Prentice-Hall of Japan, Inc., *Tokyo*
Prentice-Hall of Southeast Asia Pte. Ltd., *Singapore*
Whitehall Books Limited, *Wellington, New Zealand*
Editora Prentice-Hall do Brasil Ltda., *Rio de Janeiro*

G. WILLIAM DOMHOFF

Who Rules AMERICA Now?

A View for the '80s

A SPECTRUM BOOK

PRENTICE-HALL, INC., Englewood Cliffs, New Jersey 07632

Library of Congress Cataloging in Publication Data

Domhoff, G. William.
  Who rules America now?

  "A Spectrum Book."
  Includes bibliographical references and index.
    1. Elite (Social sciences)—United States.   2. Power
(Social sciences)   I. Title.
HN90.E4D652 1983   305.5'2'0973   83-3104
ISBN 0-13-958413-7
ISBN 0-13-958405-6 (pbk.)

To Lynne, Lori, Bill, and Joel

© 1983 by Prentice-Hall, Inc., Englewood Cliffs, New Jersey 07632.
All rights reserved. No part of this book may be reproduced in any form
or by any means without permission in writing from the publisher.
A Spectrum Book. Printed in the United States of America.

10 9 8 7 6 5 4 3 2 1

ISBN 0-13-958413-7

ISBN 0-13-958405-6 {PBK.}

Editorial/production supervision by Chris McMorrow
Cover design by Hal Siegel
Manufacturing buyers: Christine Johnston and Doreen Cavallo

This book is available at a special discount when ordered in
bulk quantities. Contact Prentice-Hall, Inc., General
Publishing Division, Special Sales, Englewood Cliffs, N.J. 07632.

G. WILLIAM DOMHOFF

Who Rules AMERICA Now?

A View for the '80s

A SPECTRUM BOOK

PRENTICE-HALL, INC., Englewood Cliffs, New Jersey 07632

Library of Congress Cataloging in Publication Data

Domhoff, G. William.
   Who rules America now?

   "A Spectrum Book."
   Includes bibliographical references and index.
   1. Elite (Social sciences)—United States.   2. Power
(Social sciences)   I. Title.
HN90.E4D652 1983   305.5'2'0973   83-3104
ISBN 0-13-958413-7
ISBN 0-13-958405-6 (pbk.)

To Lynne, Lori, Bill, and Joel

© 1983 by Prentice-Hall, Inc., Englewood Cliffs, New Jersey 07632.
All rights reserved. No part of this book may be reproduced in any form
or by any means without permission in writing from the publisher.
A Spectrum Book. Printed in the United States of America.

10 9 8 7 6 5 4 3 2 1

ISBN 0-13-958413-7

ISBN 0-13-958405-6 {PBK.}

Editorial/production supervision by Chris McMorrow
Cover design by Hal Siegel
Manufacturing buyers: Christine Johnston and Doreen Cavallo

This book is available at a special discount when ordered in
bulk quantities. Contact Prentice-Hall, Inc., General
Publishing Division, Special Sales, Englewood Cliffs, N.J. 07632.

Contents

Contents

Preface

This book is a sequel to *Who Rules America?*, a book published in 1967. As a sequel, it is far more than an update. It includes many new ideas and much new information on the basic issues of power in America that were addressed in the first book.

Who Rules America Now? can now be read without a prior reading of *Who Rules America?* It is meant to stand by itself. Indeed, it assumes no knowledge of the subject matter from any source on the part of the reader until it turns to more general theoretical issues in the final chapter. The aim of the present book is nothing less than a complete restatement of the original argument in the same basic format but I hope in a more convincing fashion, thanks to better data on some problems and better arguments where I now think I had it a little wrong. It is always nice to have a second chance when it comes to correcting mistakes.

Although I finished writing *Who Rules America?* in the summer of 1965, friendly critics convinced me it was only a first draft, and it was rewritten the following summer. Even with all the revisions, however, I thought I could do better almost as soon as I read the comments of critical reviewers, and that feeling provided the impetus for several books that appeared in the 1970s. In each of those books I tried to deal in greater depth with specific issues that were only touched on in *Who Rules America?* In this book I have tried to bring together and add to the results of those specialized efforts for a second consideration of the overall picture. The feeling that I had reached the point at which I wanted to try another general synthesis made this a very exciting and challenging book to write.

The actual writing of a book is a very solitary experience that has to take place in considerable isolation, but I am deeply aware that the preparation for such writing is a highly social process. It is dependent on the support of sympathetic friends and family, understanding colleagues, and helpful students and research assistants. Aside from the hundreds of people from whose published work I have benefited, as expressed in footnotes and references in this and earlier books, many people have been of great help and stimulation in sharing their ideas, commenting on all or parts of the manuscript, and providing suggestions and encouragement.

In particular, I want to thank Calvin S. Hall, Michael Kimmel, and two anonymous reviewers for Prentice-Hall for their many suggestions on the whole manuscript; Cynthia R. Margolin for her very helpful reading of Chapter 2; and Harvey Molotch and Clarence Stone for their comments on Chapter 6. I also want to thank my student reseach assistants for their invaluable help with data analysis and bibliography. Beth Ghiloni, Robert Marsh, Elizabeth Sholes, Jack Trumpbour, and Kathryn Weesner contributed greatly to this book, and over a dozen others did important work in the past. Their contribution is further acknowledged in the text by the use of the word *we* in presenting some of our findings down through the years.

Who Rules America? was written when I was the proud father of three very young children, and a fourth arrived a year after the book appeared. Today I am the even prouder father of four young adults and teen-agers—Lynne, Lori, Bill, and Joel—who are developing their own understanding of American society as they travel, go to college, and make their way through the school system. Two of them, Lynne and Lori, aided in the completion of this book as part-time research assistants. My gratitude to my children for the pleasure they have given me over the years is expressed by my dedicating the book to them.

Among many surprising things I have learned since the publication of *Who Rules America?* is that two books by the same title preceded it, one a small pamphlet in 1899 by a retired Army lieutenant, the other a full-length book in 1934 by a journalist. Neither has the same thesis as my 1967 book, and they do not seem very perceptive in retrospect. But their existence raises the possibility that yet another *Who Rules America?* will be written in the second decade of the twenty-first century by an author who later stumbles across my 1967 and 1983 versions, only to come to similar negative conclusions about them. I hope that such future oblivion is not to be the fate of either the *Who Rules America?* of 1967 or the *Who Rules America Now?* of 1983, but only time will tell on these matters, as it does on so many questions. For now, I will be satisfied if this book is thought by its readers to have enough redeeming features to make it as worthy of their attention in the 1980s as the first *Who Rules America?* was in the 1960s and 1970s.

Quotations from C. Wright Mills, *The Power Elite,* © Oxford University Press, Inc., 1956, are reprinted with permission.

The excerpt from David Halberstram's *The Best and the Brightest,* © 1969, 1971, 1972 by David Halberstram, is used by permission of Random House.

Excerpts from Grant McConnell's *Private Power and American Democracy,* © 1966 by Alfred A. Knopf, Inc., are used by permission.

Scattered excerpts from Leonard Silk and David Vogel, *Ethics and Profits,* copyright © 1976 by the Conference Board, are reprinted by permission of Simon & Schuster, a Division of Gulf & Western Corporation.

Quotations from Robert Dahl, "A Critique of the Ruling Elite Model," *American Political Science Review,* June 1958, copyright American Political Science Association, are used by permission.

The excerpt taken from Andrew Hacker, "What Rules America?", *New York Review of Books,* May 1, 1975, is reprinted with permission from *The New York Review of Books.* Copyright © 1975 Nyrev, Inc.

Quotations from Robert A. Dahl, *Dilemmas of Pluralist Democracy,* are reprinted by permission of the Yale University Press.

Quotations from an article by Harvey Molotch, "The City as a Growth Machine," *American Journal of Sociology,* September 1976, © 1976 University of Chicago Press, are used by permission.

Excerpts from Nathan Straus, *The Seven Myths of Housing,* are used by permission of Brandeis University.

1

The Issue of
Class and Power
in America

INTRODUCTION

Class and *power* are terms that make Americans a little uneasy, and concepts such as *ruling class* and *power elite* immediately put people on guard. The idea that a relatively fixed group of privileged people might dominate the economy and government goes against the American grain and the founding principles of the country. People may differ in their social levels, and some people may have more influence than others, but there can be no ruling class or power elite when power is constitutionally lodged in all the people, when there is democratic participation through elections and lobbying, and when the evidence of upward social mobility is everywhere apparent. If the question is asked, Who rules in the United States? the answer is likely to be in terms of interest groups, elected officials, and the people in general.

Contrary to this pluralistic view of power, it is the purpose of this book to present systematic evidence that suggests there is a social upper class in the United States that is a ruling class by virtue of its dominant role in the economy and government. It will be shown that this ruling class is socially cohesive, has its basis in the large corporations and banks, plays a major role in shaping the social and political climate, and dominates the federal government through a variety of organizations and methods.

The upper class as a whole does not do this ruling. Instead, class rule is manifested through the activities of a wide variety of organizations and institutions. These organizations and institutions are financed and directed by those members of the upper class who have the interest and ability to involve themselves in protecting and enhancing the privileged social position of their class. Leaders within the upper class join with high-level employees in the organizations they control to make up what will be called the *power elite*. This power elite is the leadership group of the upper class as a whole, but it is not the same thing as the upper class, for not all members of the upper class are members of the power elite and not all members of the power elite are part of the upper class. It is members of the power elite who take part in the processes that maintain the class structure.

The argument presented in this book, although contrary to the pluralist theory of power so prevalent in the American social sciences, does not deny that everyone is equal before the law and that there are opportunities for social mobility. It does not deny that there is freedom of expression, open political participation, and public conflict over significant issues. Nor is the argument one that ignores fundamental changes in the United States over the centuries. It does not deny that the basic form of private property has evolved from personal ownership and partnerships to corporate stock ownership, that the basis of social cohesion has shifted in part from the family and church to schools and clubs, or that the responsibility for policy formation has transferred from informal caucuses and political parties to foundations, formal policy-planning groups, and think tanks. Indeed, to begin with the premise that the class system is an open and changing one, and the political system a democratic one, is to state the aim of the book more clearly, which is to demonstrate that a ruling class can continue to exist amid the conflict and change that are so apparent in American society.

Moreover, to claim that there is an upper class with enough power to be considered a ruling class does not imply that other levels of society are totally powerless. Domination does not mean total control, but the ability to set the terms under which other groups and classes must operate. Highly trained professionals with an interest in environmental and consumer issues have been able to couple their technical information and their understanding of the legislative process with well-timed publicity to win governmental restrictions on some corporation practices. Wage and salary workers, when they are organized into unions, have been able to gain concessions on wages, hours, and working conditions. Even the most powerless of people, the very poor and those discriminated against, sometimes develop the capacity to disrupt the system through strikes, riots, or other forms of coercion, and there is evidence that such activities do bring about some redress of grievances, at least for a short time.[1]

Most of all, there is also the fact that people can vote. Although one basic theme of the book is a critique of the pluralist notion that voting necessarily makes government responsive to the will of the majority, it does not deny that under certain circumstances the electorate has been able to place restraints on the actions of the power elite as a whole, or to determine which leaders within the power elite will have the greatest influence on policy. This is especially a possibility when there are disagreements within the ruling class, as has been pointed out by several political theorists in the past.[2]

Because the argument and evidence of this book challenge basic American beliefs as well as the conventional wisdom of American social sciences, it is necessary to proceed in a step-by-step fashion, defining each concept as it is introduced and providing empirical examples of how each part of the system works. An attempt is made to begin at the level of appearances—at what seems to everyone to be obvious—and then show how this level connects to others that may not be immediately apparent. By approaching the problem in this fashion, readers can draw their own conclusions at each step of the way and decide for themselves if they think the argument fails at some point.

THE IDEA OF SOCIAL CLASS

American dislike for the idea of class is deeply rooted in the colonial and revolutionary experiences of this first new nation of the modern era. As a rapidly expanding frontier country lacking a feudal aristocracy and settled largely by people who wanted to escape the fixed stations that were their fate in Europe, colonial America seemed very different from other countries to its new inhabitants. That difference was only heightened by the need for solidarity among all classes in the nationalistic fight for freedom from England. If revolutionary leaders from the higher classes were going to win independence for the country they wished to create, they would have to gain the support of common people through a program that offered greater freedom and equality for everyone. As historian Robert R. Palmer succinctly stated in explaining the increased equality brought about by the revolutionary struggle, "Leaders who did not fight for equality accepted it in order to win."[3]

Although there existed sharp differences in wealth, income, and life-style in revolutionary America, particularly in port cities and the South, these well-understood differences were usually explained away or downplayed by members of the middle classes as well as by the merchants, plantation owners, and lawyers who were called "gentlemen" and who stood at the top of the social ladder. As a detailed historical study of diaries, letters, newspapers, and other documents of the period demonstrates, Americans instead emphasized and took pride in the fact that "class distinctions were minor in comparison with Europe." They recognized that there were rich and poor, and that 20 percent of the population was held in slavery, but they preferred to think of their country "as one of equality and proudly pointed to such features as the large middle class, the absence of beggars, the comfortable circumstances of most people, and the limitless opportunities for those who worked hard and saved their money."[4]

Even members of the upper class had come to prefer this more democratic class system to what had existed for many centuries in Europe. To emphasize this point, Palmer begins his two-volume work on "the age of the democratic revolution" in North America and Europe with a letter written from Europe in 1788 by a young adult member of a prominent American upper-class family. After noting his disgust with the hereditary titles and pomp of the European class system, and with the obsequiousness of the lower classes, the young man stated his conviction that "a certain degree of equality is essential to human bliss." He then went on to argue that the greatness of the United States was that it had provided this degree of equality "without destroying the necessary subordination."[5] As if to make sure the limits of his argument were clear, he underlined the words *a certain degree of equality*.

Two hundred years later, in response to sociologists who wanted to know what social class meant to Americans, a representative sample of the citizenry in Boston and Kansas City expressed ideas similar to those of the first Americans. Although most people were keenly aware of differences in social standing and judged status levels primarily in terms of income, occupations, and education (but especially income), they emphasized the openness of the system and the opportunity for advancement. They also argued that a person's social standing was in good part determined by such individual qualities as initiative and the motivation to work hard. Moreover, many of them felt that the importance of class was declining. This belief was partly due to their conviction that people of all ethnic and religious backgrounds were being treated with greater respect and decency whatever their occupational and educational levels, but even more to what they saw as material evidence for social advancement in the occupations and salaries of their families and friends. In the

words of sociologists, social mobility and a formal system of equality in all areas of political and social life make class a relatively unimportant idea for Americans. People are very aware of basic economic and educational differences, and they can size up social standing fairly well from such outward signs as speech patterns, mannerisms, and style of dress, but the existence of social classes is nonetheless passed over as quickly as possible.[6]

People of the highest social status share the general distaste for talking about social class in an open and direct way. In a classic study of social levels in New Haven, Connecticut, a person who fits into the top category in terms of neighborhood residence and educational background seemed startled when asked what class she was part of. After regaining her composure, she then replied: "One does not speak of classes; they are felt."[7] In the study of residents of Boston and Kansas City, an upper-class Bostonian said: "Of course social class exists—it influences your thinking." Then she added: "Maybe you shouldn't use the work 'class' for it, though—it's really a niche that each of us fits into."[8] In a study of thirty-eight upper-class women in a large midwestern city in the mid-1970s, sociologist Susan Ostrander asked her informants directly at the end of the interview if they were members of the upper class. The answers she received had the same flavor of hesitation and denial:

> I hate [the term] upper class. It's so non–upper class to use it. I just call it "all of us," those of us who are wellborn.
> I hate to use the word "class." We're responsible, fortunate people, old families, the people who have something.
> We're not supposed to have layers. I'm embarrassed to admit to you that we do, and that I feel superior at my social level. I like being part of the upper crust.[9]

Social scientists mean much the same things by the term *social class* as do typical Americans. Their definitions recognize that class is a double-edged concept, denoting both the relationship between categories of people and the specific categories within the overall relationship. Large-scale employers and wage earners both can be considered classes, but the idea of classes also encompasses the relationship between them. In defining classes for research purposes, however, sociologists and other social scientists tend to stress the similarities and interconnections among families and individuals at a given social level more than they do the relationship between levels.

For example, in one of the first empirical investigations of social class in America, a study of caste and class in a southern city in the 1930s, the group of sociological researchers defined a social class as:

The largest group of people whose members have intimate access to one another. A class is composed of families and social cliques. The interrelationships between these families and cliques, in such informal activities as visiting, dances, receptions, teas, and larger informal affairs, constitute the structure of the social class. A person is a member of the social class with which most of his or her participations, of this intimate kind, occur.[10]

Similar definitions are provided by researchers from disciplines other than sociology. A best-selling social psychology textbook defines a social class as "a division of a society, made up of persons possessing certain common social characteristics which are taken to qualify them for intimate equal-status relations with one another, and which restrict their interaction with members of other social classes."[11] Political scientist Robert A. Dahl, one of the major representatives of the pluralist view of dispersed power, defines equal "social standing" in terms of:

the extent to which members of that circle would be willing—disregarding personal and idiosyncratic factors—to accord the conventional privileges of social intercourse and acceptance among equals; marks of social acceptability include willingness to dine together, to mingle freely in intimate social events, to accept membership in the same clubs, to use forms of courtesy considered appropriate among social equals, to intermarry, and so on.[12]

A definition of social class in terms of various types of social interactions is also proposed by Marxian social scientists, who have been major critics of the pluralists within American social science. Marxist economist Paul Sweezy, in a discussion of the general characteristics of social classes, notes that they are "obstinate facts and not mere logical categories" and that "the fundamental unit of class membership is the family and not the individual." He concludes by saying, "A social class, then, is made up of freely intermarrying families."[13]

There is a general consensus, then, on what is meant by the idea of a social class. Indeed, it may be the only concept on which there is widespread agreement when it comes to studying power in the United States. The real problem with this concept begins with the question of whether or not there exists in the United States an observable, interacting social group with identifiable boundaries that can be called a social upper class. This question will be the primary focus of the next chapter.

THE CONCEPT OF POWER

American ideas about power have their origins in the struggle for independence, but they owe as much to the conflict within each colony about the founding of a new government as they do to the war itself. It is a cliché of every textbook in civics and every Fourth of July speech that people fought in the Revolutionary War because of a desire to have a say in how they were governed, and especially in how they were taxed. But it is usually lost from sight that the average citizens were making revolutionary political demands on their political leaders as well as helping in the fight against the British.

The yeoman farmers and artisans who supported the Revolution gradually developed out of their own experience the novel idea that power is the possession of all the people and is delegated to government with their consent. They also found ways to implement the idea when they insisted that special conventions be elected to frame constitutions and that the constitutions be ratified by the vote of all free white males without regard to their property holdings. In the past, governments had been founded on the power of religious leaders, kings, self-appointed conventions, or parliaments. Those revolutionary leaders such as John Adams who drafted the constitutions for the thirteen states between 1776 and 1780 expected their handiwork to be debated and voted upon by state legislatures, but they did not think to involve the general public in a direct way.

It was members of the "middling" classes who pressured for special conventions and for the right to vote on acceptance or rejection. They were steeled in their resolve by their participation in the revolutionary struggle and by a fear of the property laws and taxation policies that might be written into the constitutions by those who were known as their "betters." "The idea of the people as the constituent power," argues Palmer, "arose locally, from the grass roots." It is for this reason that he believes the American Revolution was "a political revolution, concerned with liberty, and with power."[14] This is a judgment that can stand even though there is ample evidence that the merchants, planters, and owners of large tracts of frontier land who benefited economically from the Revolution became discontent with British rule only after the British had pushed several Indian tribes off their land in the costly French and Indian Wars of 1754 to 1763.[15]

Only in Massachusetts in 1780 did the middle-level insurgents succeed in winning both a constitutional convention of elected delegates and the right of subsequent ratification. But from that time forth it became the accepted doctrine that "power" in the United States belonged to "the people." It is for this reason that every liberal, radical, populist, and ultraconservative movement since that time has insisted that it represents "the people" in its attempt to wrest allegedly arbitrary power from the "vested interests," the "money trust," or the "bureaucrats." Even the Founding Fathers, as the leadership group in the fledgling ruling class of that era, with its members far removed from the general population in their wealth, income, education, and political experience, did not consider promulgating their new constitution designed to better protect and enhance private property and commerce without asking for the consent of the governed.

In a very profound sense, then, no group or class has "power" in America, but only "influence." Some indication of the distinction Americans still make between power and influence, however great the differences in influence, can be seen in certain of the findings from a survey conducted in Muskegon, Michigan, in the late 1960s. The survey concerned beliefs about how the political system works. Only one-fifth of the respondents from all income levels believed a statement that began with the bald assertion "Big businessmen really run the government in this country" and ended with the claim that "things in Washington go pretty much the way big businessmen want them to." Instead, three-fifths of the respondents agreed with a statement that began "No one really runs the government in this country," and went on to say that "important decisions about national policy are made by a lot of different groups." By way of contrast, when asked which of several listed groups exerted the most "influence" in Washington, most people put either "big business" or "rich people" as their top choice.[16]

If the typical American is uncomfortable with the concept of power, so, too, are most social scientists. Definitions of the term are many and varied. Some social scientists prefer to get by without using the term at all, or to define power and influence to mean the same thing. Whatever their definitions, however, all social scientists use the term in the sense of great or preponderant influence, not in the sense of absolute control. In that regard their views are similar to those of most Americans.

The most widely used definition of power in the social sciences is a variation of one suggested by a German sociologist of the early twentieth century, Max Weber. Weber wrote that "we understand by 'power' the chance of a man or a number of men to realize their own will in a social action even against the resistance of others who are participating in the action."[17] More recently, Dahl concludes his discussion of the concept of power, in which he decides to use the terms *power* and *influence* interchangeably, by noting that most definitions of the term rest on the "intuitive idea" that "A has power over B to the extent that he can get B to do something that B would not otherwise do."[18]

Despite the partiality shown to Weber's definition, it has the disadvantage, as sociologist Dennis Wrong argues, that it harbors within it the implicit theory that at bottom the basis of power is the ability to use force or coercion on the other person or group. It therefore prejudges what should be a question open to empirical study. In order to avoid the problem inherent in Weber's definition, and in many others like it, Wrong's modified version of a definition first suggested by philosopher Bertrand Russell will be used as a starting point. It was offered by Wrong after a thorough consideration of every major discussion of the subject through 1978: "Power is the capacity of some persons to produce intended and foreseen effects on others."[19]

This type of definition guards against the attempt to reduce the various types of power to one basic underlying type. As Russell wrote:

> The fundamental concept in social science is Power in the sense in which Energy is the fundamental concept in physics. Like energy, power has many forms, such as wealth, armaments, influence on opinion. No one of these can be regarded as subordinate to any other, and there is no form from which the others are derivable.[20]

Russell's perspective not only avoids the emphasis on force, but it explicitly criticizes a basic Marxian assumption as well. In the final analysis, according to Marxists, all forms of power can be derived from the economic power that comes from ownership and control of the means of production. As long as there is capitalism, for instance, the owners and managers of large capitalist properties are the ruling class by definition.

Contrary to the Marxian view, Russell believes that "the attempt to isolate any one form of power, more especially, in our day, the economic form, has been, and still is, a source of errors of great practical importance."[21] In keeping with Russell's analysis, the following chapters will attempt to show that members of the upper class have several different kinds of power at their disposal. It will be suggested that it is the cumulative and combined effects of these varying types of power that makes the upper class a ruling class.

However, to say that power is the ability to produce intended and foreseen effects on others, and that there is no one form of power that is more basic than the others, does not mean it is a simple matter to study the power of a group or social class. A formal definition does not explain how a concept is to be measured. In the case of power, it is seldom possible to observe interactions that reveal its operation even in small groups, let alone to see one "class" producing "effects" on another. It is therefore necessary to develop what are called indicators of power.

CONCEPTS AND INDICATORS

For research purposes, power can be thought of as an underlying trait or property of a collectivity. As with any social trait, it is measured by a series of indicators, or signs, that bear a probabilistic relationship to it. This means that the indicators do not necessarily appear each and every time the trait is manifesting itself. This way of thinking about such sociological concepts as power and morale was developed by social psychologist Paul Lazarsfeld. In a detailed discussion of the relationship between concepts and measurement in the social sciences, he showed that the traits of a social collectivity are similar in their logical structure to the intervening variables and personality traits utilized by psychologists to understand individual behavior and the disposition concepts and inferential concepts developed by philosophers of science in order to explain the nature of scientific theory. Whether a theorist is concerned with "magnetism," as in physics, or "friendliness," as in psychology, or "power," as in sociology, the underlying structure of the investigatory procedure is the same. In each case there is an underlying concept whose presence can be inferred only through a series of diagnostic signs or indicators that vary in their strength under differing conditions. Research proceeds, in this view, through a series of "if-then" statements. "If" a group is powerful, "then" it should be expected that certain indicators of this power will be present.[22]

The indicators of a concept such as power are not perfect. For this reason, it is especially important to have more than one indicator. Ideally, indicators will be of very different types so that the irrelevant components of each of them will cancel one another out. In the best of all possible worlds, these multiple indicators will point in the same direction, giving greater confidence that the underlying concept has been measured correctly. This point is most convincingly argued by five methodologists in social psychology and sociology in a book that was widely quoted in its first edition in 1966:

> Once a proposition has been confirmed by two or more independent measurement processes, the uncertainty of its interpretation is greatly reduced. The most persuasive evidence comes through a triangulation

of measurement processes. If a proposition can survive the onslaught of a series of imperfect measures, with all their irrelevant error, confidence should be placed in it.[23]

Working within this framework, three different types of power indicators will be used in this book. They can be called (1) who benefits? (2) who governs? and (3) who wins? In the final chapter, a fourth type of indicator, a reputation for power, will be discussed in terms of its use in several studies of city power structures. But it was not possible in this book to use this indicator on a nationwide scale.

Who Benefits?

In every society there are experiences and material objects that are highly valued. If it is assumed that everyone in the society would like to have as great a share as possible of these experiences and objects, then the distribution of values in that society can be utilized as a power indicator. Those who have the most of what people want are, by inference, the powerful. Put another way, the distribution of valued experiences and objects within a society can be viewed as the most visible and stable outcome of the operation of power within that social system.

In American society, for example, wealth and well-being are highly valued. People seek to own property, to earn high incomes, to have an interesting and safe job, to enjoy the finest in travel and leisure, and to live long and healthy lives. All of these "values" are unequally distributed, and all may be utilized as power indicators. In this book, however, the primary focus with this type of indicator will be on the wealth and income distributions. This does not mean that wealth and income are equated with power, as Dahl and other pluralists constantly charge in their misunderstanding of the logic of indicators and concepts, but that the possession of great wealth or income is one visible sign that a class has power in relation to other classes.[24]

The argument for using value distributions as power indicators is strengthened by empirical studies that show that such distributions vary from country to country depending upon the relative strength of political parties and trade unions. In one study, it was found that the degree of inequality in the income distribution in Western democracies varied inversely with the percentage of socialists who had been elected to the country's legislature since 1945. The greater the socialist presence, the greater the amount of income that went to the lower classes.[25] In another study utilizing eighteen Western democracies, it was reported that strong trade unions and successful social democratic parties were correlated with greater equality in the income distribution, progressivity in the tax structure, and a higher level of welfare spending.[26] Thus, there is evidence that value distributions do vary with the power of organizations that represent a particular social class, in this case the wage-earning class.

Who Governs?

Power also can be inferred from studies of who occupies important institutional positions and takes part in important decision-making groups.[27] If a group or class is highly overrepresented or underrepresented in relation to its proportion of the population, it can be inferred that the group is relatively powerful or powerless, as the case may be. For example, when it is found that women are in only a small percentage of the leadership positions in business and government, even though they make up a majority of the population, it is readily inferred that they are relatively powerless in these areas. Similarly, when it is determined that a minority group has only a small percentage of its members in leadership positions, even though it comprises 10 to 20 percent of the population in a given city or state, then the basic processes of power—inclusion and exclusion—are inferred to be at work.

This indicator also can be shown to vary from situation to situation. The rise and fall of classes or ethnic groups can be charted historically through their positional representation.[28] Then, too, as women and blacks became more organized in the United States in the 1960s and 1970s, their representation in positions of authority also increased.

Who Wins?

There are many issues over which groups or classes disagree. In the United States different policies are suggested by opposing groups in such "issue-areas" as foreign policy, taxation, welfare, and the environment. Power can be inferred from these issue conflicts by determining who successfully initiates, modifies, or vetoes policy alternatives. This indicator, by focusing on actions within the decision-making process, comes closest to approximating the process of power that is contained in the formal definition. It is the indicator most preferred by the pluralists. But it must be stressed that it is no less an inference to say that who wins on issues relates to the underlying concept of power than with the other two types of empirical observations used as indicators. For many reasons, it is also the most difficult to use in an accurate way. Aspects of a decision

process may remain hidden, some informants may exaggerate or play down their roles, and people's memories about who did what often became cloudy shortly after the event. These are just three among several problems.[29]

Indeed, each of these three indicators has its strengths and weaknesses, as would be expected with any indicators in the social sciences. Not only do studies of who wins and loses on specific issues have problems, but the value distributions that determine "who benefits" may be in part determined by unintended consequences or by actions of the powerful to extend some benefits downward.[30] In the case of the "who governs" indicator, people in leadership positions may sometimes have only formal authority and no "real power." However, these weaknesses present no serious problem if the perspective of multiple indicators outlined earlier is utilized. This is because each of these indicators does involve different kinds of information drawn from very different types of investigatory procedures. The case will be considered a convincing one only if all three types of indicators triangulate on one particular group or social class.

THE PLAN OF THE BOOK

Each chapter will present one step in the argument. In the next chapter evidence will be presented to demonstrate that there is a socially cohesive and clearly demarcated upper class, which is distinctive in its style of life as well as the source and amount of its income. Chapter 3 will provide evidence to suggest that the upper class is based in a tightly knit corporate community, with members benefiting as major owners and working within it as financiers, lawyers, and executives.

In Chapter 4 it will be shown that corporations and corporate leaders finance and direct a network of tax-free foundations, policy-discussion groups, think tanks, and other organizations that formulate policy alternatives and attempt to shape the social and political climate. The leaders of these groups, along with the men and women active in high-level positions in the corporate community, are the core of the power elite that is the leadership group for the upper class as a whole.

Chapter 5 will describe the three different processes through which members of the power elite bring their influence to bear on government. The chapter also will explain the way in which three major forces—the liberal-labor coalition, moderate conservatives of the power elite, and ultraconservatives of the power elite—interact with one another on crucial questions of general policy.

Chapter 6 will turn attention to the question of power in local government. Not only is community power of major concern to many citizens, but it is the level of government that has been studied most intensively by political sociologists and political scientists interested in power. In contrast to what has been suggested by most previous studies, this chapter will suggest that those who govern at the local level are not part of the national power elite and are sometimes in conflict with it.

The argument to this point will be presented with a minimum of disputation with contending viewpoints. In the final chapter, however, the implications of the study for the theoretical views of pluralists, Marxists, and other analysts will be assessed by anticipating their criticisms of what has been presented.

It will be suggested that there are major difficulties created for all traditional theories of power in American society by the arguments and findings of this study. No full-blown theory of American society will be offered to replace them, although a new one clearly is needed. However, it will be concluded that any analysis of American society that does not begin with the findings of a book such as this will be doomed to triviality and confusion from the outset. There are dozens of books by journalists, writers, and social scientists that present very interesting and insightful findings on various aspects of American society. But they remain on the surface and add up to very little in the way of an overall picture because they do not start with the underlying structure of power that is spelled out in the following chapters.

NOTES

1. Robert R. Alford and Roger Friedland, "Political Participation and Public Policy." *Annual Review of Sociology*, 1, (1975); William A. Gamson, *The Strategy of Social Protest* (Homewood, Ill.: Dorsey Press, 1975); Frances Piven and Richard Cloward, *Regulating the Poor* (New York: Pantheon, 1971); Frances Piven and Richard Cloward, *Poor People's Movements* (New York: Random House, 1977).
2. Joseph Schumpeter, *Capitalism, Socialism, and Democracy* (London: Allen & Unwin, 1942); V. O. Key, *Southern Politics* (New York: Random House, 1949), p. 180; C. B. MacPherson, *The Life and Times of Liberal Democracy* (New York: Oxford University Press, 1977), chapter IV.
3. Robert R. Palmer, *The Age of the Democratic Revolution*, vol. 1 (Princeton, N.J.: Princeton University Press, 1959), p. 203.
4. Jackson Turner Main, *The Social Structure of Revolutionary America* (Princeton, N.J.: Princeton University Press, 1965), pp. 239, 284.
5. Palmer, *Age of Democratic Revolution*, p. 3.

6. Richard P. Coleman and Lee Rainwater, *Social Standing in America* (New York: Basic Books, 1978).

7. August B. Hollingshead and Frederick C. Redlich, *Social Class and Mental Illness: A Community Study (New York: Wiley, 1958), p. 69.*

8. Coleman and Rainwater, *Social Standing in America*, p. 25.

9. Susan Ostrander, "Upper-Class Women: Class Consciousness as Conduct and Meaning," in *Power Structure Research*, ed. G. William Domhoff, Beverly Hills, Calif.: Sage Productions, 1980), pp. 78–79.

10. Allison Davis, Burleigh B. Gardner, and Mary R. Gardner, *Deep South* (Chicago: University of Chicago Press, 1941), p. 59n.

11. David Krech, Richard S. Crutchfield, and Egerton L. Ballachy, *The Individual in Society* (New York: McGraw-Hill, 1962), p. 338.

12. Robert A. Dahl, *Who Governs?* (New Haven, Conn.: Yale University Press, 1961), p. 229.

13. Paul M. Sweezy, "The American Ruling Class," Paul Sweezy (ed.), *The Present as History*, ed. (New York: Monthly Review Press, 1953), pp. 123–24. For Marxian critiques of the pluralist view of social classes because it does not include a consideration of what Marxists believe to be the inherently exploitative relationship between classes, see James Stolzman and Herbert Gambert, "Marxist Class Analysis versus Stratification Analysis as General Approaches to Social Inequality," *Berkeley Journal of Sociology*, 1973–74, and Charles H. Anderson, *The Political Economy of Social Class* (Englewood Cliffs, N.J.: Prentice-Hall, 1974).

14. Palmer, *Age of Democratic Revolutions*, pp. 222, 213.

15. David Horowitz, *The First Frontier* (New York: Simon & Schuster, 1978), Part 3.

16. Joan Huber and William Form, *Income and Ideology* (New York: Free Press, 1973), pp. 134–140.

17. Dennis Wrong, *Power: Its Forms, Bases, and Uses* (New York: Harper & Row, 1979), p. 21.

18. Robert A. Dahl, "The Concept of Power," *Behavioral Science* 2 (1957), pp. 202–3.

19. Wrong, *Power*, p. 2.

20. Bertrand Russell, *Power: A New Social Analysis* (London: George Allen & Unwin, 1938), pp. 10–11.

21. Ibid., p. 12.

22. Paul Lazarsfeld, "Concept Formation and Measurement," in *Concepts, Theory, and Explanation in the Behavioral Sciences*, ed. Gordon J. DiRenzo (New York: Random House, 1966).

23. Eugene T. Webb et al., *Nonreactive Measures in the Social Sciences*, 2d ed. (Boston: Houghton Mifflin, 1981), p. 35.

24. Robert A. Dahl, *Dilemmas of Pluralist Democracy* (New Haven, Conn.: Yale University Press, 1982), p. 17.

25. Christopher Hewitt, "The Effect of Political Democracy and Economic Democracy on Equality in Industrial Societies," *American Sociological Review* 42 (1977).

26. John Stephens, *The Transition from Capitalism to Socialism* (Atlantic Highlands, N.J.: Humanities Press, 1980), chapter 4.

27. Alford and Friedland, "Political Participation and Public Policy," limit the "who governs?" indicator to the "institutional" level of power because they have an overly rigid equation between specific indicators and specific theoretical paradigms. I continue to use this indicator to study decision-making groups at what they call the "situational" level of power, as I did in *Who Rules America?*

28. E.g., W. L. Guttsman, *The British Political Elite* (New York: Basic Books, 1963); Dahl, *Who Governs?*, chapters 1–5; Ralph Miliband, *The State in Capitalist Society* (New York: Basic Books, 1969), p. 177.

29. See G. William Domhoff, *Who Rules America?* (Englewood Cliffs, N.J.: Prentice-Hall, 1967), pp. 6–7, 144–46 and Raymond Bauer, "Social Psychology and the Study of Policy Formation," *American Psychologist* 21 (1966) for detailed comments on the difficulties of decision-making studies of power.

30. Nelson Polsby, *Community Power and Political Theory,* 2d ed. (New Haven, Conn.: Yale University Press, 1980), p. 132.

2

The American Upper Class

INTRODUCTION

If there is an American upper class, it must exist not merely as a collection of families who feel comfortable with each other and tend to exclude outsiders from their social activities. It must exist as a set of interrelated social institutions. That is, there must be patterned ways of organizing the lives of its members from infancy to old age, and there must be mechanisms for socializing both the younger generation and new adult members who have risen from lower social levels. If the class is a reality, the names and faces may change somewhat over the years, but the social institutions that underlie the upper class must persist with remarkably little change over several generations.

The main purpose of this chapter will be to show that there is an upper class in this institutional, supraindividual sense. This will be accomplished through the presentation of historical, quantitative, questionnaire, and interview data that demonstrate the interconnections among a set of schools, clubs, resorts, and social activities that are the basis of the upper class. The chapter also will attempt through more anecdotal information to describe how these various social institutions provide members of the upper class with a distinctive life-style that sharply differentiates them from the rest of society. The second task is necessary because criteria for the existence of a social class include not only in-group social interaction but a unique style of life.

In addition, marriage patterns within the upper class and the continuity of upper-class families will be discussed, and the wealth, income, and occupations of its members will be examined. The result should be a clear picture of an interacting set of families and social cliques that possesses great wealth and makes up only 0.5 percent of the population. Finally, the chapter will present a lengthy list of indicators of upper-class standing that can be used to study the involvement of upper-class members in the corporate community, the policy planning network, and the government.

THE INSTITUTIONAL INFRASTRUCTURE

Four different types of empirical studies establish the existence of an interrelated set of social institutions, organizations, and social activities that undergirds and defines the upper class. They are historical case studies, quantitative studies of biographical directories, questionnaire studies of knowledgeable observers, and interview studies with members of the upper-middle and upper classes.

The first and most detailed historical study of the upper class was completed in the 1950s by E. Digby Baltzell, a member of the upper class himself. Baltzell drew together all previous historical and anecdotal data on the subject and then turned his attention to the development of the upper class in Philadelphia. He was able to demonstrate in this way that the people of highest status and greatest wealth gradually created a set of exclusive neighborhoods, expensive private schools, restricted social clubs, and such unique social occasions as debutante balls and fox hunts that provided the basis for their day-to-day lives.[1]

Building from his Philadelphia materials, Baltzell was able to show that members of the upper class in that city began in the late nineteenth and early twentieth centuries to frequent the same resorts as the people of highest status in other eastern cities. They also began to send their children to boarding schools in New England and Virginia that catered to the wealthy from other cities across the country, and they joined the social clubs of their counterparts in other cities. Baltzell found that they were listed in great numbers in an exclusive intercity address and telephone book called the *Social Register*, symbolizing the interconnectedness of the families in many different cities.

In effect, then, Baltzell showed the relationships among these institutions and activities through demonstrating that the same few people created and belonged to all of them. To test and extend his findings, we did the same kind of study in an ahistorical and quantitative way. In this particular study we analyzed the information on school attendance and club membership that appeared in 3,000 randomly selected *Who's Who in America* biographies for the late 1960s. We also determined which of these people were listed in the *Social Register*.[2]

The pattern of memberships and affiliations generated by this search were analyzed by means of a statistical technique known as contingency analysis. It provides a means to find out whether or not there is a significant relationship between two or more affiliations by determining whether or not their appearance together is greater than would be expected by chance.[3] The findings of this study fully supported Baltzell's claim that a relationship exists between listing in the *Social Register*, attendance at one of several private high schools, and membership in one or more of several social clubs. In addition, the study added new schools and clubs to those discovered by Baltzell.

A very different method provided further support for these findings and also greatly extended the list of clubs and schools while adding a few new social directories as well. In this study a questionnaire–letter was sent to editors of women's pages and society pages of newspapers in every city in the country with a chapter of the Junior League. This exclusive women's service organization was used as a starting point because it is one of the few nationwide organizations known to have a great many upper-class members. In essence, the questionnaire–letter asked if there was a set of high-status schools and clubs in the given city and if the members of those schools and clubs were listed in the *Social Register* or any other social directory. Following these open-ended questions, it asked for an estimate of how many children from that city attended each of eleven boarding schools that were listed on the page.

In all, 128 of the 317 reports were filled out and returned. Some had very little information, but most were quite informative. In twelve cases we received replies from two different newspapers in a city, and in all but one instance there was complete agreement in the reports. The replies of these well-placed observers also produced strong agreement with the findings of Baltzell's historical study and the contingency analysis. For example, the *Social Register* was listed as a useful source on upper-class families by all eight reports from cities covered by it.[4]

A fourth and final method of establishing the existence of upper-class institutions is based on intensive interviews with a cross-section of citizens. The most detailed study of this type was conducted in Kansas City in the 1950s and published in 1971.[5] The study was concerned with people's perceptions of the social ladder as a whole, from top to bottom, but it is the top level that is of concern here. Although most people in Kansas City could point to the existence of exclusive neighborhoods in suggesting that there was a class of "blue bloods" or "big rich," it was members of the upper-middle class and the upper class itself whose reports demonstrated that clubs and other social institutions as well as neighborhoods gave the class an institutional existence.

The specific schools, clubs, and social directories uncovered by these and related investigations will be listed at the end of this chapter when they are discussed as indicators of upper-class standing. For now it is enough to say that the four different types of studies described in this section leave no doubt as to the institutional reality of an upper class in America. However, this reality remains a bit dry and abstract up to this point. In order to make the upper class more concrete, it is necessary to turn to an examination of how some of these institutions affect the lives of individual members.

THE SOCIAL REGISTER

The most quaint institution of the upper class is a little-known address and telephone book called the *Social Register* that lists about 65,000 families and single adults. Although the *Social Register* is of no importance in and of itself, Baltzell's work clearly shows that it is one of the best sources of information on the upper class that is available to social scientists.

The black and orange volumes of the *Social Register* were created as a business venture by an upper-class socialite in 1887. Although the founder had considerable personal knowledge of the people he wished to include, he did not start from scratch in his efforts. The patron's list of the National Horse Show Association provided over one-third of the listings. At one time published for as many as 24 cities all over the country, the volumes that persisted after the 1920s covered 13 of the largest cities in the nation. With the exception of San Francisco, they are all east of the Mississippi: New York, Boston, Philadelphia, Baltimore, Washington, Chicago, Saint Louis, Buffalo, Pittsburgh, Cleveland, and Cincinnati–Dayton.[6]

In 1976 the *Social Register* was purchased from distant relatives of the founder by the family of Malcolm Forbes, the multimillionaire owner of *Forbes'* magazine. A slight link to the past remained, however, for the wife of Malcolm Forbes, Jr. came from one of the families holding shares in the company. Attempts by reporters to interview any members of the Forbes family about the purchase were unsuccessful. They chose to maintain the policy of discreet silence that had been practiced for several decades by the former owners. Whatever the reason for this reticence, it adds to the mystique of the *Social Register.*

Also contributing to the mystique in an odd way is the nondescript nature of the Social Register Association's headquarters. Located at 381 Park Avenue South in New York, a distinctly unfashionable address, the office is a sparsely furnished suite that is highly uninviting to the visitor: "An opaque glass and wood partition separates the office from a small reception room, which is painted green and contains a desk with a tin ashtray, two chairs, and four plants in plastic pots."[7]

The new owners took the occasion of the ownership changeover to transform the 12 slim volumes into one large volume of 1,100 pages. This cut the cost of the entire set from over $100 to $30 but made it more like a bulky reference book in the process. A spokesperson for the Association explained the change in a not-for-attribution discussion with a *New York Times* reporter: "The editions were being consolidated because such cities as Philadelphia, Boston and New York were no longer isolated social entities. ... Young people go to school in California. They make friends in that part of the world."[8] This is indirect evidence, then, for the nationwide nature of the upper class.

Although the *Social Register* may serve as a status symbol for some of its listees, it seems likely that most of the people who fill out the biographical information blanks and buy a copy do so because of the useful information it contains, including addresses, telephone numbers, and lists of marriages and deaths for each year. As an additional feature, there is a section in the back entitled "Married Maidens." It lists all the married women in the register alphabetically by their maiden names, with married names adjacent, thereby making it possible to locate old friends. Beyond all this, there are small supplementary editions: "Dilatory Domiciles" lists temporary addresses, and the *Summer Social Register* lists summer addresses for those who supply them.

The usefulness of the *Social Register* to the listees was documented in an interview study with members of the upper class in Boston. It was noted that 8 of the 18 adults interviewed in either home or office used the *Social Register* at one point or another in the interview. Most of the time it was to find a telephone number, but it also was used to look up the first names of people's spouses. One person commented in passing, "It's great for mailing lists."[9]

Although the emphasis is on useful information, there is a place for social status information in the *Social Register* as well. Following each adult or couple's name, there may appear a set of capital letters, abbreviations, and numbers that reveal membership in clubs and ancestral societies, colleges and universities attended, and year of graduation. A family's *Social Register* listing might read as follows:

> Smith Jr. and Mrs Jas W. (Helen L. Jones)   989-8034
>   Sm., Bhm., Chi., Ncd., H'54 SL'55   45 June Lane
>   Smith Mr. Kenneth F—at Cornell   Easton, MA 02193
>   Juniors Mr. Wm C—at St. Paul's

By checking the lengthy list of abbreviations and symbols at the beginning of the book, it can be determined that Mr. Smith graduated from Harvard in 1954 and is a member of the Somerset Club in Boston and the Bohemian Club in San Francisco, and that Mrs. Smith graduated from Sarah Lawrence in 1955 and is a member of the Chilton Club in Boston and the National Society of Colonial Dames.* As for their children, it is readily apparent that one is at Cornell and the other at Saint Paul's, a boarding school. Not all the listings include as much information on clubs and ancestral societies as this hypothetical example, however. Whether those who do not list such information fail to include it or are not members is an open question.

New people are added to the *Social Register* through recommendations by those who already are listed. Some accounts suggest that applicants are screened by committees, but there is no solid evidence for this claim. Baltzell summarizes the process of new listings as follows:

> [New] families are added to the *Social Register* as a result of their making a formal application to the Social Register Association in New York. In other words, a family having personal and more or less intimate social relations (in business, church, school club, or neighborhood activities) with the various members of certain families who are members of the upper class and listed in the *Social Register* reaches a point where inclusion within the register seems expedient; someone listed in the *Social Register,* presumably a friend of the "new" family, obtains an application blank which in turn is filled out by the new family (usually by the wife) and returned to the Social Register

---

*Our analysis of 5900 family entries showed that about 9 percent of the families mention one or more of 21 ancestral societies, with the National Society of Colonial Dames, the Society of Colonial Wars, the Mayflower Descendants, and the Colonial Dames of America accounting for nearly 75 percent of the listings.

Association in New York along with several endorsements by present upper-class members as to the social acceptability of the new family; after payment of a nominal fee, the next issues of the *Social Register,* including all pertinent information on the new family, will arrive the following November.[10]

The belief that there is a vigilant screening committee is based upon the fact that some people seem to be dropped each year for reasons of divorce, unacceptable marriages, or involvement in distasteful activities. Society-page writers study each new edition to determine who has been deleted, and then speculate on the reasons. However, no pattern seems to emerge. Some divorcees are deleted, some are not. Some people who marry entertainers or other non–Social Registerites are missing the next year, others are not.

It was gossip over the abrupt absence of a daughter of Nelson Rockefeller from the 1963 edition that led to the first lengthy interview by the press with principals of the Social Register Association. Because she was married to a minister involved in the Freedom Rides into the South in 1962, there was speculation in the press that she and her husband were dropped for his highly visible involvement in this cause. Embarrassed by these allegations, the Social Register Association spoke in a not-for-attribution fashion to a *New York Times* reporter, leading to the most detailed account of the *Social Register* on record. Among other things, it was denied emphatically that Mary Rockefeller Pierson and her husband had been dropped because he was a Freedom Rider. Instead, the spokesperson claimed, they were dropped for the reason anyone might be dropped, for declining to return the yearly information blank. A subsequent interview with Mrs. Pierson confirmed this claim. She had not returned the forms. "It was not an oversight," she said. "It was lack of interest."[11]

There are other members of the upper class besides Mrs. Pierson who decline to be listed in the *Social Register.* In particular, such notable multimillionaires of the past as Alfred Gwynne Vanderbilt and John Hay Whitney refused to be listed, a fact stressed in the newspaper accounts that appear on the *Social Register* from time to time. However, such accounts do not add that Mr. Vanderbilt's brother, William H. Vanderbilt, and Mr. Whitney's sister, Joan Whitney Payson, were both listed, as were numerous other members of the intermarried Vanderbilt and Whitney families. Few other Rockefellers besides Mrs. Pierson have removed themselves; there were over 25 adult descendants of the first wealthy Rockefeller brothers, John and William, in the *Social Register* in the late 1970s. Other famous names in the history of the American upper class are equally present. There is a Theodore Roosevelt IV and a Franklin Roosevelt III among the 35 Roosevelts listed, a Willliam Howard Taft

IV and a Herbert Hoover III among the 27 Tafts and 10 Hoovers, and tens of Biddles, Cabots, Dukes, DuPonts, Harrimans, Morgans, Van Rensselears, and other descendants of great fortunes from the eighteenth and nineteenth centuries.

It must be emphasized that the Social Register Association does not decide who is and who is not a member of the upper class. Its *Social Register* is merely a telephone book with perhaps a certain snob appeal. On the other hand, the very fact that the venture has persisted since 1887 and receives biography forms yearly from tens of thousands of families is no small testament in and of itself to the existence of a great many self-conscious members of the upper class in America.

TRAINING THE YOUNG

From infancy through young adulthood, members of the upper class receive a distinctive education. This education begins early in life in preschools that frequently are attached to a neighborhood church of high social status. Schooling continues during the elementary years at a local private school called a day school. The adolescent years may see the student remain at day school, but there is a strong chance that at least one or two years will be spent away from home at a boarding school in a quiet rural setting. Higher education will be obtained at one of a small number of heavily endowed private universities. Harvard, Yale, Princeton, and Stanford head the list, followed by smaller Ivy League schools in the East and a handful of other small private schools in other parts of the country. Although some upper-class children may attend public high school if they live in a secluded suburban setting, or go to a state university if there is one of great esteem and tradition in their home state, the system of formal schooling is so insulated that many upper-class students never see the inside of a public school in all their years of education.

This separate educational system is important evidence for the distinctiveness of the mentality and life-style that exists within the upper class, for schools play a large role in transmitting the class structure to their students. Surveying and summarizing a great many studies on schools in general, sociologist Randall Collins concludes: "Schools primarily teach vocabulary and inflection, styles of dress, aesthetic tastes, values and manners."[12]

The training of upper-class children is not restricted to the formal school setting, however. Special classes and even tutors are a regular part of their extracurricular education. This informal education usually begins with dancing classes in the elementary years, which are seen as more important for learning proper manners and the social graces than for learning to dance. Tutoring in a foreign language may begin in the elementary years, and there are often lessons in horseback riding and music as well. The teen years find the children of the upper class in summer camps or on special travel tours, broadening their perspectives and polishing their social skills.

The linchpins in the upper-class educational system are the dozens of boarding schools that were developed in the last half of the nineteenth and the early part of the twentieth centuries, with the rise of a nationwide upper class whose members desired to insulate themselves from an inner city that was becoming populated by lower-class immigrants. Baltzell concludes that these schools became "surrogate families" that played a major role "in creating an upper-class subculture on almost a national scale in America."[13] The role of boarding schools in providing connections to other upper-class social institutions is also important. As one informant explained to Ostrander in her interview study of upper-class women: "Where I went to boarding school, there were girls from all over the country, so I know people from all over. It's helpful when you move to a new city and want to get invited into the local social clubs."[14]

Consciously molded after their older and more austere British counterparts, it is within these several hundred schools that a unique style of life is inculcated through such traditions as the initiatory hazing of beginning students, the wearing of school blazers or ties, compulsory attendance at chapel services, and participation in esoteric sports such as lacrosse, squash, and crew. Even a different language is adopted to distinguish these schools from public schools. The principal is a headmaster or rector, the teachers are sometimes called masters, and the students are in forms, not grades. Great emphasis is placed upon the building of "character." The role of the school in preparing the future leaders of America is emphasized through the speeches of the headmaster and the frequent mention of successful alumni.*

There are some differences in emphasis and in the composition of the student body within even the most fashionable of boarding schools. Though most are socially exclusive and extremely expensive, a few have been open to minorities and have provided scholarships for low-income students. This more meritocratic emphasis has been especially the case with Phillips Exeter Academy and Phillip Acad-

---

*The Episcopal priest who served as headmaster at Choate from 1908 to 1947 often exhorted his students: "Ask not what your school can do for you, but what you can do for your school." This line was adapted slightly by one of his students, John F. Kennedy, who in 1961 as president of the United States asked his fellow citizens in a stirring patriotic speech: "Ask not what your country can do for you, but what you can do for your country."

emy (Andover, Massachusetts), which were founded in the late eighteenth century as academies to provide the necessary education for the rural populations in southeastern New Hampshire and northern Massachusetts. They became boarding schools with a focus on college preparatory courses in the first years of the twentieth century but maintained a concern for a less structured social atmosphere and a wider range of students.[15]

A social pecking order exists within the most elite of boarding schools. Those of highest prestige are usually older, located in New England, or affiliated with the Episcopalian Church. When *Fortune* printed a list of eighteen fashionable private schools in 1936, a list that would show little or no change in the 1980s, fourteen were located in New England and six were Episcopal, including Episcopal High in Virginia. The most prestigious among these eighteen schools are in turn singled out as the "Saint Grottlesex" schools, an amalgam of Saint Paul's, Saint Mark's, Saint George's, Groton, and Middlesex.[16]

Saint Paul's, as the oldest and wealthiest of Episcopal boarding schools, is the epitome of a Saint Grottlesex school. Located in Concord, New Hampshire, its campus of 80 buildings on 2,000 acres of woods and open land more nearly resembles a small college than a secondary school. Founded in 1856 as a boys' school, it now has 495 male and female students who begin school there in the third form (ninth grade). Personal interviews are required for admission, and tuition alone was $6,800 in 1981. About one in four students receives some scholarship aid. The student–teacher ratio is about 6.3 to 1, and classes have an average of 12 students.

In 1981 the students came from 38 states and 20 foreign countries. New York provided the most students (98), followed by Massachusetts (84), New Hampshire (54), and Connecticut (39), but 45 students came from 11 states west of the Mississippi as well. As many as one-fifth to one-third of the students in any given class may be the children of alumni, and there are alumni committees actively supporting the school in 32 major cities and regions around the country. Reunions and activities at the school for alumni are frequent.

The lives of the students are regulated as much as possible but much less than was the case before student protests at the turn of the 1970s. In addition to compulsory chapel, there are four seated dinner meals during the regular week that are obligatory. Weekends away from school are limited in number and must be applied for in advance. Thus, like most boarding schools, Saint Paul's has many of the features of those highly effective socializing agents that sociologist Erving Goffman calls "total institutions," isolating its members from the outside world and providing them with a set of routines and traditions that encompass most of their waking hours.[17]

Almost all graduates of private secondary schools go on to college, and almost all do so at prestigious universities. Graduates of the New England boarding schools, for example, historically found themselves at the major Ivy League universities. However, that situation changed somewhat after World War II as the boarding schools grew and provided more scholarships. An analysis of admission patterns for graduates of 14 prestigious boarding schools between 1953 and 1967 demonstrated this shift by showing that the percentage of their graduates attending Harvard, Yale, or Princeton gradually declined over those years from 52 to 25 percent. Information on the same 14 schools for the years 1969 to 1979 showed that the figure had bottomed out at 13 percent in 1973, 1975, and 1979, with some schools showing very little change from the late 1960s and others dropping even more dramatically.[18]

Graduates of private schools outside of New England most frequently attend a prominent state university in their area, but a significant minority go to eastern Ivy League and top private universities in other parts of the country. For example, the Cate School, a boarding school near Santa Barbara, California, is modeled after its New England counterparts and draws most of its students from California and other western states. In the five years between 1966 and 1970, 49 of the 160 graduates went to one or another campus of the University of California. However, the second school on the list was Harvard with 13, and six of the other nine colleges and universities enrolling three or more Cate graduates, all private schools, were in the East as well.[19] Or, to take another example, Saint John's in Houston is a lavishly endowed day school built in the Gothic architecture typical of many universities. Between its first graduating class in 1951 and 1973, 124 of its graduates went to the University of Texas, but every other university attended by 20 or more graduates was a private one. A majority of these schools were in the East or California, including Harvard with 31, Stanford with 27, Yale and Princeton with 24, and Williams with 22.[20]

Whatever university upper-class students attend, they tend to socialize together as members of a small number of fraternities, sororities, eating clubs, and secret societies, perpetuating to some extent the separate existence of a day or boarding school. As sociologist C. Wright Mills explained, it is not merely a matter of going to a Harvard or a Yale but to the right Harvard or Yale:

> That is why in the upper social classes, it does not by itself mean much merely to have a degree from an Ivy League college. That is assumed: the point is not Harvard, but which Harvard? By Harvard, one means Porcellian, Fly, or A.D.: by Yale, one means Zeta Psi or Fence or Delta Kappa Epsilon: by Princeton, Cottage, Tifer, Cap and Gown or Ivy.[21]

From kindergarten through college, then, schooling is very different for members of the upper class from what it is for most Americans, and it teaches them to be distinctive in many ways. In a country where education is highly valued and the overwhelming majority attend public schools, less than one student in a hundred is part of this private system that primarily benefits members of the upper class and provides one of the foundations for the old-boy and old-girl networks that will be with them throughout their lives.

SOCIAL CLUBS

Just as private schools are a pervasive feature in the lives of upper-class children, so, too, are private social clubs a major point of orientation in the lives of upper-class adults. These clubs also play a role in differentiating members of the upper class from other members of society. According to Baltzell, "the club serves to place the adult members of society and their families within the social hierarchy." He quotes with approval the suggestion by historian Crane Brinton that the club "may perhaps be regarded as taking the place of those extensions of the family, such as the clan and the brotherhood, which have disappeared from advanced societies."[22] Conclusions similar to Baltzell's resulted from an interview study in Kansas City: "Ultimately, say upper-class Kansas Citians, social standing in their world reduces to one issue: where does an individual or family rank on the scale of private club memberships and informal cliques."[23]

The clubs of the upper class are many and varied, ranging from family-oriented country clubs and downtown men's and women's clubs to highly specialized clubs for yachtsmen, sportsmen, gardening enthusiasts, and fox hunters. Many families have memberships in several different types of clubs, but the days when most of the men by themselves were in a half dozen or more clubs faded before World War II. Downtown men's clubs originally were places for having lunch and dinner, and occasionally for attending an evening performance or a weekend party. But as upper-class families deserted the city for large suburban estates, a new kind of club, the country club, gradually took over some of these functions. The downtown club became almost entirely a luncheon club, a site to hold meetings, or a place to relax on a free afternoon. The country club, by contrast, became a haven for all members of the family. It offered social and sporting activities ranging from dances, parties, and banquets to golf, swimming, and tennis. Special group dinners were often arranged for all members on Thursday night, the traditional maid's night off across the United States.

Although males were the first to found formal clubs within the upper class, a parallel set of women's clubs followed closely behind. In most major cities there is at least one women's club that is similar in structure and function to the metropolitan men's clubs. Garden clubs were also formed in many of these cities. They are the major specialty clubs exclusively for women.

Sporting activities are the basis for most of the specialized clubs of the upper class. The most visible are the yachting and sailing clubs, followed by the clubs for lawn tennis or squash. The most exotic are the several dozen fox hunting clubs. They have their primary strongholds in rolling countrysides from southern Pennsylvania down into Virginia, but they exist in other parts of the country as well. Riding to hounds in pink jackets and black boots, members of the upper class sustain over 130 hunts under the banner of the Masters of Fox Hounds Association. The intricate rituals and grand feasts accompanying the event go back to the eighteenth century in the United States, including the Blessing of the Hounds by an Episcopal bishop in the eastern hunts.[24]

Initiation fees, annual dues, and expenses vary from a few thousand dollars in downtown clubs to tens of thousands of dollars in some country clubs, but money is not the primary barrier in gaining membership to a club. Each club has a very rigorous screening process before accepting new members. Most require nomination by one or more active members, letters of recommendation from three to six members, and interviews with at least some members of the membership committee. Names of prospective members are sometimes posted in the clubhouse, so all members have an opportunity to make their feelings known to the membership committee. Negative votes by two or three members of what is typically a 10-to-20-person committee often are enough to deny admission to the candidate.

The carefulness with which new members are selected extends to a guarding of club membership lists, which are usually available only to club members. Older membership lists are sometimes given to libraries by members or their surviving spouses, and some members will give lists to individual researchers, but for most clubs there are no membership lists in the public domain. Our request to 15 clubs in 1981 for membership lists for research purposes was refused by 12 of the clubs and left unanswered by the other 3.

Not every club member is an enthusiastic participant in the life of the club. Some belong out of tradition or a feeling of social necessity. One woman told Ostrander the following about her country club: "We don't feel we should withdraw our support even though we don't go much." Others mentioned a feeling of social pressure: "I've only been to [the club] once this year. I'm really a loner, but I feel I have to go and be pleasant even though I don't want to." Another volunteered: "I think half the members go because they like it and half because they think it's a social necessity."[25]

People of the upper class often belong to clubs in several cities, creating a nationwide pattern of overlapping memberships. These overlaps provide further evidence for the social cohesion within the upper class. An indication of the nature and extent of this overlapping is revealed by our study of membership lists for 20 clubs in several major cities across the country, including the Links in New York, the Century Association in New York, the Duquesne in Pittsburgh, the Chicago in Chicago, the Pacific Union in San Francisco, and the California in Los Angeles. Using a clustering technique based on Boolean algebra, the study revealed there was sufficient overlap among 18 of the 20 clubs to form three regional groupings and a fourth group that provided a bridge between the two largest regional groups. The several dozen men who were in three or more of the clubs were especially important in creating the overall pattern. At the same time, the fact that these clubs often have from 1,000 to 2,000 members makes the percentage of overlap within this small number of clubs relatively small, ranging from a high of 20 to 30 percent between clubs in the same city to as low as 1 or 2 percent in clubs at opposite ends of the country.[26]

One of the most central clubs in this network, the Bohemian Club of San Francisco, is also the most unusual and widely known club of the upper class. Its annual two-week encampment in its 2,700-acre Bohemian Grove 75 miles north of San Francisco brings together the social elite, celebrities, and government officials for relaxation and entertainment. A description of this gathering provides the best possible insight into the role of clubs in uniting the upper class.[27]

The huge forest retreat called the Bohemian Grove was purchased by the club in the 1890s. Bohemians and their guests number anywhere from 1,500 to 2,000 for the three weekends in the encampment, which is always held during the last two weeks in July, when it almost never rains in northern California. However, there may be as few as 400 men in residence in the middle of the week, for most return to their homes and jobs after the weekends. During their stay the campers are treated to plays, symphonies, concerts, lectures, and political commentaries by entertainers, musicians, scholars, and government officials. They also trapshoot, canoe, swim, drop by the Grove art gallery, and take guided tours into the outer fringe of the mountain forest. But a stay at the Bohemian Grove is mostly a time for relaxation and drinking in the modest lodges, bunkhouses, and even teepees that fit unobtrusively into the landscape along the two or three macadam roads that join the few "developed" acres within the Grove. It is like a summer camp for the power elite and their entertainers.

The men gather in little camps of about 10 to 30 members during their stay. Each of the approximately 120 camps has its own pet name, such as Sons of Toil, Cave Man, Mandalay, Toyland, Owl's Nest, Hill Billies, and Parsonage. A group of men from Los Angeles named their camp Lost Angels, and the men in the Bohemian chorus call their camp Aviary. Some camps are noted for special drinks, brunches, or luncheons, to which they invite members from other camps. The camps are a fraternity system within the larger fraternity.

There are many traditional events during the encampment, including plays called the High Jinx and the Low Jinx. But the most memorable event, celebrated every consecutive year since 1880, is the opening ceremony, called the Cremation of Care. This ceremony takes place at the base of a 40-foot Owl Shrine constructed out of poured concrete and made even more resplendent by the mottled forest mosses that cover much of it. The Owl Shrine is only one of many owl symbols and insignias to be found in the Grove and the downtown clubhouse, for the owl was adopted early in the club's history as its mascot or totem animal.

The opening ceremony is called the Cremation of Care because it involves the burning of an effigy named Dull Care, who symbolizes the burdens and responsibilities that these busy Bohemians now wish to shed temporarily. More than 60 Bohemians take part in the ceremony as priests, acolytes, torch bearers, brazier bearers, boat-men and woodland voices. After many flowery speeches and a long conversation with Dull Care, the high priest lights the fire with the flame from the Lamp of Fellowship, located on the "Altar of Bohemia" at the base of the shrine. The ceremony, which has the same initiatory functions as those of any fraternal or tribal group, ends with fire-works, shouting, and the playing of "There'll Be a Hot Time in the Old Town Tonight." The attempt to create a sense of cohesion and solidarity among the assembled is complete.

As the case of the Bohemian Grove and its symbolic ceremonies rather dramatically illustrate, there seems to be a great deal of truth to the earlier-cited suggestion by Crane Brinton that clubs may have the function within the upper class that the clan or brotherhood has in tribal societies. With their restrictive membership policies, initia-tory rituals, private ceremonials, and great emphasis on tradition, clubs carry on the heritage of primitive secret societies. They create within their members an attitude of prideful exclusiveness that contributes greatly to an in-group feeling and a sense of fraternity within the upper class.

THE DEBUTANTE SEASON

The debutante season is a series of parties, teas, and dances, culminating in one or more grand balls. It announces the arrival of young women of the upper class into adult society with the utmost of formality and elegance. These highly expensive rituals, in which great attention is lavished on every detail of the food, decorations, and entertainment, have a long history in the upper class. Making their appearance in Philadelphia in 1748 and Charleston, South Carolina, in 1762, they vary only slightly from city to city across the country. They are a central focus of the Christmas social season just about everywhere, but in some cities debutante balls are held in the spring as well.

Dozens of people are involved in planning the private parties that most debutantes have before the grand ball. Parents, with the help of upper-class women who work as social secretaries and social consultants, spend many hours with dress designers, caterers, florists, decorators, band leaders, and champagne importers, deciding on just the right motif for their daughter's coming out. Most parties probably do not cost more than $15,000 to $25,000, but sometimes the occasion is made so extraordinary that it draws newspaper attention. In 1959 Henry Ford II spent $250,000 on a debutante party for one of his daughters, hiring a Paris designer to redo the Country Club of Detroit in an eighteenth-century château motif and flying in 2 million magnolia boughs from Mississippi to cover the walls of the corridor leading to the reception room. In 1965 a Texas oil and real estate family chartered a Braniff jet for a party that began in Dallas and ended with an all-night visit to the clubs in the French Quarter of New Orleans.[28]

The debutante balls themselves are usually sponsored by local social clubs. Sometimes there is an organization whose primary purpose is the selection of debutantes and the staging of the ball, such as the Saint Cecelia Society in Charleston, South Carolina, and the Allegro Club in Houston, Texas. Adding to the solemnity of the occasion, the selection of the season's debutantes is often made by the most prominent and visible upper-class males in the city, often through such secret societies as the Veiled Prophet in Saint Louis or the Mardi Gras Krewes in New Orleans.

Proceeds from the balls are usually given to a prominent local charity that is sponsored by members of the upper class. "Doing something for charity makes the participants feel better about spending," explains Mrs. Stephen Van Rensselear Strong, a social press agent in New York and herself a member of the upper class.[29] It also makes part of the expense of the occasion tax deductible.

Whatever the expense of the individual parties and teas, no cost is spared on the ball that officially introduces the several dozen 19- to-21-year-olds to their elders. Dressed in individually designed white gowns and wearing traditional long white gloves, they are treated to a party that is usually described in careful detail on the women's pages of the local paper. The account of the 1973 San Francisco Cotillion provides a typical example:

> On the red-carpeted stages, on which the girls were presented, large magnolia trees towered over pyramid topiary trees of ivy, which twinkled with tiny lights. Around the floor, pink-clothed tables held small arrangements of pink carnations, pink candles, and small yellow and white spider chrysanthemums.
>
> After the 10 o'clock presentation, a buffet was served to the approximately 1300 guests. The traditional dishes included Senegalese soup and cold consomme, oysters Rockefeller, Kirkpatrick and Casino, diced chicken saute, filet of beef, ham, cold decorated salmon, rice pilaf, various salads, coupe Mona Lisa, petit fours and French pastries.[30]

Evidence for the great traditional importance attached to the debut is to be found in the comments Ostrander received from women who thought the whole process unimportant but made their daughters go through it anyhow: "I think it's passé, and I don't care about it, but it's just something that's done," explained one woman. Another commented: "Her father wanted her to do it. We do have a family image to maintain. It was important to the grandparents, and I felt it was an obligation to her family to do it." When people begin to talk about doing something out of tradition or to uphold an image, suggests Ostrander, then the unspoken rules that dictate class-oriented behavior are being revealed.[31]

Despite the great importance placed upon the debut by upper-class parents, the debutante season came into considerable disfavor among young women as the social upheavals of the late 1960s and early 1970s reached their climax. Although enough young women participated to keep the tradition alive, the refusal to take part by a significant minority led to the cancellation of some balls and the curtailment of many others. Stories appeared on the women's pages across the country telling of debutantes who thought the whole process was "silly" or that the money should be given to a good cause.

By 1973, however, the situation began to change again, and by the mid-1970s things were back to normal.[32]

The decline of the debutante season and its subsequent resurgence in times of domestic tranquillity reveal very clearly that one of its latent functions is to help perpetuate the upper class from generation to generation. When the underlying values of the class were questioned by a few of its younger members, the institution went into decline. Attitudes toward such social institutions as the debutante ball are one indicator of whether or not adult members of the upper class have succeeded in insulating their children from the rest of society.

MARRIAGE AND FAMILY CONTINUITY

The institution of marriage is as important in the upper class as it is in any level of America society, and it does not differ greatly from other levels in its patterns and rituals. Only the exclusive site of the occasion and the lavishness of the reception distinguish upper-class marriages.

The prevailing wisdom within the upper class is that children should marry someone of their own social class. The women interviewed by Ostrander, for example, felt that marriage was difficult enough without differences in "interests" and "background," which seemed to be the code words for class in discussions of marriage. Marriages outside the class were seen as likely to end in divorce.[33]

The original purpose of the debutante season was to introduce the highly sheltered young women of the upper class to eligible marriage partners. It was an attempt to corral what Baltzell calls "the democratic whims of romantic love," which "often play havoc with class solidarity."[34] But the day when the debut could play such a role was long past even by the 1940s. The function of directing romantic love into acceptable channels was taken over by fraternities and sororities, bachelor and spinster clubs, and exclusive summer resorts.

However, in spite of parental concerns and institutionalized efforts to provide proper marriage partners, some upper-class people marry members of the upper-middle and middle classes. Although there are no completely satisfactory studies, what information is available suggests that members of the upper class are no more likely to marrry within their class than people of other social levels. The most frequently cited evidence on upper-class marriage patterns appears as part of biographical studies of prominent families. Though these studies demonstrate that a great many marriages take place within the class, and often between scions of very large fortunes, they also show that some marriages are to sons and daughters of middle-class professionals and managers. In any case, no systematic conclusions can be drawn from these examples.

Another source of evidence on this question is the wedding announcements that appear in major newspapers, but only those appearing in the *New York Times* have been examined by social scientists. In a study covering prominent wedding stories on the society pages on Sundays in June for the years 1962 and 1972, it was found that 70 percent of the grooms and 84 percent of the brides had attended a private secondary school. Two thirds of the weddings involved at least one participant who was listed in the *Social Register*, with both bride and groom listed in the *Social Register* in 24 percent of the cases.[35] However, those who marry far below their station may be less likely to have wedding announcements prominently displayed, so such studies must be interpreted with caution.

A study that used the *Social Register* as its starting point may be indicative of rates of intermarriage within the upper class, but it is very limited in its scope and therefore can only be considered suggestive. It began with a compilation of all the marriages listed in the Philadelphia *Social Register* for 1940 and 1960. Since the decision to list these announcements may be a voluntary one, a check of the marriage announcements in the *Philadelphia Bulletin* for those years was made to see if there were any marriages involving listees in the *Social Register* that had not been included, but none were found. One in every three marriages for 1940 and one in five for 1961 involved partners who were both listed in the *Social Register*. When private-school attendance and social club membership as well as the *Social Register* were used as evidence for upper-class standing, the rate of intermarriage averaged 50 percent for the two years. This figure is very similar to that for other social levels.[36]

The general picture for social class and marriage in the United States is suggested in a statistical study of neighborhoods and marriage patterns in the San Francisco area. Its results are very similar to the Philadelphia study using the *Social Register*. Of 80 grooms randomly selected from the highest-level neighborhoods, court records showed that 51 percent married brides of a comparable level. The rest married women from middle-level neighborhoods; only one or two married women from lower-level residential areas. Conversely, 63 percent of 81 grooms from the lowest-level neighborhoods married women from comparable areas, with under 3 percent having brides from even the lower end of the group of top neighborhoods. Completing the picture, most of the 82 men from middle-level areas married women from the same types of neighborhoods, but about 10 percent married into higher-level neighborhoods. Patterns of intermarriage, then, suggest both stability and some upward mobility through marriage into the upper class.[37]

Turning from marriage patterns, there is evidence that the continuity of families within the upper class is very great from generation to generation. This finding conflicts with the oft-repeated folk wisdom that there is a large turnover at the top of the American social ladder. Once in the upper class, families tend to stay there even as they are joined in each generation by new families and by middle-class brides and grooms who marry into their families. One study demonstrating this point began with a list of 12 families who were among the top wealth-holders in Detroit for 1860, 1892, and 1902. After demonstrating their high social standing as well as their wealth, it traced their Detroit-based descendants to 1970. Nine of the 12 families still had members in the Detroit social elite, and members of 6 families were directors of top corporations in the city. The study cast light on some of the reasons why the continuity is not even greater. One of the top wealth-holders of 1860 had only one child, who in turn had no children. Another family dropped out of sight after the six children of the original 1860 wealth-holder's only child went to court to divide the dwindling estate of $250,000 into six equal parts. A third family persisted into a fourth generation of four great-grand-daughters, all of whom married outside of Detroit.[38]

Comprehensive evidence on the issue of continuity was developed in a study of iron and steel manufacturers of the late nineteenth century. Using a directory of iron and steel manufacturing plants for the years 1874 to 1901 to identify 696 steel manufacturers in six midwestern cities, historian John Ingham studied their social origins as well as tracing their descendants into the mid-twentieth century. Seventy percent of the men in the sample were the sons of well-to-do businesspeople and another 13 percent were the sons of professional men. Only 10 percent were the sons of blue collar workers, and only 6 percent the sons of farmers. Although there are some variations from city to city, these overall findings are very similar to earlier studies on the social origins of nineteenth-century business leaders.

Tracing the families of the steel executives into the twentieth century, Ingham determined that they were listed in the *Social Register*, were members of the most exclusive social clubs, lived in elite neighborhoods, and sent their children to Ivy League universities. He concludes that "there has been more continuity than change among the business elites and upper classes in America," and he contrasts his results with the claims made by several generations

of impressionistic historians that there has been a decline of aristocracy, the rise of a new plutocracy, or a passing of the old order.[39]

It seems likely, then, that the American upper class is a mixture
of old and new members. There is both continuity and social mobility,
with the newer members being assimilated into the life-style of the
class through participation in the schools, clubs, and other social
institutions described in this chapter. There may be some tensions
between those newly arrived and those of established status, as
novelists and journalists love to point out, but what they have in
common soon outweighs their differences. This point is well demonstrated in the social affiliations and attitudes of highly successful
Jewish businessmen, who become part of the upper class as they rise
in the corporate community.[40]

THE PREOCCUPATIONS
OF THE UPPER CLASS

Members of the upper class do not spend all their time in social
activities. Contrary to stereotypes, most members of the upper class
are and have been hardworking people, even at the richest levels. In a
study of the 90 richest men for 1950, for example, Mills found that
only 26 percent were men of leisure.[41]

By far the most frequent preoccupation of men of the upper class
is business and finance. This point is most clearly demonstrated
through studying the occupations of boarding school alumni. A
classification of the occupations of a sample of the graduates of four
private schools—Saint Mark's, Groton, Hotchkiss, and Andover—for
the years 1906 and 1926 showed that the most frequent occupation for
all but the Andover graduates was some facet of finance and banking.
Others became presidents of medium-size businesses or practiced
corporation law with a large firm. Only a small handful went to work
as executives for major national corporations. Andover, with a more
open curriculum and a far greater number of scholarship students at
the time, produced many more people who ended up in middle
management, particularly in 1926, when 44 percent of the graduates
were in such positions. The second area of concentration for the
Andover alumni was as owners or presidents of medium-size businesses. Only 8 percent went into banking and finance, and only 4
percent into law.[42]

The business-oriented preoccupations of upper-class men is
demonstrated in greater detail in a study of the careers of all those
who graduated from Hotchkiss between 1940 and 1950. Using the
school's alumni files, one researcher followed the careers of 228

graduates from their date of graduation until 1970. Fifty-six percent of the sample were either bankers or business executives, with 80 of the 91 businessmen serving as president, vice-president, or partner in their firms. Another 10 percent of the sample were lawyers, mostly as partners in large firms closely affiliated with the business community. Outside the world of business, the most frequent occupations of the remaining one third of the Hotchkiss graduates studied were physician (7 percent), engineer (6 percent), and public official (3 percent).[43]

Although finance, business, and law are the most typical occupations of upper-class males, there is no absence of physicians, architects, museum officials, and other professional occupations. This fact was demonstrated most systematically in Baltzell's study of the Philadelphians listed in Who's Who in America for 1940; 39 percent of the Philadelphia architects and physicians listed in Who's Who for that year were also listed in the Social Register, as were 35 percent of the museum officials. These figures are close to the 51 percent for lawyers and the 42 percent for businessmen, although they are far below the 75 percent for bankers, clearly the most elite profession in Philadelphia at that time.[44]

Less systematic studies also suggest this wide range of professional occupations. Our classification of the occupations listed by Saint Paul's alumni in the spring 1965 issue of the alumni journal found 7 physicians, 7 academic scholars, and 4 authors in addition to the 20 financiers and 16 businessmen, which were once again the most frequent occupations. The remainder of the sample was divided among small numbers of ministers (5), government officials (4), private school teachers (4), military officers (2), architects (2), playwrights (1), and lawyers (1). Although this study can be considered no more than a set of examples, it is consistent with the findings of Baltzell on Philadelphia 25 years earlier.

The feminine half of the upper class has different preoccupations than those of men. Our study of a large sample of the upper-class women included in Who's Who in American Women for 1965 showed the most frequent activity of upper-class women to be that of civic worker or volunteer, which includes a wide range of welfare, cultural, and civic activities. Second on the list was author or artist followed by a career in journalism, where upper-class women are involved in both the management and writing of newspapers and magazines. Finally, women of the upper class were found in academic positions as teachers, administrators, and trustees at leading boarding schools and colleges for women.[45]

The most informative and intimate look at the preoccupations of the feminine half of the upper class is provided in Ostrander's interview study. It revealed the women to be people of both power and subservience, playing decision-making roles in numerous cultural and civic organizations, but also accepting traditional roles at home vis-a-vis their husbands and children. By asking the women to describe a typical day and to explain which activities were most important to them, Ostrander found that the role of community volunteer is a central preoccupation of upper-class women, having significance as a family tradition and as an opportunity to fulfill an obligation to the community. One elderly woman involved for several decades in both the arts and human services explained: "If you're privileged, you have a certain responsibility. This was part of my upbringing; it's a tradition, a pattern of life that my brothers and sisters do too."[46]

This volunteer role is institutionalized in the training programs and activities of a variety of service organizations, in particular the Junior League, founded at the turn of the century to contribute to the reforms of the Progressive Era. Designed for women between 20 and 40 years of age, the youngest members usually join shortly after their debuts. However, there are a great many upper-middle-class women, particularly in the smaller cities so prominent in the League structure since World War II, who join in their middle or late 20s. "Voluntarism is crucial and the Junior League is the quintessence of volunteer work," said one woman. "Everything the League does improves the situation but doesn't rock the boat. It fits into existing institutions."[47]

Quite unexpectedly, Ostrander also found that many of the women serving as volunteers, fund-raisers, and board members for charitable and civic organizations viewed their work as a protection of the American way of life against the further encroachment of government into areas of social welfare. Some even saw themselves as bulwarks against socialism. "There must always be people to do volunteer work," one said. "If you have a society where no one is willing, then you may as well have communism where it's all done by the government." Another commented: "It would mean that the government would take over, and it would all be regimented. If there are no volunteers, we would live in a completely managed society which is quite the opposite to our history of freedom." Another equated government support with socialism: "You'd have to go into government funds. That's socialism. The more we can keep independent and under private control, the better it is."[48]

Despite this emphasis on volunteer work, the women placed high value on family life. They arranged their schedules to be home when children came home from school (30 of the 38 had three or more children), and they emphasized that their primary concern was to provide a good home for their husbands. Several of them wanted to have greater decision-making power over their inherited wealth, but almost all of them wanted to be in the traditional roles of wife and mother, at least until their children were grown.

Not all men and women of the upper class fit the usual molds. It is these exceptions, when they come to public attention, who often are used by pluralists to claim that the upper class is not cohesive enough to be a ruling class. Indeed, some members of the upper class do become playboys and jet-setters who draw faded European royalty and entertainers into their worldwide party life, and incidentally provide leisure settings for working members of the upper class. Others turn to a bohemian life-style with an interest in music or writing that takes them away from their old haunts, and a few become critics of the upper class, often taking leadership roles within radical circles.

However, contrary to a few longstanding exceptions, the anecdotal evidence also suggests that many of the young rebels return to more familiar pathways. Lucy Cochrane, a daughter of upper-class Bostonians, emerged as a celebrity in the early 1940s because she became a dancer in the Ziegfeld Follies and then ran off to Mexico, where she posed in the nude for a portrait by Diego Rivera. By 1947, when she dropped from media attention, she had settled back into the upper class as the wife of a wealthy New Yorker, raising horses and dogs, tending several houses, and gaining attention in the 1970s for her beautiful gardens.[49] Walter Lippmann, the only son of an upper-class family in New York, was an enthusiastic socialist as a Harvard undergraduate and the secretary to the reform socialist mayor of Schenectady in 1912. By 1915 he was back to the life that had been waiting for him and went on to be one of the most respected opinion leaders in the upper class for a 40-year period as a columnist, author, and adviser to presidents.[50]

Our impressionistic evidence from a few individual cases suggests that even most of those who persist for a few years beyond college as social critics and radicals are gradually pushed back into their own class by their differences from members of other classes. Because they are unable to overcome the subtle effects of their socialization on their bearing and manner, there is often tension between them and their working-class allies, who become suspicious of their motives and envious of their backgrounds. In turn, the upper-class radicals become weary of being mistrusted and grow impatient with the hesitancy of the constituency they are trying to lead.

Numerous anecdotal examples also show that some members of the upper class even lead lives of failure, despite all the opportunities available to them. Although members of the upper class are trained for leadership and given every opportunity to develop feelings of self-confidence, there are some who fail in school, become involved with drugs and alcohol, or become mentally disturbed. Once again, however, this cannot be seen as evidence for a lack of cohesion in the upper class, for there are bound to be individual failures of this nature in any group.

Deviants and failures do exist within the upper class, then, but it seems likely that a majority of its male members are at work in business, finance, and corporate law, and that most of the female members are equally busy as civic volunteers and homemakers. Members of both sexes have plenty of time for clubs, vacations, and party going, but their major preoccupations are in the world of work.

THE WEALTH AND INCOME
OF THE UPPER CLASS

Whatever the precise occupations and preoccupations of specific members of the upper class, it is obvious that members of the upper class must have a considerable amount of money to afford the tuition at private schools, the fees at country clubs, and the very high expenses of an elegant social life. Just how much they have, however, is a difficult matter to determine, for the Internal Revenue Service does not release information on individuals and most people are not willing to volunteer details on this subject.

Direct questions about a person's money are frowned upon in America, even in the upper class. One young member of the upper class in Boston told an interviewer: "Money was never talked about. I still don't know how much the family is worth. I have no idea."[51] Nor are the adult members of the upper class likely to talk about their wealth or the distribution of wealth in general. After presenting figures on the wealth distribution, an upper-class society writer notes that "I have never heard a dinner conversation in which figures such as these have been discussed."[52] Instead, she reports, any conversation concerning money is more likely to concern the outrageous starting salaries of subway drivers, policemen, and other working people. Even people with millions of dollars are likely to deny they are rich if they are asked directly. This reaction is in part genuine, for they always know someone else who has much more money and makes them feel poor by comparison. This phenomenon is well known to social psychologists from studies of other social comparisons.

In considering the distribution of wealth and income in the United States, it must be stressed that the two distributions are different matters. The wealth distribution has to do with the concentration of ownership of marketable assets, which may include "such tangible things as land, buildings, machinery, raw materials, goods in process, and animals, and such intangible things as franchises, patent rights, copyrights, and good will."[53] The income distribution, on the other hand, has to do with the percentage of wages, dividends, interest, and rents paid out each year to individuals or families at various income levels. In theory, those who own a great deal may or may not have high incomes, depending on the returns they receive from their wealth, but in reality those at the very top of the wealth distribution also tend to have the highest incomes, mostly from dividends and interest.

Two different types of studies provide estimates of the distribution of wealth in the United States. The first, called the *estate-multipler method,* is based on studies of the estates of deceased individuals worth $60,000 or more, the figure at which inheritance taxes came into play for many decades. In this method, the estates of the deceased are treated as a sample of wealthy people. Estimates based on the death rates for the year are used to determine how wealth probably is distributed among the living. Studies utilizing this method suggest that just 0.5 percent of all people in the United States own from 20 to 25 percent of all wealth, and that the figure has remained relatively unchanged throughout the century.[54]

A study estimating the wealth distribution for 1962 by means of a detailed survey of a large sample of households led to very similar findings. In this study, the top 0.5 percent of "consumer units" (families and single individuals living alone) were found to have 25.8 percent of the wealth, a little higher than the finding from the estate-multipler method. The top 1 percent had 34 percent, the top 10 percent had 62 percent, and the top 30 percent held about 85 percent.[55]

Compared with the wealth distribution, much more is known about the income distribution. This is because there are yearly surveys of approximately 47,000 households by the Census Bureau, which are of use to government officials, economists, and businesspeople. These studies reveal considerable stability over the decades and slightly less concentration in the top few percent. Since the 1950s the top 5 percent of income earners, most of whom are wealthy to begin with, have received 14 to 16 percent of all money income in the United States.[56] There is only one study, however, that attempts to estimate the percentage of yearly income that goes to the very wealthy. In that study, for the year 1958, it was estimated that the top 1.5 percent of wealth-holders, those with assets of $60,000 or more, received 13 percent of the total income for that year. The percentage rose to 24 percent if the income that could have been realized from capital gains (increases in the value of stock) is included. The estimate is considered a conservative one for several reasons, including the allocation of all Social Security income to the lower 98.5 percent of wealth-holders.[57]

These figures on income distribution may underestimate concentration for several reasons. Most important, the Census Bureau studies found that the people who are most likely to have the highest incomes, well-educated or self-employed white males, are also the respondents most likely to decline to answer all questions. It is also likely that they underestimate their incomes from interest and dividends. When the Census Bureau compared its estimates for 1976 with aggregate figures on specific types of income that it obtained from other government agencies, it found that its study had included 97 percent of wages and salaries and 91 percent of Social Security payments, but only 53 percent of dividends and 42 percent of interest payments.[58] There is also the problem that reimbursements from expense accounts for meals, entertainment, and travel are not counted as income, and this amount, which is actually the same as income, can be considerable for top-level business executives. By the 1980s, it was estimated that executive perquisites added another one-third to corporate salaries.[59]

As noted earlier in this section, none of the studies on the wealth and income distribution include the names of individuals. This means studies have to be done to demonstrate that people of wealth and high income are in fact members of the upper class. The most detailed study of this kind is Baltzell's historical work on Philadelphia, which showed that the wealthiest people are also those who send their children to private schools, live in exclusive neighborhoods, and are listed in the *Social Register*. On the national level Baltzell reported that nine of the ten wealthiest financiers at the turn of the century had descendants in the *Social Register*, that over 75 percent of the wealthy families in Ferdinand Lundberg's 1937 classic, *America's Sixty Families*, had descendants in the *Social Register*, and that 87 of the wealthy men in Gustavus Myer's *History of the Great American Fortunes* also had descendants in those volumes.[60] Supplementing these findings, Mills found that at least one-half of the 90 richest men of 1900 had descendants in the *Social Register*, and our study of 90 corporation directors worth $10 million or more in 1960 found that 74 percent met criteria of upper-class membership.[61] However, the question has attracted little further research because the answer seems so obvious to most people.

There are newly rich people who are not yet assimilated into the upper class, and there are wealthy crime figures who may never be accepted. There are highly paid professionals, entertainers, and athletes who for a few years make more in a year than many members of the upper class. However, for the most part it is safe to conclude that the people of greatest wealth and highest income are part of—or are becoming part of— the upper class.

UPPER-CLASS INDICATORS

In order to study the involvement of upper-class people in the important economic, cultural, political, and governmental institutions of society, it is necessary to have indicators of upper-class standing. These indicators are in effect criteria by which it can be determined in a general way how many people in a given group, organization, or agency are members of the upper class. The development of upper-class indicators began with Baltzell's detailed historical work on the Philadelphia upper class, which established that a handful of private schools and clubs, along with the *Social Register*, were the most useful upper-class indicators for studies that had to rely on information in biographical sources rather than field observations or interviews. Building on the work of Baltzell, and using the earlier-discussed combination of statistical, questionnaire, and interview methods, our studies have extended the list of indicators to other schools, clubs, and social directories across the country.[62]

People are considered to be members of the upper class if they, their parents, their in-laws, or any of their siblings are listed in, belong to, or attended any of following:

Registers or Blue Books
The Social Register
Detroit *Social Secretary*
Houston *Social Register*
Los Angeles *Blue Book*
New Orleans *Social Register*
Seattle *Blue Book*

Coed and Boys' Schools
Asheville (Asheville, N.C.)
Buckley (New York, N.Y.)
Cate (Carpinteria, Calif.)
Catlin Gabel (Portland, Oreg.)
Choate (Wallingford, Conn.)
Country Day School (St. Louis, Mo.)
Cranbrook (Bloomfield Hills, Mich.)
Deerfield (Deerfield, Mass.)
Episcopal High (Alexandria, Va.)
Gilman (Baltimore, Md.)

Groton (Groton, Mass.)
Hill (Pottstown, Pa.)
Hotchkiss (Lakeville, Conn.)
Kent (Kent, Conn.)
Kingswood (Hartford, Conn.)
Lake Forest (Lake Forest, Ill.)
Lakeside (Seattle, Wash.)
Lawrenceville (Lawrenceville, N.J.)
Middlesex (Concord, Mass.)
Milton (Milton, Mass.)
Moses Brown (Providence, R.I.)
Pomfret (Pomfret, Conn.)
Ponahou (Honolulu, Hawaii)
Portsmouth Priority (Portsmouth, R.I.)
St. Andrew's (Middlebury, Del.)
St. Christopher's (Richmond, Va.)
St. George's (Newport, R.I.)
St. Mark's (Southborough, Mass.)
St. Paul's (Concord, N.H.)
Shattuck (Fairbault, Minn.)
Taft (Watertown, Conn.)
Thatcher (Ojai, Calif.)
University School (Cleveland, Ohio)
University School (Milwaukee, Wis.)
Webb (Bell Buckle, Tenn.)
Westminster (Atlanta, Ga.)
Woodberry Forest (Woodberry Forest, Va.)

Girls' Schools
Abbot Academy (Andover, Mass.)
Agnes Irwin (Wynnewood, Pa.)
Anna Head (Berkeley, Calif.)
Annie Wright (Tacoma, Wash.)
Ashley Hall (Charleston, S.C.)
Baldwin (Bryn Mawr, Pa.)
Beaver Country Day (Chestnut Hill, Mass.)
Berkeley Institute (Brooklyn, N.Y.)
Bishop's (La Jolla, Calif.)
Brearly (New York, N.Y.)
Brimmer's and May (Chestnut Hill, Mass.)
Brooke Hill (Birmingham, Ala.)
Bryn Mawr (Baltimore, Md.)
Chapin (New York, N.Y.)
Chatham Hall (Chatham, Va.)
Collegiate (Richmond, Va.)
Concord Academy (Concord, Mass.)
Convent of the Sacred Heart (New York, N.Y.)
Dalton (New York, N.Y.)
Dana Hall (Wellesley, Mass.)
Emma Willard (Troy, N.Y.)
Ethel Walker (Simsbury, Conn.)
Foxcroft (Middleburg, Va.)

Garrison Forest (Garrison, Md.)
Hathaway Brown (Cleveland, Ohio)
Hockaday (Dallas, Tex.)
Katherine Branson (Ross, Calif.)
Kent (Kent, Conn.)
Kent Place (Summit, N.J.)
Kingswood (Bloomfield Hills, Mich.)
Kinkaid (Houston, Tex.)
Lake Forest Country Day (Lake Forest, Ill.)
Latin School of Chicago (Chicago, Ill.)
Laurel (Cleveland, Ohio)
Lenox (New York, N.Y.)
Louise S. McGehee (New Orleans, La.)
Madeira (Greenway, Va.)
Marlborough (Los Angeles, Calif.)
Mary Institute (St. Louis, Mo.)
Marymount Secondary (Tarrytown, N.Y.)
Master's (Dobbs Ferry, N.Y.)
Milwaukee Downer Seminary (Milwaukee, Wis.)
Miss Hall's (Pittsfield, Mass.)
Miss Hewitt's (New York, N.Y.)
Miss Porter's (Farmington, Conn.)
Mt. Vernon Seminary (Washington, D.C.)
Oldfield's (Glencoe, Md.)
Packer Collegiate (Brooklyn, N.Y.)
Radford (El Paso, Tex.)
Rosemary Hall (Greenwich, Conn.)
Roycemore (Evanston, Ill.)
Salem Academy (Winston-Salem, N.C.)
Shipley (Bryn Mawr, Pa.)
Spence (New York, N.Y.)
St. Agnes Episcopal (Alexandria, Va.)
St. Catherine's (Richmond, Va.)
St. Katherine's (Davenport, Iowa)
St. Mary's Hall (San Antonio, Tex.)
St. Nicholas (Seattle, Wash.)
St. Timothy's (Stevenson, Md.)
Stuart Hall (Staunton, Va.)
Walnut Hill (Natick, Mass.)
Westminster (Atlanta, Ga.)
Westover (Middlebury, Conn.)
Westridge (Pasadena, Calif.)
Winsor (Boston, Mass.)

Country and Men's Clubs

Arlington (Portland, Oreg.)
Bohemian (San Francisco, Calif.)
Boston (New Orleans, La.)
Brook (New York, N.Y.)
Burlingame Country Club (San Francisco, Calif.)
California (Los Angeles, Calif.)
Casino (Chicago, Ill.)

Century (New York, N.Y.)
Chagrin Valley Hunt (Cleveland, Ohio)
Charleston (Charleston, S.C.)
Chicago (Chicago, Ill.)
Cuyamuca (San Diego, Calif.)
Denver (Denver, Colo.)
Detroit (Detroit, Mich.)
Eagle Lake (Houston, Tex.)
Everglades (Palm Beach, Calif.)
Hartford (Hartford, Conn.)
Hope (Providence, R.I.)
Idlewild (Dallas, Tex.)
Knickerbocker (New York, N.Y.)
Links (New York, N.Y.)
Maryland (Baltimore, Md.)
Milwaukee (Milwaukee, Wis.)
Minneapolis (Minneapolis, Minn.)
New Haven Lawn Club (New Haven, Conn.)
Pacific Union (San Francisco, Calif.)
Philadelphia (Philadelphia, Pa.)
Piedmont Driving (Atlanta, Ga.)
Piping Rock (New York, N.Y.)
Racquet Club (St. Louis, Mo.)
Rainier (Seattle, Wash.)
Richmond German (Richmond, Va.)
Rittenhouse (Philadelphia, Pa.)
River (New York, N.Y.)
Rolling Rock (Pittsburgh, Pa.)
Saturn (Buffalo, N.Y.)
St. Cecelia (Charleston, S.C.)
St. Louis County Club (St. Louis, Mo.)
Somerset (Boston, Mass.)
Union (Cleveland, Ohio)
Woodhill Country Club (Minneapolis, Minn.)

Women's Clubs
Mt. Vernon Club (Baltimore, Md.)
Society of Colonial Dames
Sulgrave (Washington, D.C.)
Sunset (Seattle, Wash.)
Vincent (Boston, Mass.)
Acorn (Philadelphia, Pa.)
Chilton (Boston, Mass.)
Colony (New York, N.Y.)
Fortnightly (Chicago, Ill.)
Friday (Chicago, Ill.)

As noted in the first chapter, no indicators in the social sciences are perfect, and these indicators of upper-class standing are no exception. As Baltzell emphasizes, constructing any set of indicators involves "simplifications." Indicators must be seen as "only a convenient tool which is constructed to approximate" the concept being studied.[63] In this particular instance, their usefulness is primarily in determining the general involvement of upper-class people in a group or organization, not in establishing with certainty whether any given individual is or is not a member of the upper class. When applied to individuals, the indicators are subject to two different kinds of errors that tend to cancel each other out in group data.

"False positives" are those people who qualify as members of the upper class according to the indicators even though further investigation would show that they are not "really" members. Scholarship students at private secondary schools are one example of a false positive. Honorary and performing members of such clubs as the Bohemian Club, who usually are members of the middle class, are another important type of "false positive."

"False negatives" are people who do not seem to meet any of the criteria of upper-class standing but are in fact members of the upper class. Surprisingly, such people probably are much more prevalent in studies of the upper class than are false positives. This is due to the fact that researchers are dependent upon published biographical sources and newspapers that may or may not include the necessary information on the person's schools and clubs. Private schools are especially underreported. Prominent political figures of the past such as Averell Harriman, Adlai Stevenson, John F. Kennedy, and John V. Lindsay never listed their private secondary schools in *Who's Who in America*, for example, and George Bush, Vice-President during the Reagan administration, removed his from the 1980–1981 edition. More generally, our study of 168 Hotchkiss alumni listed in *Who's Who in America* for 1968–1969 found that 37 percent did not list their graduation from that school.[64] Similar findings are reported in a study of corporate officers and directors listed in *Who's Who in America*, 1976–1977. Of 177 executives and directors on the alumni lists of 11 high-prestige private schools, 55 percent did not list their private school affiliation in *Who's Who in America*.[65]

Membership in social clubs may also go unreported. Neither President Ronald Reagan nor Vice-President Bush ever listed the fact of his membership in the Bohemian Club in *Who's Who in America* or other standard biographical sources. But they are not the only Bohemians who omit this information. Of the 326 Bohemian Club members listed in *Who's Who in America* for 1980–1981, 29 percent did not include this affiliation.

There are other problems that produce false negatives. Social registers and social directories exist for only a relative handful of cities, and there are some people, such as those mentioned in the earlier section on the *Social Register*, who choose not to be included for the cities that do have such directories. Then, too, a substantial number of people prefer to keep their children close to home in small private schools that are little known and hardly ever listed in standard biographical sources. In a few exclusive neighborhoods the suburban high schools are considered quite adequate for upper-class children, and only more subtle cues, such as debutante parties, socially separate the upper-middle from the upper class. Finally, some upper-class people belong only to small, specialized clubs for fox hunting or horse showing, which are not uncovered in statistical attempts to establish upper-class indicators.

None of these points casts any doubt on the usefulness of the indicators, however. They only show that the indicators must be used with caution. Moreover, these points all raise interesting empirical questions that are deserving of systematic studies. Why are scholarship students sought by some private schools, and are such students likely to become part of the upper class? Why aren't private schools and clubs listed in biographical sources by some members of the upper class? Why are some middle-class people taken into upper-class clubs? Why do some upper-class people decline to be listed in a social directory? Merely to ask these questions is to suggest the complex social and psychological reality that lies beneath this seemingly dry catalogue of upper-class indicators.

These indicators are the beginning, not the end, of sociological studies of the upper class. They could be expanded greatly by a computerized analysis of all the major biographical sources using the statistical technique of contingency analysis. They could be made even more accurate by assigning weights to each indicator through factor analysis or discriminate analysis. However, until a mathematical sociologist develops a deep interest in research on power, they are more than adequate for most studies of the upper class.

CONCLUSION

The evidence in this chapter suggests that there is an interacting and intermarrying upper social stratum or social elite in America that is distinctive enough in its institutions, source and amount of income, and life-style to be called an "upper class." This upper class makes up about 0.5 percent of the population, a rough estimate that is based upon the number of students attending independent private schools, the number of listings in past *Social Registers* for several cities, and detailed interview studies in Kansas City and Boston.[66]

Not everyone in this nationwide upper class knows everyone else, but everybody knows somebody who knows someone in other areas of the country thanks to a common school experience, a summer at the same resort, or membership in the same social club. With the social institutions described in this chapter as the under-girding, the upper class at any given historical moment consists of a complex network of overlapping social circles that are knit together by the members they have in common and by the numerous signs of equal social status that emerge from a similar life-style. Viewed from the standpoint of social psychology, the upper class is made up of innumerable face-to-face small groups that are constantly changing in theircompositionas people move from one social setting to another.

Research work in both sociology and social psychology demonstrates that constant interaction in small-group settings leads to the social cohesion that is considered to be an important dimension of a social class.[67] This social cohesion does not in and of itself demonstrate that members of the upper class are able to agree among themselves on general issues of economic and government policy. But it is important to stress that social cohesion is one of the factors that makes it possible for policy coordination to develop. Indeed, research in social psychology demonstrates that members of socially cohesive groups are eager to reach agreement on issues of common concern to them. They are more receptive to what other members are saying, more likely to trust each other, and more willing to compromise, which are no small matters in any collection of human beings trying to get something accomplished.[68]

The more extravagant social activities of the upper class—the debutante balls, the expensive parties, the jet-setting to spas and vacation spots all over the world, the involvement with exotic entertainers—are often viewed by pluralists and Marxists alike as superfluous trivialities best left to society page writers. However, there is reason to believe that these activities play a role both in solidifying the upper class and in maintaining the class structure. Within the class, these occasions provide an opportunity for members to show each other that they are similar to each other and superior to the average citizen. As political scientist Gabriel Almond suggested in his 1941 study of the New York upper class and its involvement in city politics: "The elaborate private life of the plutocracy serves in considerable measure to separate them out in their own consciousness as a superior, more refined element."[69] Then, too, the values upon which the class system is based are conveyed to the rest of the population in this conspicuous consumption. Such activities make clear that there is a gulf between members of the upper class and ordinary citizens, reminding everyone of the hierarchical nature of the society. Social extravanganzas bring home to everyone that there are great rewards for success, helping to stir up the personal envy that can be a goad to competitive striving.

In sociological terms, the upper class comes to serve as a "reference group." Sociologist Harold Hodges, in a discussion of his findings concerning social classes in the suburban areas south of San Francisco, expresses the power of the upper class as a reference group in the following way: "Numerically insignificant—less than one in every 500 Peninsula families is listed in the pages of the *Social Register*—the upper class is nonetheless highly influential as a 'reference group': a membership to which many aspire and which infinitely more consciously or unconsciously imitate."[70]

Exhibiting high social status, in other words, is a way of exercising power. It is a form of power rooted in fascination and enchantment. It operates by creating respect, envy, and deference in others. Considered less important than force or economic power by social scientists who regard themselves as tough-minded and realistic, its role as a method of control in modern society goes relatively unnoticed despite the fact that power was originally in the domain of the sacred and the magical.[71]

Whatever the importance that is attached to prestige and social status as mechanisms of power, this chapter has demonstrated the power of the upper class through the disproportionate amount of wealth and income that its members possess. As argued in the previous chapter, such disparities are evidence for class power if it is assumed that wealth and income are highly valued in American society. However, the case for the hypothesis that the American upper class is a ruling class will not rest solely on reference group power and inequalities in the wealth and income distributions. The following chapters will present other types of evidence for the power of this small tip of the social hierarchy.

NOTES

1. E. Digby Baltzell, *Philadelphia Gentlemen: The Making of a National Upper Class* (Glencoe, Ill.: Free Press, 1958). See also his *The Protestant Establishment*. (New York: Random House, 1964).
2. G. William Domhoff, *The Higher Circles* (New York: Random House, 1970), pp. 11–14.
3. Charles Osgood, "The Representation Model and Relevant Research Methods," in *Trends in Content Analysis*; I. de Sola Pool ed. (Urbana, Ill.: University of Illinois Press, 1959), pp. 55–78.
4. Domhoff, *Higher Circles*, pp. 14–17.
5. Richard P. Coleman and Bernice L. Neugarten, *Social Status in the City* (San Francisco: Jossey-Bass, 1971), chapters 2 and 6.
6. Baltzell, *Philadelphia Gentlemen*, pp. 33–41; Milton Bracker, "The Social Register Explains Its Policy on 'Dropping' Listings," *New York Times*, April 7, 1963, p. E-120.

7. Dee Wedemeyer, "Bowing to a Mobile Society, the Social Register Consolidates," *New York Times*, October 31, 1976, p. 66.

8. Ibid.

9. Gary Tamkins, "Being Special: A Study of the Upper Class" (Ph.D. diss., Northwestern University, 1974), pp. 15–18.

10. E. Digby Baltzell, "'Who's Who in America' and 'The Social Register'," in *Class, Status, and Power*, ed. Reinhard Bendix and Seymour M. Lipset, 2d ed. (New York: Free Press, 1966), p. 272.

11. Bracker, "Social Register Explains Its Policy," p. E-120.

12. Randall Collins, "Functional and Conflict Theories of Educational Stratification," *American Sociological Review* 36 (1971), p. 1010.

13. Baltzell, *Philadelphia Gentlemen*, p. 339.

14. Susan Ostrander, "A Study of Upper Class Women" (book manuscript to be published by Temple University Press, 1984) p. 174.

15. Steven B. Levine, "The Rise of the American Boarding Schools" (senior honors thesis, Harvard University, 1978), pp. 5–6.

16. "Boys' Schools," *Fortune*, January 1936.

17. Erving Goffman, *Asylums* (Chicago: Aldine, 1961).

18. Michael Gordon, "Changing Patterns of Prep School Placements," *Pacific Sociological Review*, Spring 1969; Jack Trumpbour, "Private Schools" (research memo, 1980).

19. Peter J. Nelligan, "The Cate School and the Upper Class" (term paper, University of California at Santa Barbara, 1971).

20. G. William Domhoff, "The Women's Page as a Window on the Ruling Class," in *Hearth and Home: Images of Women in the Mass Media*, ed. Gaye Tuchman, Arlene K. Daniels, and James Benet (New York: Oxford University Press, 1978).

21. C. Wright Mills, *The Power Elite* (New York: Oxford University Press, 1956), p. 67.

22. Baltzell, *Philadelphia Gentlemen*, p. 373.

23. Richard P. Coleman and Lee Rainwater, *Social Standing in America* (New York: Basic Books, 1978), p. 144.

24. Sophy Burnham, *The Landed Gentry* (New York: G. P. Putnam's Sons, 1978).

25. Ostrander, "A Study of Upper Class Women," p. 204.

26. Philip Bonacich and G. William Domhoff, "Latent Classes and Group Membership," *Social Networks* 3 (1981). The analysis also includes policy groups of the kind that will be discussed in chapter 4. For an earlier analysis of this matrix using a technique developed by Bonacich that is based on matrix algebra, see G. William Domhoff, "Social Clubs, Political Groups, and Corporations: A Network Study of Ruling-Class Cohesiveness," *The Insurgent Sociologist*, Spring 1975.

27. G. William Domhoff, *The Bohemian Grove and Other Retreats* (New York: Harper & Row, 1974); G. William Domhoff, "Politics among the Redwoods," *The Progressive*, January 1981.

28. Gay Pauley, "Coming-out Party: It's Back in Style," *Los Angeles Times*, March 13, 1977, section 4, p. 22; "Debs Put Party on Jet," *San Francisco Chronicle*, December 18, 1965, p. 2.

29. Pauley, "Coming-out Party."

30. "A Radiant Cotillion," *San Francisco Chronicle*, December 22, 1973, p. 14.

31. Susan Ostrander, "Upper-Class Women: Class Consciousness as Conduct and Meaning," in *Power Structure Research*, ed. G. William Domhoff (Beverly Hills, Calif.: Sage Publications, 1980), pp. 93–94; Ostrander, "A Study of Upper Class Women," pp. 183–188.

32. "The Debut Tradition: A Subjective View of What It's All About," *New Orleans Times-Picayune*, August 29, 1976, section 4, p. 13; Tia Gidnick, "On Being 18 in '78: Deb Balls Back in Fashion," *Los Angeles Times*, November 24, 1978, Part 4, p. 1; Virginia Lee Warren, "Many Young Socialites Want Simpler Debutante Party, or None," *New York Times*, July 2, 1972, p. 34; Mary Lou Loper, "The Society Ball: Tradition in an Era of Change," *Los Angeles Times*, October 28, 1973, Part 4, p.1.

33. Ostrander, "A Study of Upper Class Women," p. 169.

34. Baltzell, *Philadelphia Gentlemen*, p. 26.

35. Paul M. Blumberg and P. W. Paul, "Continuities and Discontinuities in Upper-Class Marriages," *Journal of Marriage and the Family*, February 1975; David L. Hatch and Mary A. Hatch, "Criteria of Social Status as Derived from Marriage Announcements in the New York Times," *American Sociological Review*, August 1947.

36. Lawrence Rosen and Rober R. Bell, "Mate Selection in the Upper Class," *Sociological Quarterly*, Spring 1966. I supplemented the original study by adding the information on schools.

37. Robert C. Tryon, "Identification of Social Areas by Cluster Analysis: A General Method with an Application to the San Francisco Bay Area," *University of California Publications in Psychology* 8 (1955); Robert C. Tryon, "Predicting Group Differences in Cluster Analysis: The Social Areas Problem" *Multivariate Behavioral Research* 2 (1967).

38. T. D. Schuby, "Class Power, Kinship, and Social Cohesion: A Case Study of a Local Elite," *Sociological Focus* 8, no. 3 (August 1975), pp. 243–255; T. D. Schuby, "The Divine Right of Property: An Analysis of the Transmission of Positional Power by the Established Upper Socio-Economic Class of Detroit, 1860–1970" (Masters thesis, Wayne State University, 1974).

39. John Ingham, *The Iron Barons* (Westport, Conn.: Greenwood Press, 1978), pp. 230–231.

40. Richard L. Zweigenhaft and G. William Domhoff, *Jews in the Protestant Establishment* (New York: Praeger, 1982).

41. Mills, *Power Elite*, p. 108.

42. Levine, "Rise of the American Boarding Schools," pp. 128–130.

43. Christopher F. Armstrong, "Privilege and Productivity: The Cases of Two Private Schools and Their Graduates" (Ph.D. diss., University of Pennsylvania, 1974), pp. 162–163. (The second school in Armstrong's study was Putney, a much newer, smaller, and more liberal school in Vermont.)

44. Baltzell, *Philadelphia Gentlemen*, pp. 51–65.

45. Domhoff, *Higher Circles*, pp. 41–43.

46. Ostrander, "A Study of Upper Class Women," p. xx.

47. Ibid., p. 56; Domhoff, *Higher Circles*, pp. 39–41.

48. Ostrander, "Upper-Class Women," p. 84; Ostrander, "A Study of Upper Class Women," pp. 100–1.

49. Sally Quinn, "C. Z. Guest: The Rich Fight Back," *Post*, May 1, 1977, p. M-1; Cleveland Amory, *The Proper Bostonians* (New York: Dutton, 1947), p. 347.

50. Ronald Steel, *Walter Lippman and the American Century* (Boston: Little, Brown, 1980).

51. Tamkins, "Being Special," p. 60.

52. Burnham, *Landed Gentry*, p. 205.

53. Robert Lampman, *The Share of Top Wealth-Holders in National Wealth* (Princeton, N.J.: Princeton University Press, 1962), p. 2.

54. Ibid., p. 24; James D. Smith and Stephen D. Franklin, "The Concentration of Personal Wealth, 1922–1969," *American Economic Review*, May 1974, p. 166.

55. Dorothy S. Projector and Gertrude S. Weiss, *Survey of Financial Characteristics of Consumers* (Washington, D.C.: Board of Governors of the Federal Reserve System, 1966).

56. Jonathan H. Turner and Charles E. Stains, *Inequality: Privilege and Poverty in America* (Santa Monica, Calif: Goodyear, 1976), p. 51, table 2.

57. James D. Smith, "An Estimate of the Income of the Very Rich," *Papers in Quantitative Economics* (Lawrence, Kans.: University of Kansas Press, 1968).

58. "Income Distribution: Whistling in the Dark," *Dollars and Sense*, no. 29 (September 1977).

59. Gabriel Kolko, *Wealth and Power in America* (New York: Praeger, 1962); Paul Blumberg, "Another Day, Another $3,000," *Dissent* 25 (1978); Mark Green, "Richer Than All Their Tribe," *The New Republic*, January 6–13, 1982; "Perks for Executives Losing Their Luster," *San Francisco Examiner*, July 5, 1982, p. C-3.

60. Baltzell, *Philadelphia Gentlemen*, pp. 36–40.

61. Mills, *Power Elite*, p. 117; G. William Domhoff, *Who Rules America?* (Englewood Cliffs, N.J.: Prentice-Hall, 1967), p. 47.

62. Domhoff, *Higher Circles*, chapter 1, for details and qualifications.

63. Baltzell, *Philadelphia Gentlemen*, p. 44.

64. Domhoff, *Higher Circles*, p. 31.

65. Michael Useem, personal communication, September 26, 1979.

66. Domhoff, *Who Rules America?* pp. 7n–8n; "Private Schools Search for a New Social Role," *National Observer*, August 26, 1968, p. 5; Coleman and Rainwater, *Social Standing in America*, p. 148. For a summary of many studies that concludes that "Capital S Society" in the United States includes "probably no more than four-tenths of one percent in large cities, and even a smaller proportion in smaller communities," see Coleman and Neugarten, *Social Status in the City*, p. 270.

67. Domhoff, *Bohemian Grove*, pp. 89–90, for a summary of this research.

68. Dorwin Cartwright and Alvin Zander, *Group Dynamics* (New York: Harper & Row, 1960), p. 89; Albert J. Lott and Bernice E. Lott, "Group Cohesiveness as Interpersonal Attraction," *Psychological Bulletin* 64 (1965): 291–296; Michael Argyle, *Social Interaction* (Chicago: Aldine, 1969), pp. 220–223.

69. Gabriel Almond, "Plutocracy and Politics in New York City: (Ph.D. diss., University of Chicago, 1941), p. 108.

70. Harold M. Hodges, Jr., "Peninsula People: Social Stratification in a Metropolitan Complex," in *Education and Society*, ed. Warren Kallenbach and Harold M. Hodges,Jr. (Columbus, Ohio: Merrill, 1963), p. 414.

71. See Norman O. Brown, *Life Against Death* (London: Routledge & Kegan Paul, 1959), pp. 242, 249–252, for a breathtaking argument on the roots of power in the sacred and the psychological. For one attempt to apply the argument to the class structure, see G. William Domhoff, "Historical Materialism, Cultural Determinism, and the Origin of the Ruling Classes," *Psychoanalytical Review*, no. 2 (1969). For a discussion that rightly announces itself as "the first extensive treatise on prestige as a social control system," see William J. Goode, *The Celebration of Heroes: Prestige as a Social Control System* (Berkeley, Calif.: University of California Press, 1978).

3

The Control
of the
Corporate
Community

INTRODUCTION

Most sectors of the American economy are dominated by a relative handful of large corporations. These corporations, in turn, are linked in a variety of ways to create a corporate community. At an economic level, the ties within the corporate community are manifested in ownership of common stock on the part of both families and other corporations, as well as in joint ventures among corporations and in the common sources of bank loans that most corporations share. At a more sociological level, the corporate community is joined together by the use of the same legal, accounting, and consulting firms and by the similar experiences of executives working in the bureaucratic structure of a large organization. Then too, the large corporations come together as a business community because they share the same values and goals—in particular, the profit motive. Finally, and not least, the common goals of the corporations lead them to have common enemies in the labor movement and middle-class reformers, which gives them a further sense of a shared identity.

It will be the purpose of this chapter to demonstrate that the most important corporations, commercial banks, investment banks, and law firms at the heart of this corporate community are controlled by members of the upper class and that the corporate community is therefore the primary financial basis for the upper class. Although

56

information presented in the previous chapter showed that upper-class people are heavily involved in financial and business pursuits, such information does not demonstrate automatically that members of the upper class are leaders in the corporate community. It may be that they are involved in smaller businesses, less important sectors of the economy, or in less important positions in large corporations.

In fact, there are a great many pluralists among American social scientists who deny that members of the upper class have control positions within the corporate community. They believe that the growth of the corporation has led to the dispersal of stock ownership on the one hand and the rise in importance of highly trained professional managers with no class allegiance on the other. There has been a "breakup of family capitalism" in the often quoted words of sociologist Daniel Bell, a "separation of ownership and control," in the even more frequently cited words of lawyer A. A. Berle, Jr., and economist Gardner Means.[1] According to this view, the upper class continues to exist as a high-status social group due to dividends from general stock ownership, but this upper class has lost its community of economic interest and its power now that its members no longer control major businesses. By way of contrast, managers of the large corporations are said to have power without property.

The idea that the upper class is cut off from a determinate role in the corporate community is one of the major objections to the claim that the upper class is a ruling class. In order to deal with this issue, this chapter will present four types of information to show that (1) members of the upper class own a majority of all privately held corporate stock in the United States; (2) many large stockholders and stockholding families continue to be involved in the direction of major corporations; (3) members of the upper class are disproportionately represented on the boards of large corporations in general; and (4) the professional managers of middle-level origins who rise to the top of the corporations are assimilated into the upper class both socially and economically and share the values of upper-class owners.

THE CONCENTRATION
OF STOCK OWNERSHIP

It is often emphasized in advertising campaigns that there are many millions of stockholders in the United States. In the 1950s the New York Stock Exchange publicized the large number of stockholders by calling the system "people's capitalism," and in the 1960s and 1970s individual companies ran magazine and television advertising that included information on their tens of thousands of stockholders.

During the late 1970s the stocks owned by pension funds were sometimes included in these claims, swelling the number of worker-owners higher than ever before. Management consultant Peter Drucker went so far as to say that the "unseen revolution" of pension fund socialism had brought to America "a more radical shift in ownership than Soviet communism," a claim that was pointed out to be quite inaccurate by economists and lawyers. A pension fund is only a promise to pay a certain amount of money to people of a certain age after a certain number of years of work, not ownership of stock by workers by which they can reap the benefit of any appreciation in its value or exercise its voting power to affect corporate policy.[2]

Whatever the actual number of stockholders, systematic studies show that most of them own very little stock. Robert Lampman's studies using the estate-multiplier method for six different years between 1922 and 1953 estimated that the top 1 percent of all adults held from 61.5 to 76 percent of all privately held stock. Using the same method, James D. Smith found the percentage to be 51 percent for the top 1 percent in 1969.[3] Smith's work also demonstrates that stock is even more dramatically concentrated within the hands of a few thousand major owners. One-twentieth of 1 percent of American adults have one-fifth of the corporate stock, and 0.2 percent have one-third of it. Sociologist Maurice Zeitlin makes this concentration more graphic by pointing out that "the Rose Bowl's 104,696 seats would still be half empty if only every American who owns $1 million or more in corporate stock came to cheer."[4]

Research employing other methods leads to comparable results. A study using stock portfolios obtained from a sample of wealthy individuals came to the conclusion that just 0.2 percent of all "spending units" (families, generally speaking) held 65 to 71 percent of the stock in the early 1950s. This figure is very close to Lampman's estimate of 76 percent for the top 1 percent.[5] The household survey for 1962 that was cited in the previous chapter estimated that the top 1 percent of wealth-holders owned 62 percent of all publicly held corporate stock; the top 5 percent had 86 percent and the richest 20 percent held 97 percent.[6] Similarly, a study utilizing random samples of individual income tax returns obtained from the Internal Revenue Service for 1960 and 1971 found that the 1 percent of families with the highest income controlled 51 percent of the market value of all stock owned by families. There was virtually no change in concentration over the eleven-year period.[7]

These different estimates vary somewhat due to the fact they employ different data bases, and they may underestimate the degree of concentration because of the difficulty in obtaining solid information. But they all make the important point that the distribution of stock ownership is even more highly concentrated than the wealth distribution in general. Among all types of assets studied by Lampman and others, only the ownership of tax-free state and local bonds is more concentrated in the hands of the rich than corporate stock. In terms of privately held stock, Mills seems to be correct that "at the very most, 0.2% or 0.3% of the adult population own the bulk, the pay-off shares, of the corporate world."[8]

However, this concentration of stock ownership within the upper class in general does not answer the question of corporate control satisfactorily. It may be that the stock is widely dispersed within the class as a whole, leading to a situation where no one family or group of investors could use its ownership of stock to influence or replace management. It therefore becomes necessary to consider the question of ownership and control more closely, for what has been demonstrated so far only shows that upper-class ownership of corporate stock may act as a general constraint upon top executives.

OWNERSHIP AND CONTROL

The control of a corporation, generally speaking, is demonstrated in three different ways. The first is the ability to replace top management. The second is the ability to maintain active involvement on the board of directors of the corporation. The third is the ability to have an influential part in major decisions concerning such matters as mergers, acquisitions, and large-scale changes in the growth and profit strategies of the corporation.

Except for the top several hundred publicly held corporations, there is every reason to believe that the relationship between ownership and control is very close by these criteria. This is obviously the case for hundreds of very large corporations that are privately owned by a family or group of families. The size and extent of such corporations is often overlooked in discussions of the modern corporation. In 1976 *Forbes* estimated that there were over 350 such companies with sales above $100 million a year.[9] Then, too, in some manufacturing industries that are less concentrated, such as printing, furniture, and clothing, privately held firms account for over two-thirds of sales, and privately held firms are even more important in such nonmanufacturing sectors as wholesaling, retailing, and construction.[10] Moreover, the close relationship between ownership and control also holds for many large publicly held corporations that are just below the 200 or 300 largest firms; in most such firms, large percentages of stock are held by a few owners who also serve as directors and top managers.

The problem of the relationship between ownership and control thus arises only for the very largest of corporations in the corporate community. Little direct information on their owners was available between 1938, when a thorough government study was conducted, and the 1970s, when new government studies and improvements in the laws on the reporting of ownership information again made systematic analysis possible. For the 30-year period between, studies by pluralists that took at face value the meager information provided by official sources often concluded that the role of big owners within corporations was declining. This conclusion could not be shaken by the many examples to the contrary that would emerge in the business press from time to time.

However, even within the large corporations where no large owners seem apparent at first glance, there are ways in which families or wealthy individuals in fact continue to play significant roles. The most important of these methods are the family office and the holding company.

The Family Office

A family office is most often an informal entity through which members of a family or group of families agree to pool some of their resources in order to hire people to provide them with advice on investments, charitable giving, and even political donations in some cases. Family offices often handle all financial transactions and legal matters as well. Journalist Shelby White, one of the few people to inquire about these offices at any length, writes that "to a large extent, the wealthy families of America have managed their money by setting up private offices, which then take care of family finances from cradle to grave: activating trusts, dispensing allowances to the younger generations, helping obtain divorces for older family members, and ultimately, managing their estates." However, her strongest emphasis is on the office as a cohesive force in keeping the family a significant economic unit:

> But most of all, family offices have served as a unifying force, keeping the money intact as the families have moved out of the entrepreneurial, risk-taking businesses that formed the basis of the wealth. Without a central office, the fortune would lose its power as it was dispersed over generations. Though each member of a family might be worth several million dollars, it is the collective use of the money that gives the offices the leverage to buy companies, create tax shelters and invest in oil drilling, real estate and the myriad of other ventures favored by the very rich.[11]

It is likely that there are at least several hundred family offices across the country, but no reliable estimate is available. Only a few offices have been studied in any detail. One, that of the Phipps family, heirs of a Pittsburgh steel baron, became known to journalists in the 1960s because one of the founder's grandsons brought suit against the rest of the family and the office for allegedly mismanaging a family holding company and family trusts.[12] Another, that of the descendants of John D. Rockefeller, Jr., was studied by physicist Charles Schwartz as part of his work on investors in advanced technology corporations. This Rockefeller family office also was subjected to close congressional scrutiny when Nelson Rockefeller was nominated by President Gerald Ford to be Vice-President in 1974.[13]

The Phipps family office is called Bessemer Trust Company. In 1960 it managed 38 different family trusts worth an estimated $250 million. It made loans to individual family members, provided investment advice, and paid $2 million worth of family bills. The largest family investments were channeled through the family holding company, Bessemer Securities Corporation, a separate entity but managed from the same office.* The hired manager of Bessemer Securities also sat on the boards of several large corporations to oversee family investments in them.

In the late 1960s the office began to manage the money of a few nonfamily members as well, but they were not invited to participate in major new investment opportunities. By the late 1970s, it was estimated that the office had over $1 billion in assets under its management—70 percent of it Phipps money. In addition to corporate investments, the Phipps family is said to have the largest real estate holdings on the East Coast.[14]

Rockefeller Family and Associates, as that family office is called, occupies three floors of the Rockefeller Center in New York and has a staff of over 150 people providing accounting, legal, investment, and tax services to the 84 descendants of John D. Rockefeller, Jr. Several of these employees sit on corporate boards for the Rockefellers. In particular, the head of the office, former investment banker J. Richardson Dilworth, an upper-class Philadelphian, served on the boards of the Chase Manhattan Bank, Chrysler Corporation, IBEC Corporation, and Rockefeller Center in the 1970s as part of his work for the family. Some members of the wealthy Mellon family of Pittsburgh also use a family office to coordinate their holdings. Located in the Mellon Bank Building, Richard K. Mellon & Sons

---

*A personal or family holding company is a company that is owned by a small number of people and exists to own stock in operating companies.

employed two nonfamily vice-presidents to represent it on the boards
of First Boston, General Reinsurance, Gulf Oil, Aluminum Company
of America (Alcoa), Carborundum, and Koppers during the 1970s.[15]

The most detailed account of a family office is provided by
sociologist Marvin Dunn in his study of a Weyerhauser family of Saint
Paul, Minnesota, and Tacoma, Washington, whose great wealth is
concentrated in the lumber industry. Through assembling a family
genealogy chart that covered five generations, and then interviewing
several members of the family, Dunn determined that a family office
called Fiduciary Counselors, Inc., aided the family in maintaining a
central role in several major corporations. By demonstrating that
there were many Weyerhausers on the boards of these companies who
were not known to be Weyerhausers by previous investigators, and by
aggregating the stock holdings that were managed out of the family
office, Dunn was able to show that Potlatch and Arcata National,
thought to be no longer dominated by the Weyerhausers, continued to
be under the family's control through the mid-1970s.[16]

Fiduciary Counselors, Inc., also housed the offices of two
Weyerhauser holding companies, called the Rock Island Corporation
and the Green Valley Corporation. These companies were used to
make investments for family members as a group and to own shares
in new companies that were being created by the family. Although the
primary focus of the Weyerhauser family office was economic matters,
the office served other functions as well. It kept the books for 15
different charitable foundations of varying sizes and purposes
through which family members give money, and it coordinated
political donations by family members all over the country to both
candidates and political action committees.

As Dunn rightly concludes, his findings raise the possibility that
more such studies of family offices might provide a means to determine the full extent of upper-class involvement in major corporations
and other aspects of American society. Following sociologists Maurice
Zeitlin, Richard Ratcliff, and Lynda Ann Ewen, whose studies of the
ownership and control of large corporations in Chile in the 1960s
revealed extensive control by interconnected families, Dunn suggests
that many corporations in America may be controlled by "kinecon
groups." Kinecon groups are defined by Zeitlin, Ratcliff, and Ewen as
"a complex kinship unit in which economic interests and kinship
bonds are inextricably intertwined."[17] If the earlier accounts on the
Phipps, Rockefeller, and Mellon offices are any indication, Dunn's
findings on the Weyerhausers are not an isolated case of a kinecon
group in the United States.

Holding Companies

Holding companies alone can serve the economic functions of a family office if the family is still small and tight-knit. They have the advantage of being incorporated entities that can buy and sell stock in their own names. Because they are privately held, they need report on their activities only to tax authorities. The role of a family holding company can be seen in the case of the Hillman family of Pittsburgh, worth about $300 million in the late 1960s. Through the Hillman Company, Henry L. Hillman and his family, in the words of *Forbes*, "own, control or otherwise influence enough other companies to make most conglomerators green with envy." Moreover, the family also controlled several other companies in diverse industries through stock purchases by Pittsburgh Coke and Chemical, an operating company that in turn is 90 percent owned by the Hillman Company.[18]

Sometimes holding companies make it difficult to trace ownership. When South African Anton E. Rupert decided to buy control of Liggett & Myers, Inc., a cigarette manufacturer, in 1974, he did so by purchasing stock under "street names" (anonymous customer accounts in brokerage firms). The money came from Rothmans of London, a holding company set up for the sole purpose of buying L&M stock. Rothman's, in turn, was owned by Rupert Group Holdings. Other properties owned by Rupert were controlled through the Luxembourg-based Rupert Foundation and Rembrandt Group, Ltd., in South Africa, making it almost impossible to determine the full extent of his personal wealth and corporate involvements.[19] Other families use slightly different types of organizational devices to exert influence or control. The Lindner family of Cincinnati uses a financial holding company, American Financial Corporation, which controls banks, savings and loans, and insurance companies, to take large ownership positions in a variety of companies. In 1980 the family was among the top five stockholders in 6 of the largest 500 industrials through purchases by this company. American Financial also owns a major newspaper, the *Cincinnati Enquirer.*[20]

Family Ownership

Three different studies provide detailed evidence on the extent of family involvement in the largest American corporations. The factual information provided by these studies concerns the concentration of stock ownership in specific families and the number of people from these families who serve as corporate directors. In the past this information was sometimes looked upon as inconclusive by skeptics, who argued that the studies provided no evidence of family coordination. However, the work by Dunn, Schwartz, and others on family offices and holding companies greatly strengthens the possibility that these concentrations of stock can be used for control purposes.

The first of these studies, by political scientist Philip Burch, used both official documents and the informal—but often more informative—findings of the business press for the years 1950 to 1970 as its sources of information. Classifying companies as "probably" under family control if a family or group of families had 4 to 5 percent of the stock and longstanding representation on the board of directors, Burch concluded that, as of the mid-1960s, 40 percent of the top 300 industrials were probably under family control, and that another 15 percent were "possibly" under family control.[21]

Analyzing the more useful official records that became available in the 1970s, a team of researchers at Corporate Data Exchange, led by Stephen Abrecht and Michael Locker, provided detailed information on the major owners of most of the top 500 industrials for 1980. This study showed that significant individual and family ownership continues to exist for all but the very largest of corporations.[22] Our classification of their findings reveals that one individual or family was a top stockholder, with at least 5 percent of the stock, in 44 percent of the 423 profiled corporations that were not controlled by other corporations or foreign interests. From two to four families held at least 5 percent of the stock and had representation on the board of directors in another 7 percent. The figures were much lower among the 50 largest, however, where only 17 percent of the 47 companies included in the study met our criteria of major family involvement.

These findings on the small percentage of the very largest industrials under individual or family control concur with those in a third study, that by economist Edward S. Herman for the 200 largest corporations among all nonfinancial corporations for 1974–1975. Using slightly more stringent criteria than in our classification, and including public utilities that are highly unlikely to be controlled by families, he found that only 14 percent of the companies in his sample were under ownership control. There were another 7.5 percent where outside ownership was a significant influence.[23] Despite the slight differences in criteria, however, there was strong agreement between the Herman findings and our analysis of the Corporate Data Exchange information. Of the 104 companies common to the two studies, there were only four disagreements in classifying the nature of their control structure, and some of those may be due to changes in ownership patterns between 1974 and 1980.

The difference between the ownership patterns in family-dominated and management-controlled corporations is usually readily apparent in the information provided by the Corporate Data Exchange. A comparison of two companies within the bottom half of the top 100 demonstrates this point. In the Weyerhauser Corporation, for example, the Weyerhauser family is the largest stockholder with 9.84 percent of the stock, followed by a family with a 2.98 percent holding that became a major owner by merging its company into Weyerhauser. The third largest stockholder, with 2.19 percent, is actually another Weyerhauser, although only access to Marvin Dunn's Weyerhauser genealogy chart, published after the Corporate Data Exchange analysis was completed, revealed this fact. Thus, over 15 percent of the stock, a very large block in a corporation of this size, is in the hands of just two families. By way of contract, Georgia-Pacific, another large lumber company, has no families or individuals among its top ten stockholders. The largest stockholder, with 2.4 percent of the stock, is the company's bonus trust plan, and it is followed by such investors as Prudential Insurance, Brown Brothers, Harriman & Company, Bank of California, and the California Public Employees and Teachers Retirement System. Among the 71 top stockholders listed for the company, only three are individuals, and only one has even 1 percent of the stock.[24]

Despite the clarity of different ownership patterns, the generalizations drawn from stock figures must be treated with some caution when it comes to actual control in any given situation. There are instances where very large stockholders, even founders or heirs of founders, have been replaced at the helm of a corporation by the combined efforts of smaller stockholders, and there are examples of corporations that are controlled by heirs who have less than 5 percent of the stock. As a further reason for caution, even the figures from the careful studies by Burch, Herman, and Corporate Data Exchange may be underestimates in some instances. A specific example of this point can be seen in the case of Arcata Corporation, one of the Weyerhauser firms studied by Dunn. According to the company, the three Weyerhausers on the board in 1975 held about 7.5 percent of the stock. Corporate Data Exchange determined the figure to be about 5 percent for 1980. However, when the company decided to buy up outstanding shares and become a private corporation in 1981, it was reported that members of the Weyerhauser family owned "about 30% of Arcata's common stock."[25] Comparisons of public records with what comes out at the time of a merger or takeover battle often show similar disparities.

These findings on family offices, holding companies, and family ownership in large industrial corporations suggest that a significant number of large corporations continue to be controlled by major owners. Through careful probing it is sometimes possible to demonstrate the role of large stockholders where no concentration of ownership or family influence seemed to exist. Such findings demonstrate that each corporation's ownership structure, board of directors, and history of family involvement must be studied in detail to determine how it is controlled. However, the fact still remains that in many of the very largest corporations in several sectors of the economy there is no large ownership stake by individuals or families, whether through family offices, holding companies, or other devices.

In these companies the stock is widely dispersed. The largest owners, in blocks of a few percent, are pension funds, bank trust departments, investment companies, and mutual funds. Moreover, interview studies suggest that these fiduciary institutions very rarely take any role in influencing the management of the corporations in which they invest.[26] Nor are representatives of original family owners or of the various institutional investors to be found on the board of directors. To understand upper-class involvement in these corporations, it is necessary to study the general composition of boards of directors.

THE BOARD OF DIRECTORS

The board of directors is the official governing body of the corporation. Usually composed of from 10 to 15 members, but including as many as 25 in the case of commercial banks, it meets for a day or two at a time about ten times a year. A smaller executive committee of the board often meets more frequently, and some of the individual members are in even closer contact with the top management, which handles the affairs of the corporation from day to day. The most important duty of the board of directors is to hire and fire top management, but it also is responsible for accepting or rejecting major policy changes. Boards seem to play their most important role when there is conflict within management, the corporation is in economic distress, or there is the possibility of a merger or acquisition.

Although the board is the official governing body, it is often the case that the company executives on the board, who are called "inside directors," play a great role in shaping the board's decisions. These inside directors, perhaps in conjunction with two or three of the nonmanagement directors (called "outside directors"), are able to set the agenda for meetings, shape board thinking on policy decisions, and select new outside directors. In those situations, the board becomes little more than a rubber stamp for management, with the top managers having great influence in naming their successors in running the company.

Whatever the role of the board in any given corporation, boards of directors embody the complex power relations within the corporate community. Their importance manifests itself in a number of ways. They speak for the corporation to the rest of the corporate community and to the public at large. New owners demand seats on boards to consolidate their positions and to have a "listening post." Conflicts over hostile merger attempts may be concluded by electing top officers of each corporation to the former rivals' respective boards. Commercial bankers desire seats on boards to keep track of their loans and to ensure that future business will be directed their way. Corporate executives from other companies are willing to take time from their busy schedules to be on two or three outside boards because it is a visible sign that their advice is respected outside their home company, and it provides them with general intelligence on the state of the business world as well. Then, too, the presence of investment bankers, corporate lawyers, and academic experts on a board is a sign that their expertise is respected by the corporations. The appointment of a university president, former government official, well-known woman, or highly visible minority group leader is a sign that their high status and respectability are regarded as valuable to the image of the corporation.

There is evidence that corporate officials recognize the symbolic importance of the board of directors. As one president told business professor Myles Mace in his interview study with top executives in the late 1960s:

> When I look at a company, I look at who is on the board. I don't know how good a criterion it is, but I form a judgment—is it a responsible kind of outfit, or is it a marginal high-flyer. The type of people on a board does in a series of informal and intangible ways, have a great deal to do with what the character of a company is.[27]

Another said: "You want to communicate to the various publics that if any large company is good enough to attract the president of a large New York bank as a director, for example, it just has to be a great company."[28]

There have been numerous studies of the social class origins of the corporate executives who serve on boards of directors. These studies use varying criteria of class origin, but they most frequently focus on the occupation of the executive's father in making this determination. These studies show, as Michael Useem suggests in a detailed synthesis of work on the corporate elite, that "between 40% and 70% of all large corporation directors and managers were raised in business families, which comprised only a tiny fraction of the families of the era."[29] One of the studies he cites, completed in the late

1950s, compared business leaders at thirty-year intervals over the century and found that the percentage whose fathers also were businessmen remained constant at about 65 percent.[30] A study of several hundred executives for 1975 found that the homogeneity of their backgrounds may be increasing since those earlier studies:

> The rather surprising result of all this digging through library materials and comparing of data is that the executives of 1975 form a more homogeneous group than those from earlier periods. Indeed, a more uniform profile is reflected than the one of the supposedly "conforming 1950's" In addition to being exclusively male and Caucasian, predominantly Protestant, Republican, and of eastern U.S. origin, from relatively affluent families, and educated at one of a handful of select universities, as had been the case in the past, the executives in our sample share some new characteristics. Most significantly, the executives are closer together in age, and most of them have little or no work experience outside their companies.[31]

In one of the most ambitious studies of corporate directors to date, political scientist Thomas R. Dye investigated the social origins of several thousand directors from the largest corporations of 1970. Using as his class indicators parental occupations as well as the parents' listing in the *Social Register*, attendance at a prestigious private school, and membership in upper-class clubs, Dye estimates that 30 percent of the corporate elite are upper class in origin. Approximately 59 percent came from the middle class, which comprises about 21 percent of the population by Dye's definition. Three percent came from the remaining 79 percent of the population, and 8 percent of the sample was not classifiable.[32]

Several studies using one or more of the criteria of upper-class standing outlined in the previous chapter focus on the class standing of the top executives themselves. They reach very similar conclusions to the studies of social origins. For example, a study of the chairmen and outside directors of the top 20 industrials for 1963 found that one-third were listed in the *Social Register*. A study of all directors for the 15 largest insurance companies for 1963 produced similar results.[33] Thirty percent of the 468 partners in the 20 largest New York law firms, in effect the directors of these firms, were in the *Social Register* in the late 1950s, and a study of 399 investment bankers listed in *Who's Who in America* in 1970–1971 found that 30 percent were listed in the *Social Register*.[34] All these figures, based on this one indicator alone, are many times greater than the number of upper-class persons that could be expected to be in these positions if positions in the corporate world were not associated with class membership.

The involvement of upper-class people on board of directors is demonstrated in our study of all Saint Paul's alumni over the age of 45 in 1980. Using *Poor's Register of Corporations, Directors and Executives,* and *Who's Who in America,* we found that 303 of these several thousand men were serving as officers or directors in corporations in general, and that 102 were directors of 97 corporations in the Fortune 800. Their involvement was especially great in the financial sector. Most striking of all, 21 graduates of Saint Paul's were either officers or directors at Morgan Guaranty Trust, one of the five largest banks in the country. This finding suggests that the alumni of particular schools may tend to cluster at specific banks or corporations.

The social ties of corporate directors to the upper class are also revealed in their club memberships. For example, in the 1960s we examined the club memberships listed in *Who's Who in America* for chairmen and outside directors of the 20 largest industrial corporations. The overlaps with upper-class clubs in general were ubiquitous, but the concentration of directors in a few clubs was especially notable. At least one director from 12 of the 20 corporations was a member of the Links Club, which Baltzell calls "the New York rendezvous of the national corporate establishment."[35] Seven of General Electric's directors were members, as were four from Chrysler, four from Westinghouse, three from IBM, and two from U.S. Steel. In addition to the Links, several other clubs had directors from four or more corporations. The Century Association in New York had directors from 8 of the 20; the Duquesne in Pittsburgh from 7; the Chicago Club in Chicago from 7; the Philadelphia Club in Philadelphia from 5; and the Pacific Union in San Francisco from 5.

These findings were confirmed and extended in our more detailed and wide-ranging study of corporate directors for 1970. It used membership lists from 11 prestigious clubs in different parts of the country. A majority of the top 25 corporations in every major sector of the economy had directors in at least one of these clubs, and several had many more. For example, all of the 25 largest industrials had one or more directors in these clubs. The Links in New York, with 79 connections to 21 corporations, and the Century Association in New York, with 24 connections to 14 corporations, had the most corporate members. The results were very similar for banking: 23 of the top 25 had directors in at least one of these clubs. The Links again headed the list, with 113 connections to 20 banks, but it was followed this time by the Chicago Club, with 70 connections to 16 banks. The findings were only slightly less impressive for other sectors. Twenty-three of the top 25 were connected at least once to these clubs for both insurance and transportation companies, but there were less connections overall. Retail firms were at the bottom of the list, with 18 firms connected to one or more of the clubs.

Some corporations had many more connections to this club network than did others. In part this is a reflection of the restricted number of clubs, for some of the least-connected corporations have their headquarters in cities far from any of these club locations. However, the results to some extent reflect the status of the corporation as well. Venerable companies within the corporate community, such as General Electric and Mobil Oil, were the industrials with the most connections, for example. General Electric's board had 21 connections into 8 of the 11 clubs, and Mobil Oil had 12 into 6 of the clubs. The best-connected company among the utilities was AT&T, with 20 connections to 8 clubs, and Southern Pacific led among transportation firms, with 32 connections to 8 clubs. Among retails, only Safeway, with 15 connections to 6 clubs, and Sears, Roebuck with 13 connections to 4 clubs, had more than a few overlaps with the club network.

Our analysis of the members and guests at the Bohemian Grove in 1970 and 1980 demonstrates the way in which one club intertwines the upper class with the entire corporate community. In 1970 29 percent of the top 800 corporations had at least one officer or director at the Bohemian Grove festivities; in 1980 the figure was 30 percent. As might be expected, the overlap was especially great among the largest corporations, with 23 of the top 25 industrials represented in 1970, 15 of 25 in 1980. Twenty of the 25 largest banks had at least one officer or director in attendance in both 1970 and 1980. Other business sectors were represented somewhat less. For 1980 the figures were 11 of 25 in insurance, 13 of 25 in transportation, and only 4 of 25 in retails. The findings for these sectors were very similar for 1970.[36]

The companies with the most directors present tended to be located on the West Coast, with Bank of America (10), Southern Pacific (9), Wells Fargo (9), and Pacific Gas and Electric (6) leading the way. However, such New York–based banks as Citicorp (6), Chase Manhattan (5) and Bankers Trust (5) were among 11 companies with 5 or more directors present in 1980.

The Inner Group

The findings from the various studies of directors as a whole show that the general direction of the corporate community is in the hands of upper-class people to a significant degree. However, this point can be made more sharply if we focus on the small number of directors who sit on two or more corporate boards. In 1970, for example, there were 8,623 people on the boards of the 800 largest corporations, but only 11 percent sat on two boards, 4 percent on three boards, and 3 percent on four or more boards. The multiple directorships of these 1,572 people create a complex pattern of interlocking corporations that encompasses most of the corporate community; 90 percent of the top corporations join together into a single network. Most of the corporations that are not directly connected are only one or two steps from each other, the equivalent of knowing someone who knows someone on the individual level.[37]

This network, which dates back to the turn of the century in roughly its present form, includes a few longstanding working relationships between specific banks and their customers, and some small cliques of corporations.[38] However, most of the connections within it are symptomatic of the overall closeness within the corporate community, not of historical ties between large cliques of corporations, as was previously thought. This fact is shown most readily in the findings on new directors in two separate studies. When the tie between two corporations is broken by the death or retirement of an interlocking director, it is seldom replaced by a person who restores the relationship. Only when there are two or three interlocks between the two corporate entities is there much likelihood that the broken tie will be replaced. Instead, new directors are drawn from the corporate community in general.[39]

Due to their multiple directorships, the people who form these interlocking directorates are in a somewhat different position within the corporate community than are single directors. They are likely to know more people, to have a better overview of the business world as a whole, and to have general information of interest to their fellow directors. The very fact that they hold several directorships suggests that they are people with either the money and power to command positions on several boards, or the respect as executives, lawyers, or advisors that makes them sought-after persons for board memberships. Such people make up what Useem calls the "inner group" or "inner circle" of the corporate community. He argues that such people are the leadership group within the corporate community as a whole and presents evidence that they are more likely than single directors to serve on the boards of nonbusiness organizations as well.[40]

Several studies have demonstrated the greater frequency of upper-class members within the inner group. Information about interlocks in a study of a sample of directors from the top 200 industrial corporations in 1965 showed that those with two or more directorships were twice as likely as single directors to be in the *Social Register*, attend a prestigious private school, or belong to an elite social club.[41] Another study, comparing samples of executives who were also university trustees, found that 57 percent of those on three or more boards were in elite social clubs as compared with 25 percent of those on one or two boards and only 16 percent of those who were executives but served on no boards.[42] In a study using 1970 interlock data, it was reported that 72 percent of those with four or more directorships were in one of the top social clubs, compared with 49 percent of those on three boards, 44 percent of those on two boards, and only 17 percent for those on a single board.[43]

Members of the inner group are very often bankers, wealthy individuals who include a bank as one of their boards, or top corporate executives who sit on bank boards. For this reason, commercial banks are the center of the networks formed by interlocking directors, and they have been so since the turn of the century.[44] Banks thereby become the settings that bring together the most powerful and visible members of the corporate community for face-to-face meetings. Whether or not banks are centers of great power within the corporate community is a matter of dispute among social scientists. But they are at the very least important centers of communication about the general state of business, and they are recognized as such by corporate leaders. As an outside director for a large bank told Useem in the late 1970s: "The bank board, for instance, is involved in general discussions of economic circumstances, and it's helpful background information. Put it this way: direct involvement in other companies' affairs replaces an awful lot of reading."[45]

An analysis of the boards of major banks shows that they are more likely to include upper-class members than are boards in other sectors of the economy. Our study of the boards of the top 15 banks in 1963 found that 62 percent met one or more criteria of upper-class standings, a figure that was higher by 10 to 20 percentage points than what we found for other sectors. Similar high percentages were found for the largest banks in Boston, Cleveland, and Philadelphia, none of which were in the top 15; the *Social Register* figures alone were 46 percent, 41 percent, and 52 percent, respectively.[46]

THE ASSIMILATION
OF RISING EXECUTIVES

Whatever the exact number of owning families and upper-class individuals who play significant roles in the corporate community, there are a great many top executives in corporations who came from middle-level origins and slowly worked their way up the corporate ladder. The number of such people may be somewhat exaggerated because relevant information on schools and clubs is not always included in biographical sources, but their role within the corporate community is a large one even by conservative estimates.

As noted at the outset of the chapter, these facts have been used by many pluralists as part of their argument that ownership and control have been separated in the large corporations. Not only is stock ownership dispersed, with no one family owning a controlling interest, but the leadership is provided by middle-class experts or technocrats whose primary concern is not with profits, which is the main interest of the upper-class owners, but with balancing the demands of workers, consumers, and owners. In this view professional managers are a group distinct from upper-class owners and directors in social origins, skills, and motivations. Contrary to this claim, the evidence to be presented in this section will show that rising executives are assimilated into the upper class and come to share its values, thereby cementing the relationship between the upper class and the corporate community rather than severing it. The aspirations of professional managers for themselves and for their offspring lead them into the upper class in behavior, values, and style of life, not away from it.

Whatever the social origins of corporate executives, they are educated and trained in a small number of private universities and business schools. Useem summarizes the results of several different studies by concluding that "approximately one-third of those who oversee the nation's largest firms attended Harvard, Yale, or Princeton, and two-thirds studied at one of the twelve (most heavily endowed) schools."[47] It is in these schools that people of middle-class origins receive their introduction to the values of the upper class and the corporate community, mingling for the first time with men and women of the upper class to some extent, and sometimes with upper-class teachers and administrators who serve as role models. This modeling becomes even more intense in the graduate schools of business that many of them attend before joining the corporation.

The conformist atmosphere within the corporations themselves furthers this socialization into upper-class styles and values. As sociologist Rosabeth Kanter explains in her study of managers and secretaries in a large East Coast corporation, the great uncertainty and latitude for decision-making in positions at the top of complex organizations creates a situation in which trust among leaders is absolutely essential. That need for trust is what creates a pressure toward social conformity:

> It is the uncertainty quotient in managerial work, as it has come to be defined in the large modern corporations, that causes management to

become so socially restricting; to develop tight inner circles excluding social strangers; to keep control in the hands of socially homogeneous peers; to stress conformity and insist upon a diffuse, unbounded loyalty; and to prefer ease of communication and thus social certainty over the strains of dealing with people who are "different."[48]

In this kind of an atmosphere, it quickly becomes apparent to new managers that they must demonstrate their loyalty to the senior management by working extra hours, tailoring their appearance to that of their superiors, and attempting to conform in their attitudes and behavior. They come to believe that they have to be part of the "old-boy network" in order to succeed in the company. Although there are competence criteria for the promotion of managers, they are vague enough or hard enough to apply that most managers become convinced that social factors are critical as well.

Executives who are successful in winning acceptance into the inner circle of their home corporations are also invited by their superiors to join social institutions that assimilate them into the upper class. The first invitations are often to charitable and cultural organizations, where they serve as fund raisers and as organizers of special events. The wives of rising executives, whose social acceptability is thought to be a factor in managers' careers, experience their first extensive involvement with members of the upper class through these same organizations. Then, too, social clubs are among the socializing agents for the rising executive. An interview and questionnaire study with several hundred corporate executives on the West Coast concluded that "the clubs are a repository of the values held by the upper-level prestige groups in the community and are a means by which these values are transferred to the business community."[49]

The role played by clubs in assimilating rising executives can be seen in a study of corporate presidents in 1958. It found that the typical president for one of the 100 largest industrial firms of that year was born in a middle-class home; about two-thirds attended a public high school, for example.[50] Though the author stresses the nonelite origins of these executives, further analysis suggests that many of these men became members of upper-class clubs as they moved up the corporate hierarchy. Using both *Who's Who in America* and several available membership lists, we found that 70 percent of these men were in one or more upper-class clubs, most becoming members before they were studied in 1958, but some in the early 1960s.

Upwardly mobile executives also become intertwined with members of the upper class through the educational careers of their children. As the children go to day schools and boarding schools, the executives take part in evening and weekend events for parents, participate in fund-raising activities, and sometimes become directors or trustees in their own right. The fact that the children of successful managers become involved in upper-class institutions can also be seen in their patterns of college attendance. This is demonstrated very clearly in the 1958 study of executives. Whereas only 29 percent of the corporate presidents went to an Ivy League college, 70 percent of their sons and daughters did so.[51]

Rising executives are assimilated economically at the same time that they are assimilated socially. The most important of these assimilatory mechanisms is the stock option, an arrangement by which the executive is allowed to buy company stock at any time within a future time period at the price of the stock when the option is granted. If the price of the stock rises, the executive purchases it at the original low price, often with the help of a low-interest or interest-free loan from the corporation. He or she then may sell the stock at the market value, realizing a large capital gain that was taxed at a maximum rate of 25 percent in the first two or three decades after World War II. The importance of stock-option plans and several similar programs can be seen in a study of executive compensation in 50 large manufacturing companies in the early 1960s. It showed that the after-tax income from stock dividends, capital gains from selling stocks, and stock-based bonuses was over six times the executive salaries.[52]

Stock-purchasing plans, in conjunction with salaries and bonuses of several hundred thousand dollars, allow top executives to earn from 10 to 40 times more than the average wage earner each year. In the mid-1970s the chief executives of large corporations were making an average of $3,000 per day.[53] These high levels of remuneration enable upwardly mobile corporate leaders to become millionaires in their own right. They do not usually accumulate a significant percentage of stock in the giant corporations they manage, but the many thousands of shares they own are substantial in terms of their own standard of living and the future economic security of their families.

The assimilation of professional executives into the upper class can also be seen in the emphasis they put on profits, the most important of ownership objectives. This manifests itself most directly in the performance of the corporations they manage. Several studies that compare owner-controlled companies with companies that have professional managers at the top show no differences in their profitability.[54] Corporations differ in their profitability, but this fact does not seem to be due to a difference in economic values between upper-class owners and rising corporate executives. As Herman concluded after a very detailed consideration of all the issues and a presentation of his own comparisons among 72 large firms for the years 1967–1976:

The frequently assumed decline in managerial interest in profits, which supposedly should result from the decreased importance of direct owner control, has not in fact, been proved. The empirical evidence has been shown here to be inconclusive. This should not be surprising, given the weakness of the case that has been made for a transformation in corporate objectives—a case that has rested on the comparison of an unswervingly profit-oriented entrepreneurial corporation which never existed, to a vision of a managerial corporation that is equally removed from reality by different oversimplifying assumptions. In fact, organizational changes, continued technical progress and competitive pressures, and the "brooding omnipresence" of ownership interest, operating through both market and non-market forces, have led to an internalization of profitable growth criteria in corporate psyches and in the rules of large managerial corporations. There are expense preference tendencies and other substantial deviations from profitability criteria in their operations, but such deviations existed, and still exist, under owner control.[55]

No studies have asked American executives directly about the emphasis they put on profits as compared with other objectives, but a survey of professional managers in Great Britain, where the corporate structure is very similar, determined that profit was their highest priority.[56] Although no one has asked American managers directly about their values, the question has been approached by studying the content of the speeches by managers of owner-controlled and management-controlled firms. Utilizing a compendium called *Vital Speeches* for the years 1956 to 1970, this study found that executives from managerially controlled firms were no more likely to give speeches emphasizing the social responsibility of the corporation than those from owner-controlled companies. Nor were there differences in their attitudes toward government regulation, government spending, or labor relations. Instead, the content of the speeches tended to differ by industrial sector. Executives whose companies dealt directly with the general public were more likely to speak in terms of a social responsibility ethic.[57]

By any indication, then, the presence of hired executives does not contradict the notion that the upper class and the corporate community are closely related. In terms of their wealth, their social contacts, and their values, successful managers become part of the upper class as they rise in the corporate hierarchy.

CONCLUSION

The overall findings on stock concentration, overrepresentation of upper-class people, and the socialization of rising executives lead to the conclusion that the upper social stratum is a business class based in the ownership and control of large corporations. Contrary to the view that there has been a separation of ownership and control in large corporations, it seems more likely that there has been a gradual reorganization of the upper class into a "corporate rich" that includes top-level executives as well as major owners. Such was the conclusion of Mills from an examination of the data available in the 1950s, and it seems even more correct in the light of the information on ownership and on executive behavior that has been developed since that time:

> The propertied class, in the age of corporate property, has become a corporate rich, and in becoming corporate has consolidated its power and drawn to its defense new men of more executive and more political stance. Its members have become self-conscious in terms of the corporate world they represent. As men of status they have secured their privileges and prerogatives in the most stable private institutions of American society. They are a corporate rich because they depend directly, as well as indirectly, for their money, their privileges, their securities, their advantages, their powers on the world of the big corporations.[58]

The fact that the upper class is also intertwined with the corporate community adds a second dimension to the nature of its cohesiveness. The cohesion is not only social, based on school and club affiliations, but economic, rooted in common stock ownership and most visibly manifested in the complex pattern of interlocking directorships that unites the corporate community and creates a dense and flexible communication network.

The societal power exercised by the corporate rich through the corporate community is considerable. Corporate leaders can invest money where and when they choose; expand, close, or move their factories and offices at a moment's notice; and hire, promote, and fire employees as they see fit. These powers give them a direct influence over the great majority of Americans, who are dependent upon wages and salaries for their incomes. They also give the corporate rich indirect influence over elected and appointed officials, for the growth and stability of a city, state, or the country as a whole can be jeopardized by a lack of business confidence in government.

One of the clearest statements of the way in which economic power influences government is by economist Charles Lindblom in an article entitled "Why Government Must Cater to Business." The crux of this argument is that in "our kind of society" the "big tasks of shaping and doing" have been entrusted to businesspeople who cannot be "commanded to perform their functions." Instead, they have to be "induced," which means they have to be given whatever they want, generally speaking, if there is to be prosperity. Therefore, the main job of government officials, elected and appointed, is to cater to business. If they do not do this job, there will be economic difficulties that will lead people to desire new political leadership: "These ills are not only deeply distressing to the population as a whole, but suicidal for public officials. That is because political leaders lose their positions if they cannot maintain a relatively healthy economy."[59]

As useful as this straightforward argument is in explaining one of the ways in which members of the corporate rich exercise power in America, it is not sufficient. It does not take into consideration the possibility that government officials might turn to nonbusiness constituencies to support new economic arrangements or that the voting public might elect leaders mandated to change the economic system. In other words, contrary to the shortsightedness of such pluralists as Lindblom, it is not only political leaders who face the possibility of losing their positions when the economy is in distress. In such situations, the business leaders may need government to protect their private property. As Bertrand Russell notes in criticizing the "undue emphasis on economics" in understanding power: "The power of the industrialist rests, in the last analysis, upon the lockout, that is to say, upon the fact that the owner of a factory can call upon the forces of the State to prevent unauthorized persons from entering it."[60]

Because there is no guarantee that the underlying population and government officials will accept the corporate viewpoint under all circumstances, it is necessary to consider the ways in which the personnel and the economic resources of the upper class and the corporate community are involved in an effort to shape the thinking of the American polity and to influence the federal government directly. These processes will be the subject of the next two chapters.

NOTES

1. Daniel Bell, "The Break-up of Family Capitalism," in *The End of Ideology*, ed. Daniel Bell (New York: Free Press, 1960); A. A. Berle, Jr., and Gardner C. Means, *The Modern Corporation and Private Property* (New York: MacMillan, 1932); A. A. Berle, Jr., *Power Without Property* (New York: Harcourt, Brace, 1959).
2. Peter Drucker, *The Unseen Revolution* (New York: Harper & Row, 1976), as quoted in Maurice Zeitlin, "Who Owns America?" *The Progressive*, June 1978, p. 14. For one excellent critique of Drucker's claims, see Michael R. Darby, "Should Pension Funds Be Cause for Concern?" *Business Week*, July 19, 1976, p. 6.

3. Robert Lampman, *The Share of Top-Wealthholders in National Health* (Princeton, N.J.: Princeton University Press, 1962), p. 209; James D. Smith and Stephen D. Franklin, "The Concentration of Personal Wealth, 1922–1969," *American Economic Review,* May 1974.

4. Zeitlin, "Who Owns America?" p. 15.

5. Keith Butters, Lawrence E. Thompson, and Lynn L. Bollinger, *The Effect of Taxation on Investments by Individuals* (Cambridge, Mass.: Riverside Press, 1953), p. 400.

6. Dorothy S. Projector and Gertrude S. Weiss, *Survey of Financial Characteristics of Consumers* (Washington, D.C.: Board of Governors of the Federal Reserve System, 1966).

7. Marshall E. Blume, Jean Crockett, and Irwin Friend, "Stock Ownership in the United States: Characteristics and Trends," *Survey of Current Business,* November 1974.

8. C. Wright Mills, *The Power Elite* (New York: Oxford University Press, 1956), p. 122.

9. Lawrence Minard, "In Privacy They Thrive," *Forbes,* November 1, 1976.

10. Roger A. Strang and Roy A. Herberger, Jr., *Privately-Held Firms: Neglected Force in the Free Enterprise System* (Los Angeles: Center for the Study of Private Enterprise, University of Southern California, 1980).

11. Shelby White, "Cradle to Grave: Family Offices Manage Money for the Very Rich," *Barron's,* March 20, 1978, p. 9.

12. R. A. Smith, "The Heir Who Turned on the House of Phipps," *Fortune,* October and November, 1960.

13. Charles L. Schwartz and G. William Domhoff, "Probing the Rockefeller Fortune," testimony and report in House Hearings before the Committee on the Judiciary, 93d Congress, 2d Session, Nomination of Nelson A. Rockefeller to be Vice President of the United States (Washington, D.C.: U.S. Government Printing Office, 1974), pp. 717–72.

14. White, "Cradle to Grave."

15. David E. Koskoff, *The Mellons* (New York: Crowell, 1978), pp. 476, 478, 493, 496, 556–559.

16. Marvin G. Dunn, "The Family Office: Coordinating Mechanism of the Ruling Class," in *Power Structure Research,* ed. G. William Domhoff (Beverly Hills, Calif.: Sage Publications, 1980).

17. Maurice Zeitlin, Lynda Ann Ewen, and Richard E. Ratcliff, "New Princes for Old? The Large Corporation and the Capitalist Class in Chile," *American Journal of Sociology,* July 1974, p. 109.

18. "The Hillmans of Pittsburgh," *Forbes,* September 15, 1969, p. 41.

19. "South Africa's Mystery Man: Anton E. Rupert," *Business Week,* September 28, 1974, p. 80.

20. "American Financial Moves into the Big Time," *Business Week,* March 3, 1973, p. 72; Stephen Abrecht and Michael Locker, eds., *CDE Stock Ownership Directory: Fortune 500* (New York: Corporate Data Exchange, 1981), p. 208.

21. Philip H. Burch, Jr., *The Managerial Revolution Reassessed* (Lexington, Mass.: Heath, 1972), pp. 29–30, 70.

22. Abrecht and Locker, *CDE Stock Ownership Directory.*

23. Edward S. Herman, *Corporate Control, Corporate Power* (New York: Cambridge University Press, 1981), pp. 54–65, appendix A.
24. Abrecht and Locker, *CDE Stock Ownership Directory*, pp. 88–89, 193–94.
25. Timothy C. Gartner, "Arcata Takes Steps to Go Private," *San Francisco Chronicle*, September 30, 1981, p. 29.
26. Edward S. Herman, *Conflicts of Interest: Commercial Bank Trust Departments* (New York: Twentieth Century Fund, 1975); Herman, *Corporate Control, Corporate Power*, chapter 4.
27. Myles Mace, *Directors: Myth and Reality* (Boston: Harvard University Press, 1971), p. 90.
28. Ibid.
29. Michael Useem, "Corporations and the Corporate Elite," *Annual Review of Sociology*, 6 (1980): 64.
30. Seymour M. Lipset and Reinhard Bendix, *Social Mobility in Industrial Society* (Berkeley, Calif.: University of California Press, 1959), pp. 121–128.
31. Frederick Sturdivant and Roy Adler, "Executive Origins: Still a Gray Flannel World?" *Harvard Business Review*, November–December 1976, p. 129.
32. Thomas R. Dye, *Who's Running America?*(Englewood Cliffs, N.J.: Prentice-Hall, 1976), pp. 151–2.
33. G. William Domhoff, *Who Rules America?* (Englewood Cliffs, N.J.: Prentice-Hall, 1967), pp. 53–55.
34. Erwin O. Smigel, *The Wall Street Lawyer* (New York: Free Press, 1964), p. 74; Lawrence Chaitkin, "The Social Organization of Investment Banking" (Ph.D. diss., University of Pennsylvania, 1974).
35. Domhoff, *Who Rules America?* p. 26; E. Digby Baltzell, *The Protestant Establishment* (New York: Random House, 1964), p. 371.
36. G. William Domhoff, *The Bohemian Grove and Other Retreats* (New York: Harper & Row, 1974), pp. 31–32.
37. Peter Mariolis, "Interlocking Directorates and Control of Corporations: The Theory of Bank Control," *Social Sciences Quarterly* 56 (1975).
38. David Bunting and James Barbour, "Interlocking Directorates in Large American Corporations, 1896–1964," *Business History Review*, Autumn 1971; Mark S. Mizruchi and David Bunting, "Influence in Corporate Networks: An Examination of Four Measures," *Administrative Science Quarterly*, September, 1981; Mark S. Mizruchi, *The Structure of the American Corporate Network, 1904–1974* (Beverly Hills, Calif.: Sage Publications, 1982).
39. Donald Palmer, "Broken Ties: A Theoretical and Methodological Critique of Corporate Interlock Research" (Ph.D. diss. State University of New York, Stony Brook, 1980); Thomas Koenig and Robert Gogel, "Interlocking Directorates as a Social Network," *American Journal of Economics and Sociology* 40 (1981).
40. Michael Useem, "The Inner Group of the American Capitalist Class," *Social Problems* 25 (February 1978); idem, "The Social Organization of the American Business Elite and the Participation of Corporate Directors in the Governance of American Institutions," *American Sociological Review*, August 1979; idem, "Which Business Leaders Help Govern?" in *Power Structure Research*, ed. G. William Domhoff (Beverly Hills, Calif.; Sage Publications, 1980), pp. 199–225.

41. Michael Soref, "The Finance Capitalists," in *Class, Conflict, and the State,* ed. Maurice Zeitlin (Cambridge, Mass.: Winthrop, 1980), p. 72.

42. Useem, "The Inner Group," p. 232.

43. Thomas Koenig and Robert Gogel, "Models of the Significance of Inter-locking Directorates," *American Journal of Economics and Sociology* 38 (1979), p. 173.

44. Beth Mintz, "Who Controls the Corporation? A Study of Interlocking Directorates" (Ph.D. diss., State University of New York, Stony Brook, 1978); Beth Mintz and Michael Schwartz, "The Structure of Intercorpo-rate Unity in American Business," *Social Problems* 29 (1981); Beth Mintz and Michael Schwartz, "Interlocking Directorates and Interest Group Formation," *American Sociological Review,* December 1981; Mizruchi, *The Structure of the American Corporate Network, 1904–1974;* William G. Roy, "Interlocking Directorates and the Corporate Revolution, 1886–1903," *Social Science History,* May, 1983.

45. Michael Useem, "Classwide Rationality in the Politics of Managers and Directors of Large Corporations in the United States and Great Britain," *Administrative Science Quarterly,* June 1982, p. 210.

46. Domhoff, *Who Rules America?* P. 53.

47. Useem, "Corporations and the Corporate Elite," p. 57.

48. Rosabeth Kanter, *Men and Women of the Corporation* (New York: Basic Books, 1977), p. 49. For a detailed statement of this argument, see Nancy DiTomaso, "Organizational Analysis and Power Structure Research," in *Power Structure Research,* ed. G. William Domhoff (Beverly Hills, Calif.: Sage Publications, 1980), pp. 255–268.

49. Reed M. Powell, *Race, Religion, and the Promotion of the American Executive* (College of Administrative Science Monograph no. AA-3, Ohio State University, 1969), p. 50.

50. Andrew Hacker, "The Elected and the Anointed: Two American Elites," *American Political Science Review* 55 (1961).

51. Ibid., pp. 541, 544.

52. W. G. Lewellen, *The Ownership Income of Management* (New York: National Bureau of Economic Research, 1971), as quoted in Useem, "Corporations and the Corporate Elite," p. 48.

53. Paul Blumberg, "Another Day, Another $3000," *Dissent* 25 (1978); Mark Green, "Richer Than All Their Tribe," *New Republic,* January 6–13, 1982.

54. Useem, "Corporations and the Corporate Elite," pp. 50–51.

55. Herman, *Corporate Control, Corporate Power,* p. 113.

56. Useem, "Corporations and the Corporate Elite," p. 49.

57. Maynard S. Seider, "Corporate Ownership, Control, and Ideology: Sup-port for Behavioral Similarity," *Sociology and Social Research,* October 1977.

58. Mills, *The Power Elite,* p. 148.

59. Charles E. Lindblom, "Why Government Must Cater to Business," *Business and Society Review,* Fall 1978, p. 4.

60. Bertrand Russell, *Power: A New Social Analysis* (London: George Allen and Unwin, 1938), pp. 123–24.

4

The Shaping
of the
American Polity

INTRODUCTION

The purpose of this chapter is, first, to describe the ways in which leaders within the upper class and corporate community develop general policies on economic and social issues of concern to them and, second, to show how they attempt to shape public opinion on these issues. It is possible to consider these somewhat different processes at the same time because they both have their origins in the same set of interlocking policy-discussion groups, foundations, think tanks, and university institutes.

The nonprofit organizations concerned with public policy to be discussed in this chapter are necessary features of the corporate landscape because social cohesion and common economic interests are not enough in themselves to lead to agreed-upon policies without research, consultation, and deliberation. Issues of foreign policy are too complex and volatile, and the corporate economy too big and diverse, for the new policies that are often required to be deduced from some storehouse of wisdom on the functioning of corporate capitalism or to arise implicitly from the fact of a common social environment.

The effort to influence public opinion is considered necessary because average citizens do not automatically agree with the corporate community on every policy initiative. Their life situations as wage and salary earners with little or no wealth beyond a house and life insurance often lead them to see things in a light different from the corporate rich. Thus, trade unions, minority organizations, and women's groups, among others, can find independent bases of power within the general populace, and they often suggest policy alternatives opposed to those supported by leaders within the corporate community. To the degree that these groups might be able to hinder the adoption of corporate-favored policy suggestions, to that degree is it necessary for the opinion-shaping network to counter their influence.

However, for all the hundreds of millions of dollars spent each year in the effort to mold public opinion, the importance of public opinion in the functioning of the social system should not be exaggerated. The opinions of the majority on a wide range of issues have differed from those of the corporate elite for many generations without major consequences for public policy. To assume that differences in opinion will lead to political activity does not give due consideration to the fact that people's beliefs do not lead them into opposition or disruption if they have stable roles to fulfill in the society. Routine involvement in a daily round of activities, the most important of which are a job and a family, probably is a more important factor in social stability and acquiescence in corporate-supported policies than any attempts to shape public opinion. Contrary to what many Marxian analysts have claimed, what happens in the economy and in government has more impact on how people will act than what is said in the opinion-shaping process and the mass media.[1]

Members of the upper class and corporate community involve themselves in the policy-planning and opinion-shaping processes in three basic ways. First, they finance the organizations that are at the core of these efforts. Second, they provide a variety of free services for some of the organizations in the network, such as legal and accounting help or free advertising space in newspapers and magazines. Finally, they serve as the directors and trustees of these organizations, setting their general direction and selecting the people who will manage their day-to-day operations.

The nonbusiness trustees and executives of the organizations to be discussed in this chapter, who are not infrequently members of the upper class themselves, join with members of the corporate community in forming the power elite. As stated earlier, the power elite is defined as the leadership group for the upper class as a whole, transcending to some degree the business-oriented perspective of those who are involved only in corporate activities. The core of the power elite is the inner group of the corporate community. Its members sit on the boards of foundations, universities, cultural organizations, and numerous other organizations. However, the policy specialists are an essential complement to members of the inner group in bringing long-range political considerations and issues concerning social stability to their attention.

THE POLICY-PLANNING NETWORK

The policy-planning process begins in corporate board rooms, where problems are informally identified as "issues" to be solved by new policies. It ends in government, where policies are enacted and implemented. In between, however, there is a complex network of people and institutions that plays an important role in sharpening the issues and weighing the alternatives. This network has four main components—policy groups, foundations, think tanks, and university research institutes.

The policy-discussion organizations are nonpartisan groups, bringing together corporate executives, lawyers, academic experts, university administrators, and media specialists to discuss such general problems as foreign aid, tariffs, taxes, and welfare policies. In discussion groups of varying sizes, the policy-oriented organizations provide informal and off-the-record meeting grounds in which differences of opinion on various issues can be aired and the opinions of specialists can be heard. In addition to their numerous small-group discussions, these organizations encourage general dialogue within the power elite by means of luncheon and dinner speeches, written reports, and position statements in journals and books. Taken as a whole, the several policy-discussion groups are akin to an open forum in which there is a constant debate concerning the major problems of the day and the best solutions to those problems.

Foundations are tax-free institutions that are created to give grants to both individuals and nonprofit organizations for activities that range from education, research, and the arts to support for the poor and the upkeep of exotic gardens and old mansions. They are an upper-class adaptation to inheritance and income taxes. They provide a means by which wealthy people and corporations can in effect decide how their tax payments will be spent, for they are based on money that otherwise could go to the government in taxes. From a small beginning at the turn of the century, they have become a very important factor in shaping developments in higher education and the arts, and they play a significant role in policy formation as well.

The best-known and most influential are the Ford, Rockefeller, and Carnegie foundations.

Think tanks and university research institutes are nonprofit organizations that have been developed to provide settings for experts in various academic disciplines to devote their time to the study of policy alternatives free from the teaching and departmental duties that are part of the daily routine for most members of the academic community. Supported by foundation grants and government con-tracts, they are a major source of the new ideas that are discussed in the policy-formation groups.

No one type of organization within the network is more impor-tant than the others. Nor is any one organization or group the "inner sanctum" where final decisions are made. It is the network as a whole that shapes policy alternatives, with different organizations playing different roles on different issues.

THE POLICY-DISCUSSION GROUPS

National-level discussion groups were first created at the turn of the century coterminous with the development of the corporate com-munity. The group that was to be the prototype for all the rest, the National Civic Federation, had outlived its usefulness by World War I, but the several groups that gradually replaced it—the Conference Board (1916), the Council on Foreign Relations (1921), and the Com-mittee for Economic Development (1942)—became even more impor-tant in their own right and have been functioning in tandem since the 1950s.

The Council on Foreign Relations

The largest and best-known of the policy organizations is the Council on Foreign Relations (CFR). Founded by bankers, lawyers, and acade-micians who were fully cognizant of the larger role the United States would play in world affairs as a result of World War I, the council's importance in the conduct of foreign affairs was well established by the 1930s. The council has about 1,800 members, half from the New York area, half from the rest of the country. Before 1970 the members were primarily financiers, executives, and lawyers, with a strong minority of journalists, academic experts, and government officials. Since that time there has been an effort to include a larger number of government officials, including foreign-service officers, politicians, and staff members of congressional committees concerned with foreign policy.

Several different studies demonstrate the council's connections to the upper class and corporate community. A sample of 210 New York members of the council in the mid-1960s found that 39 percent were listed in the *Social Register,* and a random sampling of the full membership in 1969 found 33 percent in that directory.[2] In both studies, directors of the council were even more likely than regular members to be members of the upper class. Council overlaps with the corporate community are equally pervasive. Twenty-two percent of the 1969 council membership and 29 percent of its directors served on the board of at least one of *Fortune*'s top 500 industrials, for example.[3] In a study of the directors of 201 large corporations in 1970, it was found that 125 of these companies had 293 positional interlocks with the council. Twenty-three of the very largest banks and corporations had four or more directors who were members.[4]

The full extent of council overlap with the corporate community and government was determined in our study of its entire membership list for 1978–1979. The analysis showed that about one in every five members was an officer or director of a business listed in *Poor's Register of Corporations, Directors, and Executives.* Membership was once again found to be greatest for the biggest industrial corporations and banks. Overall, 37 percent of the 500 top industrials had at least one officer or director who was a member, with the figure rising to 70 percent for the top 100 and 92 percent for the top 25. Twenty-one of the top 25 banks had members, as did 16 of the largest 25 insurance companies. However, only the top ten among utilities, transports, and retails were well represented. For all sectors of the economy, the companies with the most members among their officers and directors were Morgan Guaranty Trust (16), Chase Manhattan Bank (15), Citibank (10), and IBM (8).

The success of the council's effort to include more government officials in the enlarged council is reflected in this study. Two hundred and fifty members were listed in the index of the *Governmental Manual* for that year. About half were politicians and career government officials; the other half were appointees to the government who came from business, law, and the academic community. In addition, another 184 members were serving as unpaid members of federal advisory committees that year.[5]

The council receives its general funding from wealthy individuals, corporations, and subscriptions to its influential periodical, *Foreign Affairs.* For special projects, however, it often relies upon major foundations for support. In 1978–1979, for example, it received

$66,000 from the Ford and Rockefeller Foundations for its project on emerging issues in Africa, and in 1979–1980 its project on U.S.-Soviet relations received $55,000 from the Ford Foundation and $5,000 from the Mobil Oil Foundation.[6]

The council conducts an active program of luncheon and dinner speeches at its New York clubhouse, featuring government officials and national leaders from all over the world. It also encourages dialogue and disseminates information through books, pamphlets, and articles in *Foreign Affairs*. However, the most important aspects of the CFR program are its discussion groups and study groups. These small gatherings of about 15 to 25 people bring together business executives, government officials, scholars, and military officers for detailed consideration of specific topics in the area of foreign affairs. Discussion groups, which meet about once a month, are charged with exploring problems in a general way, trying to define issues and identify alternatives.

Discussion groups often lead to a study group as the next stage. Study groups revolve around the work of a council research fellow (financed by a foundation grant) or a regular staff member. The group leader and other experts present monthly papers which are discussed and criticized by the rest of the group. The goal of such study groups is a detailed statement of the problem by the scholar leading the discussion. Any book that eventuates from the group is understood to express the views of its academic author, not of the council or the members of the study group. However, the books are published with the sponsorship of the council, and the names of the people participating in the study group are listed at the beginning of the book.

Historical case studies suggest that study groups at the CFR have been at the heart of many foreign policy initiatives. For example, council groups called the War-Peace Study Groups met from 1940 to 1945 in order to develop plans for after World War II. They had a major influence in creating the International Monetary Fund, the World Bank, and the United Nations. A series of study groups in the 1940s and 1950s helped to establish the consensus wisdom that it was necessary to defend South Vietnam at all costs. Large foundation grants in the early 1960s led to study groups that reconsidered U.S. policy toward China, concluding that the policy must be changed to allow for recognition of its communist government and eventual trade relations.[7]

Council leaders reacted to the large-scale international changes of the late 1960s and early 1970s by creating a new discussion organization called the Trilateral Commission, which included 60 members from Japan and 60 from Western Europe as well as American members. Its goal was to develop closer economic and political cooperation among the industrialized democracies in dealing with economic competition among themselves and with challenges from the underdeveloped countries. The council also launched a large number of its own research projects and discussion groups under the auspices of the 1980s Project to parallel the work of the Trilateral Commission.[8]

The council is far too large for its members to issue policy proclamations as a group. Moreover, its usefulness as a neutral discussion ground would be diminished if it tried to do so. However, its leaders did help to mediate the dispute that broke out in the foreign policy establishment in the 1970s over the nature of Soviet intentions and the extent of its threat to United States interests. After holding several discussion groups and study groups on the topic, it created a special Commission on U.S.-Soviet Relations in the fall of 1980 that included representatives of both the Soviets-are-expansionists-and-dangerous view and the Soviets-can-be-worked-with view, at least to the degree that the latter view exists within respectable opinion. The discussants had worked in all recent administrations, Republican and Democrat, and they were chaired by the editor-in-chief of *Time* magazine. The report that emerged from these discussions was drafted by a specialist in international relations from a major Washington think tank. He had served as an aide to the National Security Council in the early 1970s. The 31-page report was distributed free of charge with the aid of a grant from the Ford Foundation and publicized in newspapers and magazines read by members of the power elite.[9]

Time described the commission's recommendations as "tough-minded." The participants agreed that the Soviets were a "vastly more formidable foe" than had been thought a decade earlier and that their intentions were relentlessly hostile to Western interests. The report called for an even bigger defense buildup than either presidential candidate had advocated in the 1980 elections, and it branded the volunteer army a failure.[10] Commentators during the early 1980s increasingly noted that foreign policy experts were once again basically in agreement in their overall view of the world situation. It is likely that the ongoing debate at the council and the report of its commission played a major role in maintaining dialogue between the opposing camps.

The Committee for Economic Development

The Committee for Economic Development (CED) was founded in the early 1940s to help plan for the postwar world. The corporate leaders who were instrumental in creating this new study group had two major concerns at the time: (1) There might be another depression after the war; and (2) if businessmen did not present economic plans for the postwar era, other sectors of society might present plans that would not be acceptable to the corporate community. The expressed purpose of the committee was to avoid any identification with special-interest pleading for business and to concern itself with the nation as a whole: "The Committee would avoid promoting the special interests of business itself as such and would likewise refrain from speaking for any other special interests. ... The CED was to be a businessman's organization that would speak in the national interest."[11]

The CED consisted of 200 corporate leaders in its early years. Later it included a small number of university presidents among its members. In addition, leading economists and public administration experts have served as advisers to the CED and conducted research for it; many of them have gone on to serve in advisory roles in both Republican and Democratic administrations, particularly on the Council of Economic Advisors. Although there is an overlap in membership with the larger Council on Foreign Relations, the committee has a different mix of members. Unlike the council,, it has few bankers and no corporate lawyers, journalists and academic experts.

Like the council, the CED works through study groups that are aided by academic experts. The study groups have considered every conceivable issue from farm policy to government reorganization to campaign finance laws, but the greatest emphasis is on economic issues of both a domestic and international nature. The most ambitious of its projects have been financed by large foundations, but its general revenues come directly from its corporation members.

Unlike the CFR, the results of committee study groups are released as official policy statements of the organization. The statements are published in pamphlet form and disseminated widely in business, government, and media circles. Several of the statements bear a striking similarity to government policies that were enacted at a later time.[12]

The Conference Board

The Conference Board, founded in 1916 as the National Industrial Conference Board, is the oldest of the existing policy-discussion groups. It was originally a more narrowly focused organization, with a primary interest in doing research for the corporate community itself. During the 1930s and 1940s it drifted to an extreme right-wing stance under the influence of its executive director, who often denounced other policy groups for their alleged desertion of the free enterprise system. Only with the retirement of this director in 1948 and an infusion of new members into the board of directors did the organization move back into the corporate mainstream and begin to assume a role as a major voice of the corporate community. Further changes in the 1960s were symbolized by the shortening of its name to Conference Board and the election of a CED trustee as its president.[13]

In addition to discussion groups and the publication of a variety of statistical and survey studies, the Conference Board has been innovative in developing international policy linkages. In 1961, in conjunction with the Stanford Research Institute, a West Coast think tank, the board sponsored a week-long International Industrial Conference in San Francisco, bringing together 500 leaders in industry and finance from 60 countries to hear research reports and discuss common problems. The International Industrial Conference has met every four years since that time. Along with the Trilateral Commission and the "sister" committees that the CED has encouraged in numerous nations, the International Industrial Conference is one of the major institutions in an international policy discussion network that has emerged since the 1950s.

Ultraconservative Policy Groups

The policy network is not totally homogeneous. Reflecting differences of opinion within the corporate community, there is an ultraconservative clique within the policy-planning network that has consistent and longstanding disagreements with the more moderate conservatives of the CED, CFR, and Conference Board. Historically, the most important of these organizations have been the National Association of Manufacturers and the Chamber of Commerce of the United States, but they were joined in the 1970s by the American Enterprise Institute, the Hoover Institution, the Institute for Contemporary Studies, and one or two other small groups.[14]

It is the ultraconservative organizations that are most often identified with "big business" in the eyes of social scientists and the general public. The fact that they are generally nay-sayers who often lose on highly visible issues is one of the major reasons for the belief that the corporate community is not the dominant influence in shaping government policy. What is not understood is that those setbacks are usually at the hands of their more moderate and soft-spoken brethren within the policy network and the corporate community.

The moderate conservatives and ultraconservatives have differed throughout the century on foreign policy, economic policy, and welfare legislation.[15] Historically, the moderates have favored foreign aid, low tariffs, and increased economic expansion overseas, whereas the ultraconservatives tended to see foreign aid as a giveaway and called for high tariffs. Moderates came to accept the idea that government taxation and spending policies could be used to stimulate and stabilize the economy, but ultraconservatives have continued to insist that taxes should be cut to the very minimum and that budget deficits are the work of the devil. Moderates created some welfare-state measures, or they supported such measures in the face of serious social disruption; ultraconservatives have constantly opposed any welfare spending, claiming that it destroys moral fiber and saps individual initiative as well as costing them tax money and making it harder to keep wages down.

No one factor is readily apparent as the sole basis for the division into moderate conservatives and ultraconservatives within the corporate community and power elite. There is a tendency for the moderate organizations to be directed by executives from the very largest and most internationally oriented of corporations, but there are numerous exceptions to that generalization. Moreover, there are corporations that support policy organizations within both ideological currents. Then, too, there are instances where some top officers from a corporation will be in the moderate camp, and others will be in the ultraconservative camp. However, for all their differences, leaders within the two clusters of policy organizations have a tendency to search for compromise policies due to their common membership in the corporate community and the numerous interlocks among all policy groups. When compromise is not possible, the final resolution of policy conflicts often takes place in legislative struggles in Congress that will be outlined in the next chapter.

Whatever their final success in resolving disputes among corporate leaders, the policy groups have several important functions, some inside the power elite and some in relation to society as a whole. Beyond the already-mentioned functions of familiarizing corporate leaders with general issues and providing a setting where conflicts can be discussed and compromised, the policy groups have two other important functions within the power elite:

1. They provide an informal training ground for new leadership. It is within these organizations that corporate leaders can determine in an informal fashion which of their peers are best suited for service in government and as spokespersons to other groups;

2. They provide an informal recruiting ground for determining which academic experts may be best suited for government service,

either as faceless staff aides to the corporate leaders who take government positions, or as high-level appointees in their own right.

In addition to their several functions within the power elite, the policy groups have at least two major functions vis-a-vis the rest of society:

1. These groups legitimate their members as "serious" and "expert" persons capable of government service and selfless pursuit of the national interest. This image is created because group members are portrayed as giving of their own time to take part in highly selective organizations that are nonpartisan and nonprofit in nature.

2. Through such avenues as books, journals, policy statements, press releases, and speakers, these groups influence the climate of opinion both in Washington and the country at large. This point will become apparent when the opinion-shaping process is discussed in a later section of this chapter.

FOUNDATIONS

Among the many thousands of foundations that exist in the United States, only a few hundred have the money and interest to involve themselves in funding programs that have a bearing on public policy. They are of three basic types:

1. There are 26 general-purpose foundations with an endowment of $100 million or more that were created by wealthy families. Most of them are controlled by a cross-section of leaders from the upper class and corporate community, but there remain several ultraconservative foundations in the general-purpose category that are tightly controlled by the original donors.

2. There are dozens of corporate foundations that are funded by a major corporation and directed by the officers of that corporation. Their number and importance has increased greatly since the 1960s, especially in donations to education, medical research, and the arts.

3. Many cities have community foundations that are designed to aid charities, voluntary associations, and special projects in their home cities. They receive funds from a variety of sources, including other foundations, wealthy families, and corporations, and they are directed by boards that include both corporate executives and community leaders.

Upper-class and corporate representation on the boards of the large general-purpose foundations most involved in policy-oriented grants has been documented in several studies. In a study of the 12 largest foundations in the mid-1960s, for example, it was found that half the trustees were members of the upper class. A study of corporate connections into the policy network for 1970 showed that 10 of these 12 foundations had at least one connection to the 201 largest corporations; most had many more than one connection.[16] There is also evidence of numerous interlocking memberships between foundations and policy associations. In 1971, 14 of 19 Rockefeller Foundation trustees were members of the Council on Foreign Relations, with 4 of those members also serving as directors of the council. Ten of 17 trustees of the Carnegie Corporation, as the most important of four Carnegie foundations is named, were members of the council at that time, as were 7 of 16 trustees at the Ford Foundation.[17]

By far the most extensive and revealing study of the relationship among foundations, policy groups, and think tanks was undertaken by sociologist Mary Anna Culleton Colwell, a former executive officer of a small foundation who also conducted lengthy interviews with foundation officials as part of her larger study. Starting with a sample of 77 large foundations for 1974, which included all 26 with over $100 million in assets, she found 20 foundations that gave over 5 percent of their total grants, or over $200,000, to public policy grants in either 1972 or 1975. These 20 foundations in turn led to a group of 31 recipient organizations in the policy-planning and opinion-shaping networks that received grants from three or more of these foundations.[18]

The extent of the policy-planning network revolving around these core organizations was even greater than any previous studies had led social scientists to expect. Of the 225 trustees who served on the 20 foundations between 1971 and 1977, 124 also served as trustees of 120 other foundations as well. Ten of the 20 foundations had trustee interlocks with 18 of the 31 policy-planning organizations and think tanks.[19] The Rockefeller Foundation had the largest number of trustee interlocks with other foundations (34), followed by the Sloan Foundation, the Carnegie Corporation, the Ford Foundation, Rockefeller Brothers Fund, and the Russell Sage Foundation. The Rockefeller Foundation also had the largest number of trustee connections to the policy groups it finances (14), followed by the same five foundations named in the previous sentence. Moreover, all six of these foundations tended to be involved with the same policy groups. These foundations, then, are part of the moderate-conservative portion of the network that includes the Council on Foreign Relations and the

Committee for Economic Development as its most important policy groups.

Colwell's analysis also showed that another set of foundations, led by the Pew Memorial Trust, Lilly Endowment, and Smith Richardson Foundation, gave money to policy groups and think tanks identified with ultraconservative programs—the American Enterprise Institute, the American Economic Foundation, the Hoover Institution, the Foundation for Economic Education, and Freedoms Foundation. Unlike the large foundations in the moderate part of the network, all of the very conservative foundations are under the direct control of the original donating family.* On the basis of tax records and interviews, Cowell concludes it is a "reasonable supposition" that many, if not all, of the ultraconservative organizations of nonprofit standing receive a very large percentage of their annual budgets from philanthropic foundations and corporations.[21]

Foundations often become much more than sources of money that respond to requests for funding. Some foundations set up programs that are thought to be necessary by their trustees or staff. Then they search out appropriate organizations to undertake the project or create special commissions within the foundation itself. A few foundations have become so involved in a specific issue area that they function as a policy-discussion organization on that particular issue. This is especially the case with the Carnegie Corporation and its affiliates in the area of higher education. Their study groups, commissions, and fellowship programs have been central to the history of college and university development throughout the twentieth century. For example, the Carnegie Commission on Higher Education of the late 1960s and early 1970s spent $6 million and produced 80 books with policy implications for all aspects of higher education.[22]

Similarly, the Ford Foundation became the equivalent of a policy group on the issue of urban unrest in the 1950s and 1960s. It created a wide range of programs to deal with the problems generated by urban renewal programs and by the large black migration from the South into the inner cities of the North. One of these

*The tremendous impact that just a few extremely wealthy mavericks can have within the policy process is seen in the fact that the major funding for most of the new ultra-right organizations of the 1970s and 1980s came from one extremely conservative member of the Mellon family of Pittsburgh, Richard Mellon Scaife, who was giving $10 million a year through four foundations and trusts in addition to an unknown amount of money from the income of a personal fortune estimated to be worth $150 million. On the other side of the ideological divide, the liberal and social democratic lefts, a great percentage of their much smaller budgets also came from a handful of atypical multimillionaires, but these multimillionaires were neither as wealthy nor as numerous as those on the extreme right.[20]

programs, called the Gray Areas Project, became the basis for the War on Poverty declared by the Johnson Administration in 1964 in the face of serious urban unrest.[23]

Foundations, then, are an integral part of the policy-planning process both as sources of funds and program initiators. They are not mere donors of money for charity and value-free academic research. In contrast to the general image that is held of them, they are in fact extensions of the corporate community in their origins, leadership, and goals.

THINK TANKS
AND RESEARCH INSTITUTES

The deepest and most critical thinking within the policy-planning network does not take place in the discussion groups, as many academicians who have participated in them are quick to point out. This claim may be somewhat self-serving on the part of professors, who like to assume they are smarter than businesspeople and bankers. However, the fact remains that many new initiatives are created in various think tanks and university research institutes before they are brought to the discussion groups for modification and assimilation by the corporate leaders. Among the dozens of think tanks, some highly specialized in one or two topics, the most important are the RAND Corporation, the Urban Institute, the National Bureau of Economic Research, Resources for the Future, and centers for international studies at MIT, Harvard, and Georgetown. The institutes and centers connected to universities receive much of their funding from foundations, but the larger and less specialized independent think tanks are more likely to undertake contract research for businesses or government agencies.[24]

Some organizations are hybrids that incorporate both think tank and policy-discussion functions. They do not fit neatly into one category or the other. Such is the case with the Brookings Institution, one of the most important Washington-based organizations in the policy network. Formed in 1927 with the help of foundation monies, the Brookings Institution is directed by corporate executives, but it is not a membership organization. Although it conducts some study groups, particularly for government officials, it is even more important as a kind of postgraduate school for specialists in a wide range of policy areas. Employing a very large number of social scientists, it functions as a source of new ideas and consultants for policy groups and government leaders. Its economists in particular have been prominent as advisers to both Republican and Democratic administrations. In terms of common directors, its greatest overlaps are with the Committee for Economic Development, the Council on Foreign Relations, and the American Assembly. In addition, 60 percent of its trustees were foundation trustees in the early 1970s.[25]

Several hybrid organizations function in specialized issue-areas. The Population Council was established in 1952 to fund research and develop policy on population control. Relying at the outset on large personal donations from John D. Rockefeller III as well as grants from the Ford and Rockefeller Foundations, it helped to create population research institutes at several carefully selected universities in different regions of the country that would aid in giving respectability to this area of concern. It also held conferences and publicized findings that showed that population growth was a major problem. Working closely within several other organizations, including the Population Reference Bureau and International Planned Parenthood, it had enormous success in popularizing its policy suggestions and having them implemented at both the national and international levels, as a detailed case study demonstrates.[26] The step-by-step fashion in which the population groups proceeded, including the establishment of research institutes and spreading information through the mass media before approaching government, is a classic example of the policy network in action.

Resources for the Future was founded about the same time as the Population Council, with primary funding from the Ford Foundation. In part concerned with population because population growth puts pressure on resources, it has become one of the power elite's major sources of expertise on environmental issues. Its leaders share an informal coordinating role in this issue-area with the Conservation Foundation. Both work with the National Audubon Society, the National Wildlife Federation, and Nature Conservancy in attempting to infuse an environmental consciousness into the corporate community. At the same time they try to moderate the more militant demands of the middle-class environmental movement.[27]

Two organizations, the American Law Institute and the American Judicature Society, join with committees of the American Bar Association in dealing with problems within the issue-area of the law. The focus of the American Law Institute is on such general areas of law as tax law or the penal code. Its goal is to write model acts for state legislatures to consider, or to propose revisions in areas of the law through its written documents of restatement and clarification. The Judicature Society, on the other hand, is more specifically focused on the functioning of the court system, proposing methods to improve or streamline the administrative procedures of the judicial process. As one aspect of this interest, it is concerned with the processes by which state and federal judges are selected, and it attempts to influence standards of judicial conduct.

The leadership of the American Law Institute and the American Judicature Society comes primarily from the corporate lawyers who also play the dominant role within the American Bar Association. However, this is not exclusively the case with the Judicature Society. Its chair in 1981, for example, was an economist who heads the Henry Luce Foundation and serves as a director of the Council on Foreign Relations, New York Telephone, Bristol-Myers, American Express, American Can, and Chemical Bank.

There are hybrid organizations in other specialized areas as well, including farm policy, municipal government, and the arts.[28] In each case, many of their expert members and directors are part of the larger policy organizations as well. There is hardly a think tank of note that does not include directors from the Committee for Economic Development or Conference Board, or the Ford, Rockefeller, and Carnegie foundations. In the case of the larger Council on Foreign Relations, the overlaps are of course even more numerous.

Although the experts within the think tanks and university institutes relate to other members of the power elite primarily through the policy-planning groups, they are not without their own connections to the corporate community, either as directors or consultants. This point is made most systematically in the work of Charles Schwartz. He found through careful checking of corporate documents that there are many more such connections than are mentioned by these experts in standard biographical sources. Of 55 full-time university professors who served on the President's Science Advisory Committee between 1957 and 1973, for example, over half had served as directors of a corporation with annual sales or total assets of more than $100 million. Another 15 percent had served as consultants to these large firms or as directors of smaller companies.[29] Schwartz also looked at the interconnections of corporations and university experts by studying the boards of 130 of the largest corporations for 1974. The sample consisted of the top 100 industrials and the five biggest companies in the other six economic sectors listed by *Fortune*. Just over half (66) of these corporations had university presidents and professors on their boards. More specifically, 68 people from 44 different universities held 85 directorships on these boards.[30]

The extent of the consulting relationship between university experts and corporations is difficult to determine, for such information is considered private by both the professors and the corporations. A 1969 survey for the Carnegie Commission on Higher Education reported that 17 percent of the professors at major universities had acted as consultants for a national corporation in the two previous years. A less systematic survey of the Harvard faculty in the same year suggested that nearly one-half of the senior professors had outside incomes greater than one-third of their regular salaries, with much of this money probably coming from consulting arrangements.[31] The fees for such consulting usually are several hundred dollars a day plus expenses. They usually add up to between $5,000 and $25,000 a year, but sometimes the payments are quite dramatic. In 1981, for example, it was revealed that AT&T had paid Yale law professor Eugene V. Rostow, a very prominent member of several policy groups, a total of $456,000 in consulting fees over a four-year period beginning in 1975 to help in its defense against a government antitrust suit. Another Yale professor, Merton Peck, received between $44,000 and $50,000 a year between 1977 and 1980 from the same company.[32]

Information on specific elements of the overall network aside, there are several ways in which the people and ideas of the policy-planning network reach government. These avenues will be discussed in the next chapter, where the general relationship between the power elite and government is considered. It is now time to turn to the opinion-shaping process that has its roots in the organizations that have been discussed in this section.

THE OPINION-SHAPING PROCESS

The opinion-shaping process involves a wide range of organizations and methods through which members of the power elite attempt to influence the beliefs, attitudes, and opinions of the general public. In order to prevent the development of attitudes and opinions that might interfere with the acceptance of policies created in the policy-formation process, leaders within the opinion-molding process attempt to build upon and reinforce the underlying principles of the American belief system. Academically speaking, these underlying principles are called laissez-faire liberalism, and they have their roots in such great systematizers of the past as Locke, Hume, Montesquieu, Adam Smith, and the American founding fathers. These principles emphasize individualism, free enterprise, competition, equality of opportunity, and a minimum of reliance upon government in carrying out the affairs of society. Slowly articulated during the centuries-long rise of the capitalist system in Europe, they arrived in America in nearly finished form and had no serious rivals in a nation that did not have a feudal past or an established church.[33]

Popularly speaking, these values are known to most citizens as plain "Americanism." They are seen as part of human nature or the product of good common sense, not as just another belief system that may or may not have any more validity than the dozens of others that have been developed by nations and peoples around the world. Americanism, including the all-important component of patriotism that is a fanatical constant in all tribes and nations, is the world view, or ideology, of the United States.* If Americans can be convinced that some policy or action can be justified in terms of this emotion-laden and unquestioned body of beliefs, they are likely to accept it. Thus, the organizations that make up the opinion-shaping network strive to become the arbitrators of which policies and opinions are in keeping with good Americanism, and which are "un-American," meaning foreign and treasonous at the very least. These organizations struggle to define for everyone what policies are in the "national interest" and to identify those policies with Americanism.

One of the most important goals of the opinion-shaping network is to influence public schools, churches, and voluntary associations. To that end, organizations within the network have developed numerous links to these institutions, offering them movies, television programs, books, pamphlets, speakers, advice, and financial support. However, the schools, churches, and voluntary associations are not part of the network. Rather, they are relatively autonomous settings within which the power elite must constantly contend with spokespersons of other social strata and with critics of the economic system. To assume otherwise would be to overlook the social and occupational affiliations of the members as well as the diversity of opinion that often exists in these institutions of the middle and lower levels of the social hierarchy.

Operating at the center of the opinion-shaping process are many of the same foundations, policy-planning groups, and think tanks that are part of the policy-formation process. In this context, however, these organizations are connected to a large dissemination network that includes advertising agencies, public relations firms, corporate-financed advertising councils, special committees to influence single issues, and, not least, the very large and very active public affairs and public relations departments of the giant corporations. Unlike the policy-planning process, where a relatively small number of organizations do most of the work, there are thousands of organizations within the opinion-shaping process. In addition to a few organizations that do general ideological work, there are hundreds that specialize in

---

*An ideology is the complex set of rationales and rationalizations through which a group, class, or nation interprets the world and justifies its actions within it.

public relations and education in virtually every issue area. Thus, at its point of direct contact with the general public, the opinion-molding process is extremely diverse and diffuse, thereby making a full exposition very difficult. Here it is only possible to examine selected examples from various points in this wide-ranging network.

Shaping Opinion on Foreign Policy

The opinion-shaping network achieves its clearest expression and greatest success in the area of foreign policy, where most people have little information or interest and are predisposed to agree with top leaders out of patriotism and a fear of whatever is strange or foreign. Because so few people take a serious interest in foreign policy issues, the most important efforts in opinion shaping are aimed toward a small stratum of highly interested and concerned citizens of college-educated backgrounds.[34]

The central organizations in the shaping of opinion on foreign policy are the Council on Foreign Relations and the Foreign Policy Association. However, the council does very little to influence public opinion directly. It publishes *Foreign Affairs*, the most prestigious journal in the field, and occasionally it prints pamphlets on major issues that can be used by other discussion groups. However, these efforts are primarily for consumption within the foreign-policy establishment. For local elites, the council sponsors Committees on Foreign Relations in over 35 cities across the country. These committees meet about once a month or on the occasion of the visit of a special dignitary to hear speakers that are usually provided by the council or the government. The aim of this program is to provide local leaders with the information and legitimacy in the area of foreign affairs that makes it possible for them to function as opinion leaders. A 1951 report by the council on these committees explained their role as follows:

> In speaking of public enlightenment, it is well to bear in mind that the Council has chosen as its function the enlightenment of the leaders of opinion. These in turn, each in his own sphere, spread the knowledge gained here [Committees on Foreign Relations] in ever-widening circles.[35]

The most important organization involved in shaping upper-middle-class public opinion on foreign affairs is the Foreign Policy Association, based in New York. Forty-two percent of its 74-person governing council were also members of the Council on Foreign Relations in 1972.[36] Although the association does some research and discussion work, its primary focus is on molding opinion outside the power elite, a division of labor with the Council on Foreign Relations that is well understood within foreign-policy circles. A council director of the 1930s wrote that the FPA had "breadth of influence," whereas the CFR had "depth"; he went on to say that "anyone with the slightest experience in such matters knows that you must have policy-making individuals and groups working closely in a government" as well as "the support of the electorate" made possible in part by organizations that function "as channel-ways of expression."[37] More bluntly, a retired president of the council explained to historian Laurence Shoup that the council and its Committees on Foreign Relations attempt to reach top-level leaders, whereas the Foreign Policy Association attracted the "League of Women Voters type."[38]

The association's major effort is an intensive program to provide literature and create discussion groups in middle-class organizations and on college campuses. It sponsors a yearly Great Decisions program that prepares thematic discussions each year for groups around the country. It publishes a Headline Series of pamphlets for use in discussion groups, and it attempts to place its material on radio programs and into extension courses. It works closely with local World Affairs Councils to provide speakers and written materials, and it compiles foreign-policy briefings that are sent to all incumbents and candidates for Congress.

The council and the association, in turn, are linked to other opinion-molding organizations influential in foreign affairs. Perhaps the most important of them is the United Nations Association, which attempts to build support for American involvement in that organization. Another is the American Assembly, which sponsors discussion groups around the country on a variety of issues, not all of them concerning foreign policy. There are also foreign-affairs institutes at major universities that provide books and speakers reflecting the perspectives of the power elite on foreign policy.

The established organizations are supplemented when the need arises by special committees that publicize specific issues. Perhaps the biggest effort of this type was the Committee for the Marshall Plan, formed in 1947 to combat isolationist sentiment. Chaired by a former secretary of state who had been a member of the Council on Foreign Relations since the 1920s, it enlisted two labor leaders to join with five council members on its seven-member executive committee. Working with $150,000 in private contributions, the committee ran an all-out promotional campaign:

Regional committees were promptly organized, the cooperation of national organizations enlisted, and relevant publications given wide circulation. The committee promoted broad news and editorial coverage in metropolitan newspapers, set up a speaker's bureau, and employed a news agency which arranged for press releases, a special mat service for small town and country newspapers, and national and local radio broadcasts.[39]

In addition to its media efforts, the committee circulated petitions in every congressional district, then sent the results to the elected representatives. It also created an office in Washington to lobby Congress and to help prepare supportive testimony for appearances before congressional committees.

When it comes to the general public, the most important influences on foreign-policy opinions are the actions of the president and top foreign-policy officials. Political analyst Samuel Lubell provided one of the best examples of this point by means of interviews with a wide range of people shortly after the Soviet Union surprised everyone with the launching of Sputnik in the late 1950s:

> . . . especially striking was how closely the public's reactions corresponded to the explanatory "line" which was coming from the White House. ... In talking about Sputnik, most people tended to paraphrase what Eisenhower himself had said. ... In no community did I find any tendency on the part of the public to look for leadership to anyone else—to their newspapers, or radio commentators, to Congressmen, or to men of science.[40]

Public opinion polls conducted before and after critical events in the war in Vietnam showed similar results. For example, until the bombing of Hanoi and Haiphong began in late spring 1966, the public was split fifty-fifty on whether to bomb or not. When asked in July 1966, after the bombing began, if "the administration is more right or more wrong in bombing Hanoi and Haiphong," 85 percent favored the bombing. Conversely, 51 percent of those polled in March 1968 opposed a halt to the bombing, but when asked one month later if they approved or disapproved of a decision by President Lyndon B. Johnson to stop the bombing, only 26 percent disagreed with the President. Sixty-four percent agreed and 10 percent had no opinion. College-educated adults and people in younger age groups were most likely to show this change in opinion shortly after a presidential initiative.[41]

However, even on foreign policy there are limits to the shaping of public opinion. Opposition to both the Korean and Vietnam wars grew consistently as the number of American casualties continued to mount.[42] Vehement sentiment in the case of the Vietnam War helped to limit presidential alternatives in the late 1960s, and the constant complaints between 1975 and 1980 from foreign-policy leaders about the "post Vietnam syndrome" attested to the effects of a lingering antiwar sentiment on foreign-policy options.

Shaping Opinion on Economics

Attempts to shape public opinion on domestic issues, where people feel directly involved and have their own experiences to rely upon, are far more difficult than in the area of foreign policy. This is especially the case when there is no threat of a menacing external enemy to bind people together in common economic sacrifice. One of the most important of these domestic issues concerns the functioning of the economy. Blue-collar and white-collar workers who want better salaries and less inflation are often critical of corporations in public opinion polls. They complain that corporations are operating only to produce large profits for their stockholders and care little about employees or consumers.

Corporate leaders find such opinions very annoying and potentially troublesome. They blame them in part on a lack of economic understanding, which they have labeled "economic illiteracy." They believe these negative attitudes would change if people had the facts about the functioning of corporations and the economy, and they have spent tens of millions of dollars trying to present the facts as they see them. An analysis of how the power elite attempts to shape economic understanding is a case study in how the opinion-shaping network reaches into the school system on an issue of concern to it.

The central organization in the field of economic education is the Joint Council on Economic Education. Founded in 1949 by leaders within the Committee for Economic Development, the joint council received much of its early funding from the Ford Foundation.[43] Since 1964 it has been an independent organization, although its corporate-dominated board continues to have many members in common with the CED. Most of its financial support now comes from corporations and corporate foundations; in 1975, for example, its biggest backers were the American Bankers Association, AT&T, International Paper Company Foundation, the J.M. Foundation, Northern Gas Company, and Sears, Roebuck Foundation.

The joint council has several programs to influence the teaching of economics. At the most obvious level, it publishes books, pamphlets, movies, and teaching aids and provides school systems with curriculum guides and the literature and films of affiliated corporations. Equally important, it seeks to change the views of teachers through council-sponsored classes and workshops. These efforts began in the late 1940s and early 1950s with in-service mini-courses and summer workshops. The program expanded to the point where, in 1974, for example, 17,000 teachers participated in the in-service workshops and 2,500 took part in 84 summer workshops.[44] Graduates of the early workshops provided the joint council with the basis for local and regional councils designed to give support to economic education in the schools.

However, the real backbone of the joint council's strategy is its program in the 122 council-affiliated Centers for Economic Education at colleges and universities in 48 states. By the late 1970s, over three-fourths of the teacher-training programs in the country required social studies teachers to take an economics course, and the percentage of elementary teachers taking economics courses for teachers had risen from 13 percent to over one-third.

The program of the joint council, then, begins in corporate board rooms and foundation offices, flows through affiliated councils and university centers, and ends up in teacher-training programs and public school curricula. In that regard, it is an ideal example of the several steps and organizations that are usually involved in attempts to shape public opinion on any domestic issue. However, the level of economic illiteracy, according to polls taken for the corporations, remained as high in the 1970s as it was in the 1940s.[45]

This inability to engineer whole-hearted consent to the views of the power elite on economics reveals the limits of the opinion-shaping process in general. These limits are in good part created by the work experiences and general observations of average citizens, which lead them to be skeptical about many corporate claims. Then, too, the anticorporate analyses advocated by trade unionists, liberals, socialists, and middle-class ultraconservatives also have a counteracting influence. However, this continuing disagreement does not mean that the opinion-shaping process has failed completely in its task. Although it has not been able to bring about active acceptance of all power elite policies and perspectives, on economics or most other domestic issues, it has been able to ensure that opposing opinions have remained isolated, suspect, and only partially developed. The result is not a society-wide consensus, but "confusion, fragmentation, and inconsistency in belief systems," in the words of sociologist David Sallach.[46]

In summary, the most important role of an organization such as the joint council may be to help ensure that an alternative view does not consolidate to replace the resigned acquiescence and lack of interest in policy issues that are found by pollsters and survey researchers to permeate the political and economic consciousness of Americans at the lower levels of the socioeconomic ladder.[47] In the case of the joint council, this means that even with the continuing illiteracy on many specific issues, and the continuing criticism of specific corporations and their practices, the program has helped to maintain a general acceptance of the idea of private profits as a necessary feature of the economic system. This point is made by a leader in one of the many public relations firms that constantly monitors public opinion for the large corporations:

> Our work shows that better than nine out of 10 will certainly take strong exception to any threat to free enterprise. Even as many as three out of four feel that the role of profits is very clear—it's for the good of the country—and some even reinforce their belief in profits, or the profit motive, in terms of calling it a moral thing. It's moral to have a profit system because then, truly, the deserving get rewarded.[48]

Advertising and Public Opinion

Advertising is usually thought of in terms of the efforts used by corporations to sell specific products, but it can be used to sell the corporations and the economic system as well. Many corporations attempt to sell the free-enterprise system through what is called institutional advertising. Instead of talking about their products, they tell what they have done to benefit local communities, schools, or service organizations. Other corporations promote a good image by providing funds for local charities, donating services to community organizations, or sponsoring programs on public television. The quiet sponsorship on public television is especially useful in revealing the image-building efforts that motivate such sponsorship. A sociological study of donors to the public broadcasting system in the 1970s showed that the biggest donors were those companies that were having the most problems with the general public or regulatory bodies, especially oil companies and pharmaceutical companies.[49]

However, the most pervasive and longstanding use of advertising by the leaders within the corporate community and the opinion-shaping network can be seen in the functioning of the Advertising Council.[50] Once again, the council is only a striking example, not an organization of great importance in and of itself. The Advertising Council began its institutional life as the War Advertising Council during World War II as a means to support the war effort through advertising in the mass media. Its work was judged so successful in promoting a responsible image for the corporate community that it was continued in the postwar period as an agency to support Red Cross, United Fund, conservation, population control, and other campaigns that its corporate-dominated boards and advisory committees believe to be in the public interest. With an annual budget of only a few million dollars, the council nonetheless places over $500 million worth of free advertising through radio, television, magazines, newspapers, billboards, and public transportation. After the council leaders decide on which campaigns to endorse, the specifics of the program are given to one or another Madison Avenue advertising agency, which does the work without charge.

Most council campaigns seem relatively innocuous and in a public interest that nobody would dispute. Its best-known figure for many years, Smokey the Bear, was created in the campaign against forest fires. However, as media analyst Glenn K. Hirsch demonstrates in his detailed study of these campaigns, many of them have a strong slant in favor of corporations. The council's ecology ads do not point the finger at corporations as the prime cause of a dirty environment. They suggest instead that "people start pollution, people can stop it," thereby putting the responsibility on individuals rather than a system of production that allows corporations to avoid the costs of disposing their waste products by dumping them into the air or water. A special subcommittee of the council's Industry Advisory Committee gave very explicit instructions about how this ad campaign should be formulated: "The committee emphasized that the [advertisements] should stress that each of us must be made to recognize that each of us contributes to pollution, and therefore everyone bears the responsibility."[51] Thus, the campaign was geared to deflect growing criticism of the corporate role in pollution as well as to show corporate concern about the environment.

Along with its standard support for voluntary organizations, the council also tries to create a receptive climate for new government programs that it favors. In the early 1970s, for example, it ran ads downgrading the importance of college education and praising technical education. This campaign came at a time when corporate and government officials foresaw a surplus of college graduates on the job market. It marked a turnaround from earlier ad campaigns that encouraged high school graduates to go to college because they could make more money over a lifetime with a college degree.

The council also tries to help restore order in times of crisis. Between 1965 and 1971 there was an unprecedented 95 percent growth in expenditures by the mass media in support of council campaigns, and most of this effort was directed at ghetto unrest. One set of commercial messages in 1965 urged people to "Put Your Racial Problems on the Table—Keep Them Off the Streets." In 1970 the council assembled over 100 notables from business, labor, sports, and politics to demonstrate racial harmony by joining together to sing "Let the Sun Shine" from a hit musical of the era, *Hair.* In a more sober vein, the council ran a "Crisis Series," which urged businesspeople to give jobs to ghetto blacks. This series resulted in more pages of advertisements in the business press than ever had been given to a single campaign.[52]

The effectiveness of such campaigns is open to question. It is not clear that they have a direct influence on very many opinions. Studies by social scientists suggest that advertising campaigns of a propagandistic nature work best "when used to reinforce an already existing notion or to establish a logical or emotional connection between a new idea and a social norm."[53] But even when an ad campaign can be judged a failure in this limited role, it has filled a vacuum that might have been used by a competing group. This is especially the case with television, where the council is able to capture more than 80 percent of the public-service advertising time that television networks must provide by law. Thus, Hirsch concludes his assessment of the effectiveness of the Advertising Council by stressing both its direct and indirect effects: "its commercials reinforce and channel existing values, while simultaneously preventing groups with a different ideology from presenting their interpretation of events."[54]

The Advertising Council is in some ways unique because of its prominence, massive resources, and wide range of concerns. In its major activities, however, it is typical of a wide variety of opinion-shaping organizations that function in specific areas from labor relations, where they battle union organizers, to something as far removed as the arts, where they encourage the development of the arts as a booster to the morale of those trapped in the inner city. Those functions are basically three in number:

1. They provide think-tank forums where academics, journalists, and other cultural experts can brainstorm with corporate leaders about the problems of shaping public opinion.
2. They help to create a more sophisticated corporate consciousness through forums, booklets, speeches, and awards.
3. They disseminate their version of the national interest to the general public on issues of concern to the power elite.

THE MASS MEDIA

The mass media—newspapers, magazines, television, and radio—are one outlet for much of the material generated by the organizations of the opinion-shaping network. Many social scientists believe that the media, and in particular television, play a large role in the shaping of public opinion. However, it seems more likely to me that they have a much more secondary role, reinforcing existing viewpoints and helping to set the outer limits of respectable discourse.

The mass media have a complex relationship to the upper class and corporate community. On the one hand, they are lucrative business enterprises owned by members of the upper class and directed by members of the corporate community who have extensive connections to other large corporations. On the other hand, editors and journalists, fortified by a professional code of objectivity and impartiality, have some degree of independence in what they report and write, and their opinions are sometimes at variance with those of corporate executives and policy experts. The result is a relationship between media and corporate community that is marked by tension, with corporate leaders placing part of the blame on the mass media for any negative opinions about business that are held by the general public.[55]

The differences in viewpoint between corporate leaders and media professionals is brought home in an elite opinion survey conducted in 1970–1971. Surveying leaders from business, labor, media, and minority group organizations, as well as politicians, civil servants, and leaders of both liberal and ultraconservative advocacy groups, sociologist Allan Barton and his associates found that representatives of the mass media were more liberal on foreign policy and domestic issues than corporate and conservative leaders, although not as liberal as the representatives of minority groups and liberal organizations. On questions of environment, which were very sensitive to corporate leaders during the 1970s, the media professionals held much the same liberal views as people from labor, minority, and liberal organizations. The corporate suspicion of liberals within the media is not without basis, at least for the early 1970s.[56]

The growing rift between the corporate community and the liberal elements of the mass media led to a number of corporate initiatives in the late 1970s. In 1977, for example, the Ford Foundation sponsored an off-the-record, two-day conference between business and media representatives that was designed to air mutual grievances. Programs to teach "business reporting" were created at several universities with the goal of improving the skills and judgment of reporters. Finally, corporations led by Mobil Oil began to run advertisements on opinion pages in major newspapers, and in liberal weeklies and reviews. They presented the corporations' viewpoints in their own words on a variety of issues. By 1976 corporations were spending $140 million a year on such advocacy advertising.[57]

For all the corporate community's complaints about specific stories, newspapers, or television stations within the mass media, the overall effect of the media efforts nevertheless tends to reinforce the stability of the present corporate system. First of all, as highly profitable companies whose primary goal is to sell advertising, their basic allegiance is to the corporate system. This is evidenced in the fact that their owners and directors play an active role in setting limits beyond which their reporters cannot go without facing reassignment, demotion, or firing. Then, too, editorial policies make a distinction between criticizing the system and exposing the wrongdoing of specific corporations, industries, or politicians. For example, the *Wall Street Journal*, perhaps the favorite newspaper of the corporate community and a fierce champion of the free enterprise system, has nonetheless published numerous stories exposing unacceptable behavior by corporate leaders and policy experts. Especially damning was a story in 1980 that showed that President-elect Ronald Reagan's top foreign-policy adviser, Richard Allen, a former fellow of the Hoover Institution, had worked as a paid consultant to Japanese corporations while serving as a government adviser.[58]

Finally, the media reinforce the legitimacy of the social system through the routine ways in which they accept and package events. Their style and tone always takes the statements of business and government leaders seriously, treating their claims with great respect. In the area of foreign policy, for example, the media cover events in such a way that America's diplomatic aims are always honorable, corporate involvement overseas is necessary and legitimate, and revolutionary change in most countries is undesirable and must be discouraged whatever the plight of the majority of their citizens.[59]

Whatever the exact role of the mass media, it should be clear that they are not the be-all and end-all of the opinion-shaping process that has been outlined in this section. In my view, the mass media are merely one dissemination point among many. They reach the most people, but the people they reach are those who matter least from the point of view of the opinion molders, and the message they provide is sometimes ambiguous besides.

CONCLUSION

This chapter has introduced the concept of a power elite as the leadership group of the upper class. This power elite is composed of members of the upper class who have taken on leadership roles in the corporate community and the policy network, along with high-level employees in these institutions. More formally, the power elite consists of active, working members of the upper class and high-level employees in profit and nonprofit institutions controlled by members of the upper class through stock ownership, financial support, or involvement on the board of directors.

In theory, the upper class, the corporate community, and the policy-planning network from which this power elite is drawn can be imagined as three intersecting circles. A person can be a member of one of the three, or two of the three, or all three. There can be upper-class people who are only socialites, corporate leaders who are neither upper class nor involved in policy planning, and policy experts who are neither upper class nor members of the corporate community.

As a practical matter, however, the interrelations among these three sectors are even closer than the image of three intersecting circles would indicate. Most male members of the upper class between 45 and 65 are, in fact, part of the corporate community as owners, active investors, or titled executives even if they are not directors in top corporations. Then, too, a great many members of the policy network become involved in the corporate community as consultants and advisers even if they do not rise to the level of corporate directors. Thus, the corporate community becomes the common sector that encompasses most older males within the three overlapping circles.

Although this chapter provides evidence for the existence of a network of policy-planning and opinion-shaping organizations that are extensions of the corporate community in their financing and leadership, it does not claim there is a unified power elite policy line that is readily agreed upon and then easily foisted on a hapless mass of passive citizens. Instead, it shows that the upper class and corporate community have created a complex and only partially coordinated set of institutions and organizations that often disagree among themselves about what policies are most compatible with the primary objectives of the corporate community, and that are only partially successful in convincing wage and salary earners that these policies are in everyone's interest.

Nonetheless, the weight of the emphasis has to be on the considerable similarity in viewpoint among institutions that range from moderately conservative to highly conservative in their policy suggestions and that have in their two contending camps a near monopoly of nongovernmental expertise and research support. Even if they are not able to agree completely among themselves, they have been able to discourage development of a large body of experts with a more liberal point of view. They also have been successful in keeping the few liberal programs that do exist at the fringe of serious discussion.

The chapter thus provides evidence for a form of power exercised by the upper class through its power elite—expertise. Expert power is an important complement to the subtle status power and naked economic power discussed in the two previous chapters. Since government officials with only small policy-planning staffs must often turn to foundations, policy groups, think tanks, and university institutes if they are to have new ideas for dealing with emerging problems, it is once again a form of power that can be exercised without any necessary direct involvement in government.

Indeed, status power, economic power, and expertise are formidable quite independent of any involvement in government. But they are not enough to sustain the upper class as a ruling class without the ability to influence government directly. This is because the governmental system is the primary coordinating center within the society. It has numerous functions that affect the upper class and the corporate community greatly. As the main avenue through which some redistribution of the country's wealth and income could be effected in a democratic way, it is the arena within which other groups and classes fight for new rights and benefits. It can pass laws that help or hinder profit making, and it can collect and utilize tax funds in such a way as to stimulate or discourage economic growth. It is needed to enforce the laws of the land, including the laws that keep corporate profits in a few hands. It has to be capable of defending the nation's territory, and it can play a crucial role in defending and expanding the economic interests of American corporations overseas. Perhaps just as important, if somewhat more nebulous, it is the place in the social system that legitimates new policies through the actions of elected and appointed officials.

For all these reasons, it is necessary for leaders within the upper class and corporate community to have means by which they can ensure that government decisions continue to support their basic interests, which have been summarized as the interests of economic accumulation and political legitimation by economist James O'Connor.[60] Given what is at stake, it is unlikely that any upper class has ever been content to leave governmental actions in the hands of disinterested civil servants and elected officials. If people want to be sure that individuals they know and trust are in the positions with a wide latitude of decision-making discretion within the corporations, as the work of organizational sociologists suggests, then it is likely this would be even more the case with government.

It follows, therefore, that there should be evidence of power elite involvement in the national government in America if the upper class is a ruling class. Such evidence is readily at hand, and it will be presented in the next chapter.

NOTES

1. For a strong argument against an overemphasis by Marxists on ideology and public opinion in explaining the stability of power structures, see Michael Mann, "The Ideology of Intellectuals and Other People in the Development of Capitalism," in *Stress and Contradiction in Modern Capitalism*, ed. Leon N. Lindberg, et al. (Lexington, Mass.: Lexington Books, 1975). For evidence on the differing opinions of elites and underclasses in America, see Richard Hamilton, *Class and Politics in the United States* (New York: Wiley, 1972) and Michael Mann, "The Social Cohesion of Liberal Democracy," *American Sociological Review*, June 1970.
2. G. William Domhoff, *Who Rules America?* (Englewood Cliffs, N.J.: Prentice-Hall, 1967), p. 72; Lawrence Shoup and William Minter, *Imperial Brain Trust* (New York: Monthly Review Press, 1977), p. 87.
3. Shoup and Minter, *Imperial Brain Trust*, pp. 87, 97.
4. Harold Salzman and G. William Domhoff, "The Corporate Community and Government: Do They Interlock?" in *Power Structure Research*, ed. G. William Domhoff (Beverly Hills, Calif.: Sage Publications, 1980), p. 235.
5. Dale Dunham and G. William Domhoff, "The Council on Foreign Relations in Government: Connections with the Nixon and Carter Administrations" (Paper delivered to the meetings of the International Studies Association, Los Angeles, Spring 1980).
6. Council on Foreign Relations, *Annual Reports*, 1978–79; Council on Foreign Relations, *Annual Reports*, 1979–80.
7. Shoup and Minter, *Imperial Brain Trust*, chapters 4–6.
8. Ibid., chapter 7; Lawrence Shoup, *The Carter Presidency and Beyond*. (Palo Alto, Calif.: Ramparts Press, 1980); John S. Treantafelles, "The Trilateral Commission in the Policy Planning Process" (Masters thesis, California State University, Los Angeles, 1980).
9. *The Soviet Challenge: A Policy Framework for the 1980's.* (New York: Council on Foreign Relations, 1981).
10. "Tough Response: Meeting the Soviet Threat," *Time*, May 25, 1981; "Foreign Affairs Council Advocates Arms Increase," *New York Times*, May 4, 1981, p. 10.
11. David Eakins, "The Development of Corporate Liberal Policy Research in the United States, 1885–1965" (Ph.D. diss., University of Wisconsin, 1966), p. 346.
12. *Ibid.* Karl Schriftgiesser, *Business Comes of Age.* (New York: Harper & Row, 1960); idem, *Business and Public Policy.* (Englewood Cliffs, N.J.: Prentice-Hall, 1967).
13. Eakins, "Development of Corporate Liberal Policy Research," chapter 5.

14. Wesley McCune, *Who's Behind Our Farm Policy?* (New York: Praeger, 1956); G. William Domhoff, *Fat Cats and Democrats* (Englewood Cliffs, N.J.: Prentice-Hall, 1972), pp. 158–166; Dan Morgan, "Hearts and Minds: The Conservative Network," *Washington Post*, January 4, 1981, p. A-14.

15. James Weinstein, *The Corporate Ideal in the Liberal State* (Boston: Beacon Press, 1968); David S. McLelland and Charles E. Woodhouse, "The Business Elite and Foreign Policy," *Western Political Science Quarterly*, March 1960; idem, "American Business Leaders and Foreign Policy: A Study in Perspectives," *American Journal of Economics and Sociology*, July 1966.

16. Domhoff, *Who Rules America?* p. 65; Salzman and Domhoff, "The Corporate Community and Government," p. 234.

17. Shoup and Minter, *Imperial Brain Trust*, pp. 78–79.

18. Mary Anna Culleton Colwell, "The Foundation Connection: Links among Foundations and Recipient Organizations," in *Philanthropy and Cultural Imperialism*, ed. Robert F. Arnove (Boston: Hall, 1980), pp. 418–19.

19. Ibid., pp. 419–421.

20. Karen Rothmyer, "Citizen Scaife," *Columbia Journalism Review*, July/August 1981.

21. Mary Anna Culleton Colwell, "Philanthropic Foundations and Public Policy: The Political Role of Foundations" (Ph.D. diss., University of California, Berkeley, 1980).

22. Merle Curti and Roderick Nash, *Philanthropy in the Shaping of American Higher Education* (New Brunswick, N.J.: Rutgers University Press, 1965); Frank Darknell, "The Carnegie Council for Policy Studies in Higher Education: A New Policy Group for the Ruling Class," *Insurgent Sociologist*, Spring 1975; idem, "The Carnegie Philanthropy and Private Corporate Influence on Higher Education," in *Philanthropy and Cultural Imperialism*, ed. Robert F. Arnove (Boston: Hall, 1980); David E. Weischadle, "The Carnegie Corporation and the Shaping of American Educational Policy," in *Philanthropy and Cultural Imperialism*, ed. Robert F. Arnove (Boston: Hall, 1980).

23. *Oral History, Paul Ylvisaker* (Ford Foundation Archives), p. 23; Leonard Silk and Mark Silk, *The American Establishment* (New York: Basic Books, 1980), chapter 4; Daniel Moynihan, *Maximum Feasible Misunderstanding* (New York: Free Press, 1969).
Ylvisaker's account of the general urban affairs program at the Ford Foundation shows very clearly how important the corporate trustees were in shaping this program. For example, Ylvisaker constantly mentions (pp. 15–17, 25–27, 33, 46–47) his great concern to check out initiatives with local "power structures" and "grand old sachems" because he knew the trustees would be in touch with such people in any case.
In a book that makes a major contribution to political sociology by showing that welfare payments are both a way of regulating social disruptions and enforcing work norms, Francis Piven and Richard Cloward, *Regulating the Poor* (New York: Pantheon, 1971), pp. 255–63, argue that the origins of the War on Poverty and related urban programs were in the desire of national-level Democratic politicians to bind black

voters in inner cities to the Democratic Party. The role of the Ford Foundation suggests that this view does not go far enough. The Ylvisaker oral history, for example, suggests that corporate officials had nonpolitical reasons for supporting such a program. The Democrats probably saw the program as to their benefit, but its corporate dimension should not be ignored either.

24. Paul Dickson, *Think Tanks* (New York: Atheneum, 1971).

25. Eakins, "Development of Corporate Liberal Policy Research"; Colwell, "The Foundation Connection"; Phillip Bonacich and G. William Domhoff, "Latent Classes and Group Membership," *Social Networks*, Winter 1982; Irvine Alpert and Ann Markusen, "Think Tanks and Capitalist Policy," *Power Structure Research*, ed. G. William Domhoff (Beverly Hills, Calif.: Sage Publications, 1980).

26. Phyllis T. Piotrow, *World Population Crisis: The United States Response* (New York: Praeger, 1973); William Barclay, Joseph Enright, and Reid T. Reynolds, "Population Control in the Third World," *NACLA Newsletter*, December 1970.

27. Alpert and Markusen, "Think Tanks and Capitalist Policy"; Peter Collier and David Horowitz, *The Rockefellers: An American Dynasty* (New York: Holt, 1976), pp. 84–85, 305–6, 401.

28. McCune, *Who's Behind Our Farm Policy;* Frank M. Stewart, *A Half Century of Municipal Reform* (Berkeley, Calif.: University of California Press, 1950); Arnold Gingrich, *Business and the Arts* (New York: Eriksson, 1969).

29. Charles Schwartz, "The Corporate Connection," *Bulletin of the Atomic Scientist*, October 1975.

30. Charles Schwartz, "Academics in Government and Industry" (Paper, Department of Physics, University of California at Berkeley, 1975), p. 25.

31. Ibid., pp. 2, 20.

32. Robert Walters, "Academics on AT&T's Payroll" (Syndicated column, Newspaper Enterprise Associates, New York, June 22, 1981).

33. Louis Hartz, *The Liberal Tradition in America* (New York: Harcourt, 1955); Seymour M. Lipset, *The First New Nation* (New York: Basic Books, 1963); Francis X. Sutton et al., *The American Business Creed* (Cambridge, Mass.: Harvard University Press, 1956).

34. James N. Rosenau, *Public Opinion and Foreign Policy* (New York: Random House, 1961); Bernard C. Cohen, *The Public's Impact on Foreign Policy* (Boston: Little, Brown, 1973).

35. Shoup and Minter, *Imperial Brain Trust*, p. 31.

36. Ibid., p. 72.

37. Ibid., p. 71.

38. Ibid., p. 31.

39. Harry B. Price, *The Marshall Plan and Its Meaning* (Ithaca, N.Y.: Cornell University Press, 1955), p. 56.

40. Samuel Lubell, "Sputnik and American Public Opinion," *Columbia University Forum*, Winter 1957, p. 18.

41. John E. Mueller, *War, Presidents and Public Opinion* (New York: Wiley, 1973), pp. 70 table 4.2, 72ff table 4.3.

42. Ibid. The influence of rising casualties on public opinion is the major finding of this book.

43. Schriftgiesser, *Business and Public Policy,* chapter 22. The chapter is entitled "Fighting Economic Illiteracy." See also Karl Kraeplin, "The American Upper Class and the Problem of Legitimacy: The Joint Council on Economic Education," *Insurgent Sociologist,* Winter 1979.

44. Joint Council on Economic Education, *Annual Report,* 1975, p. 3.

45. E.g., "Americans Are Economically 'Illiterate,'" *San Francisco Chronicle,* November 26, 1977, p. 44.

46. David Sallach, "Class Domination and Ideological Hegemony," *Sociological Quarterly,* Winter 1974, p. 42.

47. Mann, "The Social Cohesion of Liberal Democracy."

48. Florence R. Skelly, "The Changing Attitudes of Public Opinion," *Public Relations Journal,* November 1976, pp. 15–16. My thanks to Glenn K. Hirsch for bringing this article to my attention.

49. M. David Ermann, "The Operative Goals of Corporate Philanthropy: Contributions to the Public Broadcasting Service, 1972–1976," *Social Problems,* June 1978.

50. Glenn K. Hirsch, "Only You Can Prevent Ideological Hegemony: The Advertising Council and Its Place in the American Power Structure," *Insurgent Sociologist,* Spring 1975.

51. Ibid., p. 69.

52. Ibid., pp. 76–77.

53. Ibid., p. 78.

54. Ibid., p. 79.

55. Peter Dreier, "The Position of the Press in the American Power Structure," *Social Problems,* December 1981; Peter Dreier and Steve Weinberg, "Interlocking Directorates," *Columbia Journalism Review,* November/December 1979. The neo-Marxist analysis by Dreier presents a full picture of the complex position occupied by the mass media.

56. Allen H. Barton, "Fault Lines in American Elite Consensus," *Daedalus,* Summer 1980.

57. Peter Dreier, "Capitalists vs. the Media: An Analysis of an Ideological Mobilization among Business Leaders," *Media, Culture & Society,* April 1982.

58. Jonathan Kwitney, "The Rehabilitation of Richard Allen," *New Republic,* December 6, 1980. This article by the *Wall Street Journal* reporter who broke the story into the major mass media summarizes the issues and records the way in which the Reagan administration handled the problems. A year later Allen was relieved of his duties as Reagan's foreign-policy adviser because of adverse publicity on other possible conflicts of interest.

59. David L. Paletz and Robert M. Entman, *Media Power Politics* (New York: Free Press, 1981), chapter 13, for a good account of the role of the media in shaping opinion on foreign affairs. For other good accounts of the role of the media in reinforcing the status quo, see Gaye Tuchman, *Making News* (New York: Free Press, 1978); Herbert J. Gans, *Deciding What's News* (New York: Pantheon, 1979); and Todd Gitlin *The Whole World Is Watching* (Berkeley, Calif.: University of California Press, 1980).

60. James O'Connor, *The Fiscal Crisis of the State* (New York: St. Martin's, 1973).

5

The Power Elite
and Government

INTRODUCTION

Members of the power elite directly involve themselves in the federal government through three basic processes, each of which plays a slightly different role in ensuring access to the White House, Congress, and specific agencies, departments, and committees in the executive branch. Although some of the same people are involved in all three processes, most people specialize in one or two of the three processes. This is because each process requires slightly different knowledge, skills, and contacts. The three processes are

1. The candidate selection process, through which members of the power elite attempt to influence electoral campaigns by means of campaign finances and favors to political candidates.
2. The special-interest process, through which specific individuals, corporations, and industrial sectors realize their narrow and short-run interests on taxes, subsidies, and regulation in dealing with congressional committees, regulatory bodies, and executive departments.
3. The policy-making process, through which the general policies of the policy-planning network explained in the previous chapter are brought to the White House and Congress.

THE CANDIDATE-SELECTION PROCESS

The power elite involves itself in the candidate-selection process through the simple, direct, and often very unsubtle means of large campaign donations that far outweigh what other classes and groups can muster. Although the method of involvement is simple, the reason such a direct approach is possible requires a structural and historical understanding of why politics operate as they do in the United States. Only part of that understanding can be provided in this chapter, however.

Candidate selection at the national level takes place through a party system that is the oldest and most stable in the world as well as one of the few that has only two major parties. It is a party system that grew slowly and took its unique shape because of the basic governmental system. As political scientist Theodore Lowi summarizes, "Parties and elections are so intertwined that the very structure of parties is shaped by the electoral process."[1]

Two fundamental features of American government lead to a two-party system. The first is the election of a president, and the second is the election of senators and representatives from states and districts. The fact that only one person can win the presidency or be elected from a given state or district, which seems trivial and is taken for granted by most Americans, creates a series of "winner-take-all" elections in which a vote for a third candidate of the right or left is in effect support for the voter's least-favored candidate on the other side of the political spectrum. Because a vote for a third candidate is a vote for "your worst enemy," the most sensible strategy for those who want to avoid this fate is to form the largest possible preelection coalition, even if numerous policy preferences must be abandoned or compromised. The inevitable result is two coalitional parties that attempt to blur their differences in order to win the voters in the middle.

By way of contrast, the parliamentary systems that exist in most democratic countries create a different party system. Because a prime minister is selected by the legislature from among its members after the election, there is less pressure toward two preelectoral coalitions, thus making the existence of several issue-oriented parties possible or for a new third party to grow over the period of several elections. Even more parties are likely to exist if the parliament is elected by a system of proportional representation that abandons geographical election districts and gives each party legislative seats roughly in proportion to the percentage of the entire electorate that supports it. According to sociologist Seymour Martin Lipset, "every country which uses proportional representation has four or more parties represented in the legislature, and, except in Norway, Sweden, and Ireland in recent decades, absolute parliamentary majorities of one party have been extremely rare."[2] Thus, comparative studies of the relationship between electoral rules and the number of political parties suggest how candidate selection in the United States came to be conducted through a two-party system despite the existence of class, regional, and ethnic conflicts that have led to three or more parties in other countries. On the basis of these studies, Lipsit suggests the following relationship between electoral systems and party systems:

> If enough cases existed for analysis, the following rank-order correlation might be found between electoral systems and the number of political parties: presidential system with single-member districts and one plurality election—two parties; parliamentary system with single-member districts and one plurality election—tendency to two parties; parliamentary system with single-member districts and alternative ballot or run-off (second) election—tendency to many parties; proportional representation—many parties.[3]

Although the system of presidential elections and single-member congressional districts generates the strong tendency toward a two-party system, it was not designed with this fact in mind. The Founding Fathers wished to create a system of checks and balances that would keep power within bounds, including the potential power of an aroused and organized majority of farmers and artisans. However, the creation of a two-party system was not among their plans. Indeed, the Founding Fathers disliked the idea of parties, which they condemned as "factions" that were highly divisive. Parties were a major unintended consequence of their deliberations, and it was not until the 1830s and 1840s that a new generation of political leaders finally accommodated themselves to the idea that the two-party system was not disruptive of rule by elites.[4]

If leaders eventually came to see parties as a way of arguing about those issues over which they disagreed, pluralists came to see them as something much more, as one of the most important means by which average citizens influence governmental policies. Using an economic analogy, they likened voters to consumers and the electoral process to the marketplace. Voters could influence parties to offer their favorite policies by means of their votes in the same way that consumers could influence businesses to offer their favorite products by means of their purchases. Economist Donald Wittman, who has raised serious questions about this marketplace analogy, summarizes the typical view as follows: "Selfishness and competition by the parties are shown to lead to an optimal result. Adam Smith's 'Invisible Hand' has been applied to politics."[5]

The analysis by political scientists Nelson W. Polsby and Aaron B. Wildavsky of the way that the presidential election limits and shapes national policy embodies this general pluralist view. They begin by stating the argument in its most general form:

> The two political parties to a certain extent act as transmissions belts for policy preferences in the general population. They perform this function partly out of choice—as partisans, party leaders know more and care more about issues—but mostly out of necessity.[6]

In this view, the fear of losing office keeps politicians responsive to voters. "In a competitive two-party system such as exists in American presidential politics, the lively possibility of change provides an effective incentive for political leaders to remain in touch with followers." At the same time, Polsby and Wildavsky concede there is no direct relationship between the policy preferences of voters in a single election and the behavior of the President in office; it takes time for the relationship between policies and elections to work itself out: "Aside from casting extremists out beyond the pale, free elections and a two-party system operate to bring government policy roughly in line with intense public preferences over a reasonable span of time."[7]

Polsby and Wildavsky contrast their view with what they wrongly claim to be the power-elite perspective: "A cynical view would hold that the United States was ruled by a power elite—a small group outside the democratic process."[8] The fatal misconception in their characterization of the power-elite position is in the phrase "outside the democratic process." If there is anything to a power-elite analysis of the United States, it is in its ability to show how the power elite operates within—not outside—the democratic process, including the two-party system.

There is evidence to show that the assumptions underlying the pluralist model of how the parties operate are incorrect. The assumption that politicians will adopt the views of the majority in order to be elected is contradicted by the fact that most politicians do not subscribe to the very liberal views on economic issues that are held by a majority of the electorate.[9] Nor does a party and its candidate always try to win. There are numerous examples where party leaders have preferred to lose with a candidate who shared their views rather than win with one who seemed to be more popular with the electorate. Such was the fate of populist Democratic candidates in the Midwest in the late nineteenth century whose economic programs were disliked by wealthy Democratic leaders, and it also was the fate of antiwar candidate Eugene McCarthy at the Democratic National Convention in 1968. McCarthy was brushed aside by party officials even though polls showed he would do much better against Nixon or Rockefeller than would Hubert Humphrey.[10]

Then, too, there is evidence that the parties sometimes collude rather than compete. This is especially the case when an "unacceptable" candidate wins the nomination in one or the other of them. In 1972, for example, southern Democrats and labor Democrats openly or tacitly supported Nixon against the party's candidate, George McGovern. To reciprocate this support, "more than a hundred Republican candidates for seats held by Southern and labor-backed Democrats were simply written off by White House strategists."[11] Collusion need not be explicit, however. Wittman makes this point very clearly after showing through a game-theory argument that collusion between the two parties often makes better sense for them than competition if they are interested in rewards other than winning, as indeed they often are:

> The parties may find many ways of restricting competition with each other: bipartisanship, promotion of mutually acceptable ideologies, marginal changes in the previous administration's policies, and recruitment of those who are not antagonistic to the other party. Even the belief in the impossibility of certain platforms being able to win the election may be a form of implicit collusion if there is more fiction than substance to the belief. Thus the parties compete more *with* the voters than *for* the voters or *with each other.*[12]

Contrary to the pluralist claim, then, there is no a priori theoretical reason to believe that political parties and their candidates will reflect out of necessity the policy preferences of the majority of the voters. Candidates and parties are relatively free to say one thing and do another. Once in office the President or other elected officials have the ability to interpret their mandate just about any way they want to. Lyndon B. Johnson's landslide in 1964 obviously involved his professions of a less "warlike" policy for Southeast Asia than Barry Goldwater seemed to have, but he and his party escalated the war soon after his victory. In 1980 polls showed that Ronald Reagan's victory in part reflected the dissatisfaction with unemployment on the part of the traditional democratic voters who defected to him and a belief on their part that he would stimulate the economy and leave their "safety net" intact. But his administration claimed its success as a mandate for the policies of Calvin Coolidge and proceeded to increase unemployment and cut social welfare programs.[13]

It even may be that a two-party system discourages policy discussion, political education, and an attempt to satisfy majority preference, rather than encouraging these activities, as in the pluralist analogy with the free market. The need for a majority vote where the stakes are high, such as the presidency, may lead to campaigns in which there are no issues but personality, even when voters are extremely issue conscious. For example, journalist Jules Witcover, who covered the 1976 presidential election in great detail, saw the campaign as one of image building and issue avoiding, with both candidates asking voters to put their trust in them on the basis of their personal qualities. Meanwhile, both parties concentrated on the personal peccadilloes of the other candidate:

> It had not been what one would call an uplifting campaign for the highest office in the land. The political horizon had been cluttered with superficial matters: the valences in Clarence Kelley's apartment built by FBI carpenters; artful dodging by both Ford and Carter on the abortion issue, in blatant courtship of the Catholic vote; reports of Ford's free golfing trips [from U.S. Steel] and Carter's [free] hunting trips [from lumber companies]; Carter's dissembling on a tax-reform statement and Ford's dissembling on Carter's dissembling; disclosure that Carter lusted in his heart; and pious denunciation from presumably lustless Republicans.[14]

Then, too, there is evidence that a two-party system discourages voting, for those in a minority of even 49 percent receive nothing for their efforts. In countries where single-member districts have been abandoned for proportional representation, voting has increased considerably. It is also the case that the percentage of people voting in the United States has decreased during the twentieth century even while it remains constant or increases in most European countries.[15] Perhaps the major conclusion to be drawn about the political consequences of the two-party system is not that it allows citizens to express their policy preferences but that it creates a situation where there is very little relationship between politics and policy. As Lowi concludes: "Majorities produced by the American two-party system are simply numerical majorities; they usually have no political content whatsoever."[16]

In a system where policy preferences become blurred, the emphasis on the images of individual candidates becomes very great. Individual personalities become more important than the policies of the parties. This tendency has been increased somewhat with the rise of the mass media, in particular television, but it is a reality of American politics that has existed far longer than is understood by the many columnists and pundits who lament the "recent" decline of political parties. The executive director of a congressional watchdog organization, the National Committee for an Effective Congress, put the matter even more strongly well before the alleged deterioration of the parties become a media cliche:

> For all intents and purposes, the Democratic and Republican parties
> don't exist. There are only individuals (i.e., candidates) and profession-
> als (i.e., consultants, pollsters, and media advisers).[17]

It is because the candidate-selection process in the American two-
party system is so individualistic, and therefore dependent upon
name recognition and personal image, that it can be in good part
dominated by members of the power elite through the relatively
simple and direct means of large campaign contributions. In the roles
of both big donors and fund raisers, the same people who direct
corporations and take part in policy groups play a central role in the
careers of most politicians who advance beyond the local level in
states of any size and consequence. "Recruitment of elective elites,"
concludes political scientist Walter D. Burnham, "remains closely
associated, especially for the most important offices in the larger
states, with the candidates' wealth or access to large campaign
contributions."[18]

The role of the wealthy donor and the fund raiser seems to be
especially crucial in the nomination phase of the process. This was
the conclusion of one of the earliest systematic studies of campaign
finance:

> The necessity for obtaining essential election funds has its most
> profound importance in the choosing of candidates. The monies can
> usually be assured, and often can be withheld, by the relatively small
> corps of political specialists whose job it is to raise money. ... As a
> consequence, money probably has its greatest impact on the choice of
> public officials in the shadow land of our politics where it is decided
> who will be a candidate for a party's nomination and who will not be.
> There are many things that make an effective candidate, but there is a
> *choke point* [my italics] in our politics where vital fiscal encouragement
> can be extended or withheld.[19]

This conclusion, based on research conducted in the 1950s, is supported by the evidence of the 1960s and 1970s, when the increased use
of television, polling, computerized mailings, and political consultants made campaigning even more expensive. "Because of its
ability to buy the kinds of services that produce name recognition and
exposition of positions," writes campaign finance analyst Herbert E.
Alexander, "money wields its greatest influence on campaigns—
particularly presidential races—during the prenomination period."[20]

Several reforms in campaign finance during the 1970s that
restricted the donation of large contributors at the national level and
in some states have altered the system somewhat since Heard and
Alexander wrote. But these reforms have not diminished the influence
of the corporate community. If anything, they have increased it quite

inadvertently. In the past a handful of owners and executives would give tens or hundreds of thousands of dollars to candidates of interest to them. Now they organize luncheons and dinners at which all of their colleagues and friends are asked to give a few thousand dollars each to specific candidates and party finance committees. They also form what are called Political Action Committees (PACs) through which their stockholders and executives are asked to give up to $5,000 each year, depending upon their rank and salary in the corporate hierarchy. These committees, in turn, can contribute to all individual candidates. When a coordinated set of corporate PACs give to a candidate, the impact is considerable.

Before the changes in the campaign finance laws, there were very few corporate PACs. By 1975 there were several dozen, and in that year an additional 107 major corporations and 22 top-level banks set up such committees. By 1980 hundreds of large corporations had a PAC. There were numerous other business organizations, such as trade associations, that had PACs as well, but the potentialities of the new law were still far from being fully realized by the corporate community.[21] Thus, the effect of the reforms, although unintended, was to corporatize campaign finance and to make political money even more directly tied to the top leaders in the corporate community. Wealthy mavericks, whether extremely liberal or extremely conservative, who often gave millions of dollars to unusual candidates, had to turn their attention to more indirect ways of supporting their favorite candidates.

There are numerous other methods besides campaign donations by which members of the corporate community can give financial support to politicians. One of the most direct is to give them stock or to purchase property from them at a price well beyond the market value. In 1956, to take one example, Texas millionaires wanted one of their corporate lawyers, Robert B. Anderson, to consider becoming the vice-presidential candidate on the Republican ticket. Anderson hesitated because he did not want to lower his income. To deal with this problem, several oilmen entered into a complex transaction in which Anderson purchased royalty interests for one dollar, then sold the leases a short time later at a profit of over $900,000, leaving him a millionaire and able to carry on his political career. In the event, he did not become the vice-presidential candidate but was appointed secretary of the treasury instead.[22]

A somewhat similar case involved Ronald Reagan in 1966, just after he became governor of California. Twentieth Century-Fox purchased several hundred acres of his land adjacent to its large outdoor set in Malibu for nearly $2 million, triple its assessed market value and 30 times what he had paid for it in 1952. The land was never utilized and was later sold to the state. It was this transaction, along with $20,000-an-appearance speeches to business and conservative groups, that gave Reagan the financial security that made it possible for him to devote full time to his political career.[23]

A very direct method of benefiting the many politicians who are lawyers is to hire them or their law firms as legal consultants or to provide them with routine legal business. In the late 1960s, Citibank of New York retained the law firm of Javits and Javits, where Senator Jacob Javits of New York was a partner, to handle medium-size mortgage foreclosures. When this particular instance was exposed by a team of young lawyers working for Ralph Nader, Javits withdrew from the firm and retired from legal practice.[24] Corporations can be especially helpful to lawyer-politicians when they are between offices. William Benton, chairman of *Encyclopedia Britannica* and a campaign fund raiser for Adlai E. Stevenson throughout the 1950s, hired Stevenson as a director and consultant between 1952 and 1964. Benton did the same thing for Hubert Humphrey between 1968 and 1970.[25] Similarly, Donald M. Kendall, chairman of Pepsico, retained Richard M. Nixon as the company's lawyer after 1963 and thereafter paid for every trip Nixon made overseas in the next two years. This made it possible for Nixon to remain in the political limelight as a foreign-policy expert.[26]

Business organizations can also supplement the income of politicians by paying them large honoraria for speeches to trade associations and conventions. They can give them expensive Christmas gifts. Wealthy individuals can even use small foundations to give scholarships to the children of politicians they favor; real estate developer Louis Lurie made such grants to the children of Edmund G. Brown, Sr., when he was governor of California in the late 1950s and early 1960s.[27]

There are other sources of campaign donations and financial favors besides the corporate community, of course, but they are neither as large nor as consistent in their donations. The role of small donations, particularly those raised through direct-mail appeals, receives considerable publicity, but it is minor when compared with that of big donors. Presidential candidate George M. McGovern raised $15 million from several hundred thousand donors in 1972, but he had to spend $4.5 of this in printing and postage, leaving him a net of only $10.5 million. By way of contrast, in the same year President Nixon raised over $19.8 million from people who gave $10,000 or more. Moreover, the McGovern campaign was dependent upon large loans from several millionaires to get its fund raising off the ground.[28]

Nonbusiness sources not only provide less money than corporate sources; they also are less consistent. Middle-level groups often are able to mobilize against specific instances of military intervention or environmental pollution, but they find it difficult to sustain themselves when the issue is resolved or becomes highly routinized. It is at this point that nonbusiness and antibusiness candidates become highly vulnerable and begin to search for compromises that will make corporate groups less likely to spend large sums of money to defeat them the next time around. In the case of the House of Representatives, the members must run every two years, and most members grow weary of worrying about their seats each time. If they come to enjoy the status and modicum of power that their offices bring them, they try to accommodate to corporate pressures. As one staff member explained in the case of those on the House Banking, Finance and Urban Affairs Committee:

> These guys come to Congress in their thirties as promising $20,000–$25,000-a-year attorneys and businesspeople, with high ideals and great enthusiasm. But after six or seven years they find themselves approaching middle age with decent incomes but no real security, while their former law partners back home are secure and prosperous. They need $50,000–$150,000 to cover campaign costs every two years, just to stay in office. Since bank funds are easy to get, since bank issues are complex and therefore easy to camouflage, and since these members are socially close to the middle-level business professional leadership of their communities in which local bankers play so crucial a role, support for banker positions on the committee comes to seem entirely natural.[29]

Organized labor is a consistent source of money for the Democratic Party, but its role has not been as large as is sometimes thought. Although organized labor provides 10 to 20 percent of the funds for Democratic candidates in some states, and is often the largest single donor to that party in these states, its contributions at the national level are much less important. In 1968 organized labor gave $7.1 million at the national level and in 1972 it gave $8.5 million, with most of that going to Senate and House campaigns.[30] Since 1976, when federal financing of presidential campaigns was adopted, labor has focused all its resources on the congressional level, but it continues to be outspent by corporate PACs and trade associations. In 1980, for example, 1,095 corporate groups gave $19 million to congressional candidates, 490 trade and medical groups gave another $17 million, and 240 labor organizations provided $13 million.[31] Unions also make an indirect contribution to Democratic candidates through such officially non-partisan efforts as voter-registration drives, get-out-the-vote campaigns, and the printing of leaflets containing the voting records of Democratic and Republican candidates. However, this has not been enough to gain it a major voice in presidential politics. Contrary to conservative propaganda, the unions do not come close to matching the amount of nonpartisan political material that is distributed by the nonprofit groups within the right wing of the policy network.

In short, the campaign donations and less obvious financial favors from members of the upper class and corporate community are a central element in determining who enters politics with any hope of winning a nomination. Campaign money is not the only element in the political process, as studies of high-spending losers reveal, but it is an essential one given the nature of the two-party system and the need for name recognition. It is the need for a large amount of start-up money—to travel around the district or the country, to send out large mailings, to schedule radio and television time in advance—that gives members of the power elite a very direct role in the process right from the start and thereby provides them with personal access to politicians of both parties. Even if they do not tie specific strings to their monies, as they often do not, they are aboe to ensure a polite hearing for their views and to work against those candidates whom they do not consider sensible and approachable.

The Results of the Candidate-Selection Process

What kinds of elected officials emerge from a political process that puts such great attention on campaign finance and media recognition? The answer is available from numerous studies. Politicians, especially those who hold the highest elective offices, are first of all people from the top 10 to 15 percent of the occupational and income ladders. Only a minority are from the upper class or corporate community, but in a majority of cases they share in common a business and legal background with members of the upper class.[32]

Few twentieth-century Presidents have been from outside the very wealthiest circles. Theodore Roosevelt, William H. Taft, Franklin D. Roosevelt, and John F. Kennedy were from upper-class backgrounds. Herbert Hoover, Jimmy Carter, and Ronald Reagan were millionaires before they became deeply involved in national politics. Lyndon B. Johnson was a millionaire several times over through his wife's land dealings and his use of political leverage to gain a lucrative television license in Austin. Even Richard M. Nixon was a rich man when he finally attained the presidency in 1968, after earning high salaries as a corporate lawyer between 1963 and 1968 due to his ability to open political doors for corporate clients.

Studies of the social backgrounds and occupations of members of Congress have consistently shown that they come from the highest levels of society and are involved in the business and legal communities. A study of the Congress for 1972 found that 66 percent of the senators and 74 percent of the representatives came from the 10 percent of families with business or professional occupations, and that virtually all of the senators and representatives were themselves professional people or former business executives. Twenty percent of the senators and 5 percent of a sample of representatives were members of the upper class. Only 5 percent of the senators had been farmers or ranchers; none had been blue-collar workers. Three percent of the representatives had been farmers or ranchers, and 3 percent had union backgrounds. A comparison of these findings with a study of the Senate in the mid-1950s and the House in the early 1940s showed that there had been very little change over that time span, except for a decrease in the number of farmers and a slight increase in the number of professionals and business executives.[33]

The stringent financial disclosure laws adopted by Congress in the mid-1970s in the aftermath of Watergate and other scandals provided detailed information on the wealth and income of senators and representatives for 1978. Changes in the law since that time suggest that it may be the best information ever to become available. Still, the information is not exact because the questionnaire required disclosure only within general ranges for each category of ownership and income. In the Senate the highest point on the ownership scale was "over $5 million"; in the House it was "over $250,000."[34]

Nineteen members of the Senate were clearly millionaires, 10 from the Republican side and 9 from the Democratic. It was possible that another 13 or 14 were also millionaires, but the general categories did not permit accurate assessment in their cases. The largest income was that of the Republican senator from Pennsylvania, Henry J. Heinz III, with between $437,000 and $836,000. Democratic Senator Edward M. Kennedy of Massachusetts had dividend income between $288,000 and $581,000. In all, 95 of the senators had incomes from stocks or rent from real estate investments, and some held directorships or other positions in the business world. As one example, Thomas Eagleton, the Democratic senator from Missouri, continued to be a vice-president in his family's company, Missouri Pipe Fitting. He also received over $100,000 in dividends from all sources.

The less complete information on House members was nonetheless revealing in that one-third of House members had outside jobs, many in real estate or as bank directors, and 460 had income from stock or rent from real estate. At least 30 representatives were millionaires, and nearly 100 had outside incomes of $20,000 or more. Jack Brooks, a Democrat from Texas, received $56,000 in 1978 from two banks of which he was a director. Republican John J. Rhodes of

Arizona, the House minority leader, was paid $32,000 for his service as a vice-president in an insurance company. The conclusions drawn by the editors of *Congressional Quarterly* from these data are similar to those reached by the authors of earlier studies: "With few exceptions, members of Congress were successful lawyers or businessmen before coming to Washington. Most members kept and expanded their lucrative financial investments after election to Congress."[35]

The second general finding concerning the nature of elected officials in the United States is that a great many of them are lawyers. In 1972, for example, 70 percent of the senators and 51 percent of the representatives were lawyers, and the situation is similar for earlier times and at the state level. Of 995 elected governors for all states between 1870 and 1950, 46 percent were practicing lawyers. Twenty-five of the first 40 American Presidents were lawyers.[36] The large percentage of lawyers in the American political system is highly atypical when compared with other countries, where only 10 to 30 percent of legislators have a legal background. An insight into this overrepresentation may be provided by comparing the United States with a deviant case at the other extreme, Denmark, where only 2 percent of legislators are lawyers. The class-based nature of Danish politics since the late nineteenth century, and the fact that political careers are not pathways to judicial appointments, are thought to discourage lawyer participation in that country. The Danish situation thus suggests that the classless nature of American political parties, combined with the intimate involvement of the parties in the judicial system, creates a climate for strong lawyer involvement in the political system.[37]

Whatever the reasons for their involvement, lawyers are the occupational grouping that by training and career needs are ideal go-betweens and compromisers. They have the skills to balance the relationship between the corporate community that finances them on the one hand and the citizens who vote for them on the other. They are the supreme "pragmatists" in a nation where pragmatism is a central element in the self-deceiving ideology that the country has no ideology. They have an ability to be dispassionate about "the issues" and to discuss them in legalistic ways that are confusing to all concerned. They have been socialized to be discreet, and they can claim the cloak of "lawyer-client privilege" when questioned about work for their clients that seems to overlap with their political activities.

Though some lawyers see politics as a vocation, and indeed become lawyers because they knew the law to be the best avenue to elected office, others have been quite frank in telling social scientists that they see politics as an opportunity to make the kinds of connections that will advance their law careers. Whereas businesspeople and other professionals are hampered in their careers if they take a few years off to try their hand at politics, the nature of a legal practice makes it easy and beneficial for lawyers to go into politics. Win or lose, lawyer-politicians learn the governmental system and meet potential clients.[38] Many lawyer-legislators at the state and national level work for corporate clients while they are in office, although the practice declined dramatically at the national level after the scandals of the 1970s.[39]

Whether elected officials are lawyers or not, the third general result of the candidate-selection process is a large number of very ambitious people who are eager to "go along to get along," in the famous advice of former House speaker Sam Rayburn. To understand the behavior of a politician, concludes political scientist Joseph A. Schlesinger, "it is more important to know what he wants to be than how he got to where he is now."[40] This ambition, whether it be for wealth or higher office, makes politicians especially available to those who can help them rise, and such people are often members of the upper class and corporate community with money to contribute and connections to other districts, states, or regions where striving candidates need new friends. Thus, even the most liberal or archconservative of politicians may develop a new circle of moderate supporters as he or she moves from the local to the congressional to the presidential level, gradually becoming more and more involved with leading figures within the power elite.

However, despite the great involvement of members of the power elite with politicians in both political parties, there are still numerous liberal, labor, and proenvironment politicians who are not beholden to the corporate community. It is also the case that a certain amount of independence is often exercised, at least under some conditions and on some issues, even by those politicians who are supported by and feel sympathetic toward the corporate rich. Thus, there always is the possibility of disagreement over specific issues between elected officials and the power elite. This means that members of the power elite often have the need for other means by which they can influence government.

The next two sections will demonstrate how the power elite goes beyond the candidate-selection process to involve itself in matters of public policy.

THE SPECIAL-INTEREST PROCESS

The special-interest process, as already noted, is the means by which specific individuals, corporations, or industries gain the favors, tax breaks, regulatory rulings, and other governmental supports they need to realize their short-run interests. It depends on the efforts of such people as lobbyists, lawyers who used to serve on congressional staffs or work in regulatory agencies, employees of trade associations, and corporate executives whose explicit function is governmental liaison.

The special-interest process is based upon a great amount of personal contact, which involves varying combinations of information, pressure, gifts, friendship, and—not least—implicit promises of lucrative private jobs in the future for those who might want them. Although the most general term for this complex of activities is lobbying, the lawyers involved insist they are not lobbying but only supplying information, and the former politicians imply that many of their conversations and gifts are out of friendship, not a desire for favors for their present employers. Lobbying has the implication of pressure of an untoward nature, and few of those who operate in the special-interest process see themselves as applying pressure, any more than most politicians see the business groups as anything other than people with a legitimate interest in the issue at hand. Lobbying is what other people—opponents—do.

The special-interest process is that aspect of business-government relations described by social scientists and journalists in their case studies and exposés.[41] It is the process that was the target of the numerous investigations by consumer advocate Ralph Nader and his colleagues in the late 1960s and early 1970s, and it is constantly being scrutinized by other reform-minded groups as well.[42] It is so well known, and so often lucrative to the corporate rich, that it is often taken as the sum and substance of policy making in Washington. Moreover, the conflicts that erupt within this process, occasionally pitting one corporate sector against another, reinforce the image of widely shared and fragmented power in America, including the image of a badly divided corporate community.

Although most studies of the special-interest process recount the success of one or another corporation or trade association in receiving the favor or support it requests, there have been defeats for corporate interests within the special-interest process. In 1971, for example, environmentalists convinced Congress to end taxpayer subsidies for the construction of a supersonic transport. In 1977 a relatively strong anti-strip-mining bill was adopted over the objections of the coal industry. Laws that improved auto safety standards and that set job safety standards were passed over industry objections in the 1970s, as were standards of water cleanliness opposed by the paper and chemical industries.[43]

One of the finest summaries of the implications of the special-interest process is provided by political scientist Grant McConnell in his now-classic *Private Power and American Democracy*. After reviewing several decades of congressional investigations into lobbying, including halfhearted attempts to limit it, and numerous studies suggesting that, more often than not, regulatory agencies are "captured" by those they are supposed to regulate, he noted that "the record of exposure of this sort is one of almost tiresome repetition."[44] He concludes, in an explicit rejection of the usual pluralist image, that the ability of special interests to dominate specific committees and agencies of concern to them has given these interests considerable isolation from any countervailing pressures from other sources:

> The large extent of autonomy accorded to various fragments of government has gone far to isolate important matters of public policy from supposedly countervailing influences. Moreover, the picture of government as mediator among different interests is falsified to the extent that government itself is fragmented and the various fragments are beholden to particular interests.[45]

However, as McConnell also points out, evidence on the power of special interests does not add up to power elite domination of government as a whole. It does not show that the many different sectors of the corporate community have an interest in larger issues, let alone the unity to evolve policies on such issues. Indeed, in McConnell's view the parts of government that deal with general issues that concern the nation as a whole, such as the presidency, are not controlled by a unified power elite: "These elites do not "rule" in the sense of commanding the entire nation," he writes. "Quite the contrary, they tend to pursue a policy of non-involvement in the large issues of statesmanship, save where such issues touch their own particular concerns."[46]

In order to deal with the claim that the special interests do not come together to involve themselves in bigger policy issues, it is necessary to demonstrate how the policy-planning network described in the previous chapter involves itself in government.

THE POLICY-MAKING PROCESS AND GOVERNMENT

The policy-making process is as little known and seldom studied as the special-interest process is highly visible and constantly written about. It appears to be as detached from day-to-day events as the special-interest process is completely immersed in them. It appears as concerned with fairness and the national interest as the special-interest process seems biased and self-seeking. "Nonpartisan" and "objective" are its shibboleths, and many of its members show a mild disdain for lobbyists and trade associations. Compared with those who labor in the special-interest process, its members are much more likely to be from the "oldest" and wealthiest of families, the most prestigious of law schools and university institutes, and the highest levels of banks and corporations.

The perspectives developed in the organizations of the policy-planning network reach government in a variety of ways. On the most general level, their reports, news releases, and interviews are read by elected officials and their staffs, if not in their original form, then as they are summarized in the *Washington Post, New York Times,* and *Wall Street Journal.* Members of these organizations also testify before congressional committees and subcommittees that are writing legislation or preparing budget proposals. However, the most important involvements with government are more direct and formal in nature.

First, people from these organizations are regular members of the unpaid committees that advise specific departments of the executive branch on general policies. Second, they are prominent on the presidential commissions that have been appointed with regularity since World War II to make recommendations on a wide range of issues from foreign policy to highway construction. Third, they are members of two private organizations, the Business Council and the Business Roundtable, which are treated with the utmost respect and cordiality in Washington. Finally, they serve as informal advisors to the President in times of foreign-policy crisis, and they are appointed to government positions with a frequency far beyond what could be expected by chance. It is now time to explore some of these formal involvements in more detail.

Presidential Commissions

Presidential commissions are specially appointed temporary committees made up primarily, if not totally, of private citizens. They gather information, deliberate, and report to the President on the topic assigned to them. Their use is not without precedent in the nineteenth century, but they first came into their own in the turn-of-the-century administration of Theodore Roosevelt. Since that time there has been fairly steady growth in their employment by chief executives, especially since World War II.[47]

Commissions can serve several functions. Some are meant to cool out public opinion on an issue that has caused a sense of urgency in the general citizenry. Such was the role of various commissions which investigated ghetto uprisings in the 1960s, as well as the commission that President Gerald Ford appointed in 1975 to look at embarrassing revelations about the misdoings of the CIA. Other commissions seem to have little other purpose than to throw the President's political opposition off guard; this was one of the purposes of President Johnson's Commission on Urban Problems.[48] However, contrary to the frequent critics of the commissions, the majority of them are meant to suggest new policy initiatives or to build support for programs the President wishes to pursue. This point was established in a thorough study of all commissions appointed between 1945 and 1972, but it is evident from earlier case studies as well.[49]

Although several social scientists have recognized the significant policy influence of many presidential commissions, they have failed to grasp the intimate connection between presidential commissions and private policy groups. They merely note that the commissions have representatives from many sectors of society even while acknowledging that there is a considerable overrepresentation of older white males of business and professional backgrounds.[50]

Fifteen commissions dealing with aspects of foreign and military policy were established between 1945 and 1972. Twelve were headed by a member of the Council on Foreign Relations; two others were headed by trustees of the Committee for Economic Development. Five commissions were concerned with problems of governmental reorganization and federal salaries; four were chaired by members of the Committee for Economic Development, which has taken a special interest in such matters through its Committee for the Improvement of Management in Government. The numerous commissions dealing with diverse problems of health, education, urban housing, population, science policy, and welfare were more likely to be headed by specialists in the specific field, but even here several of the chairpersons were members of major policy groups.

Because those who have written about commissions do not link them to policy groups, they overlook their most important role, which is to legitimate the ideas that have been developed in the policy network. Then, too, it is in the commissions that a few representatives of labor, minorities, women, and other sectors of society are given a chance to participate in the policy process and introduce possible compromises. The commissions thereby give new policies a society-wide stamp of approval as well as the official sanction of a goverment commission.

The Business Council

The Business Council is a unique organization in the policy-planning network because of its close formal contact with government. It was created in 1933 as a quasi-governmental advisory group and still holds its regular consultative meetings with government officials even though it became an independent organization in 1962. Since the 1960s all of its three-day private meetings with government officials have been held in the relaxed and friendly atmosphere of the Homestead Hotel in Hot Springs, Virginia, 60 miles from Washington. During the meetings council members hear speeches by government officials, conduct panels on problems of concern to them, receive reports from their staff, and talk informally with each other and the government officials in attendance. Business sessions are alternated with social events, including golf tournaments, tennis matches, and banquet-style dinners for members, guests, and wives. The expenses for the meetings, reports, and social events are paid by the corporate leaders.[51]

The members are, with few exceptions, the chairmen or presidents of the largest corporations in the country. The centrality of the Business Council within the corporate community can be seen in our tabulation of all the directorships listed by the 154 Business Council members who were included in *Who's Who in America* for 1971–1972. This self-report information showed that these men held 730 directorships in 435 banks and corporations, as well as 49 foundation trusteeships in 36 different foundations and 125 trusteeships with 84 universities. The 435 corporations were at the heart of the corporate community; 176 of them were among the 800 largest corporations for 1970. The companies most heavily represented were Chase Manhattan Bank (11 directors), Morgan Guaranty Trust (10 directors), General Electric (10 directors), General Motors (9 directors), and Metropolitan Life (9 directors).

Business Council members were part of other policy groups as well; 49 were trustees of the Committee for Economic Development and 42 were members of the Council on Foreign Relations. Not surprisingly, then, an analysis of membership overlaps among 30 social clubs and policy groups using the mathematics of matrix algebra determined that the Business Council had the highest centrality score in the matrix. It was rivaled only by the Committee for Economic Development.[52]

A detailed study of the Business Council suggests that it had little impact on government policy during its early years.[53] Its only real domestic success throughout the New Deal was its supportive involvement in the Social Security Act, where some of its members served on important committees and all of its members offered their public support at a critical juncture when the act was attacked by the Chamber of Commerce of the United States.[54] It was not until the Eisenhower administration that it began to assume its role as a major contact point between the corporate community and government, serving as an unofficial board of directors for the inner group of the corporate community.

The Business Roundtable

The Business Roundtable is the most recent addition to the policy-planning network. Founded in 1973 by the chairmen of several dozen of the largest corporations, it is the lobbying counterpart of the Business Council, with which it has numerous common members. In 1976, for example, 33 of the 45 leaders of the Business Roundtable also were members of the Business Council.

Whereas the Business Council prefers to remain in the background and talk informally with members of the executive branch, the Business Roundtable has an activist profile. It sends its leaders to lobby members of Congress as readily as it meets privately with the President and cabinet leaders. Indeed, it was formed in part because corporate leaders came to the conclusion that the Business Council was not effective enough in pressing the corporate viewpoint on government. There was also a belief that the corporate community was relying too heavily on specific trade associations and hired lobbyists in approaching Congress. It was hoped that the direct lobbying of legislators by chief executives would have more impact.[55]

Irving S. Shapiro, chairman of both DuPont Corporation and the Business Roundtable in 1980, explained the difference between the Business Roundtable and the Business Council as follows:

> The Roundtable is only for chief executive officers. Once I'm through with that I am out. There's a counterpart to the Roundtable that you may not be familiar with, and that's the Business Council, and that you stay involved with. It is not an advocacy organization. It simply deals with public issues. The Roundtable was created to have an advocacy organization. It wasn't created by the Business Council, but by the same people. I am a member of the Council and will stay with that. People who are retired stay with it the rest of their lives if they choose to.[56]

The 150 companies in the Business Roundtable pay from $10,000 to $35,000 per year in dues, depending on their size. This provides a budget of over $3 million a year. Decisions on where the Roundtable will direct its efforts are determined by a 40-person policy committee that meets every two months to discuss current policy issues, create task forces to examine selected issues, and review position papers prepared by task forces. Task forces are asked to avoid focusing on problems in any one industry and to concentrate instead on issues that have a broad impact on business. With a staff of less than a dozen people, the Business Roundtable does not have the capability for developing its own information. However, this presents no problem because the organization has been designed so that task force members will utilize the resources of their own companies as well as the information developed in other parts of the policy network.

During the 1970s the Roundtable played a defensive role in Washington, stopping legislation rather than passing its own. It helped to kill the proposed Consumer Protection Agency during the Ford administration, which did not like the idea in any case, then did the same during the more proconsumer Carter presidency even while it worked closely with President Carter on other issues. It also is credited with watering down antitrust legislation and working out compromises on other issues.[57] However, unlike the ultraconservative National Association of Manufacturers and Chamber of Commerce of the United States, which function as general lobbying organizations as well as sites for policy discussions, the Business Roundtable is not perceived by journalists and critics as being completely negative in its orientation.

The Business Council and the Business Roundtable, then, are in effect the same small group of corporate executives taking part in two different activities. One consults with the executive branch, the other lobbies the legislative branch. By dividing these roles into two separate organizations, corporate leaders are able to protect the lofty image of the Business Council and at the same time deliver a more effective one-two punch.

Appointments to Government

Appointments to government are the final and most direct method through which members of the corporate community and the policy network influence government. Two very different types of studies in the late 1970s by Useem make this point in the most general way. Studies by several other social scientists do so by studying the occupational and directorship backgrounds of top appointees to specific administrations.

In the first study by Useem, participation rates in federal government advisory positions were determined for various kinds of business leaders. Whereas only 4 percent of small industrialists with few outside directorships served on an advisory committee, the figure was 16 percent for large industrialists with several outside directorships, and 28 percent for large industrialists with outside directorships and memberships in at least one policy-planning group. This finding, Useem suggests,

further underscores the significance of the national associations' role as a screening mechanism for the selection of businesspeople to represent business to outside institutions. Business elites, otherwise similar in location in the social organization of the capitalist class, are sharply distinguished in their propensity to serve in governance positions according to their involvement in the national business policy associations.[58]

In the second study Useem interviewed chief executives concerning the kinds of people they suggest for government positions. Their typical response was that "character and integrity" are of the greatest importance, but under further questioning Useem found that this was "defined as an executive's capacity to transcend the immediate imperatives of his or her own company to express a broader vision."[59] Most important for my theory, the people who fit these criteria were talked about in terms of their experience and leadership in policy-planning organizations. Thus, a chief executive who sat on four company boards and served in the Department of Defense for several years told Useem that the executives who best represented business "are down in Washington undertaking responsibilities beyond the requirements of their own operation ... heading the Roundtable and the Business Council, and you see them willing to step out and accept public responsibility even while they will carry out their private responsibility."[60]

The way in which Presidents rely on people from the policy groups in making appointments to government can be seen very dramatically in the varying cases of John F. Kennedy, Jimmy Carter, and Ronald Reagan. After winning an election based on promises of a "new frontier" and the image of an urbane liberalism, President-elect Kennedy called in Republican Robert Lovett, a Wall Street investment banker who was a former member of the Committee for Economic Development and the Council on Foreign Relations as well as a former Secretary of Defense. Kennedy wished to have Lovett's advice on possible appointments to the new administration. Lovett soon became, according to historian and Kennedy-aide Arthur M. Schlesinger, Jr., the "chief agent" between Kennedy and the "American Establishment." Schlesinger defined this establishment as consisting primarily of financiers and corporate lawyers who were an "arsenal of talent which had so long furnished a steady supply of always orthodox and often able people to Democratic as well as Republican administrations."[61] Lovett seemed to be an unusual adviser for a President-elect who had promised to "get the country moving again," but Kennedy needed experienced experts to run the government:

He had spent the last five years, he said ruefully, running for office, and he did not know any real public officials, people to run a government, serious men. The only ones he knew, he admitted, were politicians, and if this seemed a denigration of his own kind, it was not altogether displeasing to the older man. Politicians did need men to serve, to run the government. The implication was obvious. Politicians could run Pennsylvania and Ohio, and if they could not run Chicago, they could at least deliver it. But could politicians run the world? What did they know about the Germans, the French, the Chinese? He needed experts for that, and now he was summoning them.[62]

Kennedy first asked Lovett if he would be interested in serving as the secretary of state, defense, or treasury, but he gracefully declined for reasons of health. When talk then turned to possible people for these positions, Lovett named several. Among them were Dean Rusk, president of the Rockefeller Foundation and a member of the Council on Foreign Relations; Robert McNamara, president of the Ford Motor Company; and C. Douglas Dillon, head of the investment banking firm of Dillon, Read and a member of the Council on Foreign Relations. Kennedy solicited other names, and there was intense lobbying for some of the candidates, but in the end there was general consensus around Rusk for Secretary of State, McNamara for Secretary of Defense, and Dillon for Secretary of Treasury.

Many other members of the Kennedy administration came from the policy-planning groups. In particular, they were members of the policy network who had taken part in a special set of commissions and panels sponsored by the Rockefeller Brothers Fund in the late 1950s. These panels, whose deliberations were published as a book entitled *Prospect for America*, were designed to assess the prospects for the United States in the 1960s on such issues as foreign policy, national security, education, and the domestic economy. Among the 83 men who served on one or more of these panels and lived into the 1960s, 26 later served in the Kennedy administration. Most were consultants or advisers, but the list also included the secretary of state, the undersecretary of state, two assistant secretaries of state, and four other State Department appointees.[63]

The contrast between President Carter's campaign rhetoric and his deference to the established experts was equally great. One of his main campaign themes was that as a down-home populist he was not a part of the "mess" in Washington. He was a man of the people who would bring new faces into his administration. One of his top aides, Hamilton Jordan, went so far as to promise that two of the old faces, Cyrus Vance and Zbigniew Brzezinski, would never serve in a Carter administration: "If, after the inauguration, you find a Cy Vance as Secretary of State and Zbigniew Brzezinski as head of National Security, then I would say we failed. ... The government is going to be run by people you never heard of."[64] Indeed, Jordan added that he would quit if Carter made such establishment appointments. A few months later, two of Carter's first appointments were Cyrus Vance—a Wall Street lawyer, director of several corporations, trustee of the Rockefeller Foundation, and member of the Council on Foreign Relations—as secretary of state, and Zbigniew Brzezinski—a foreign policy analyst and a member of the Council on Foreign Relations—as White House foreign-policy adviser. Jordan stayed on as a White House aide to Carter.

The other top appointments were equally predictable. The new secretary of defense was Harold Brown, president of the California Institute of Technology, a director of several corporations, a member of the Council on Foreign Relations, and a former appointee in the Department of Defense. The secretary of treasury was W. Michael Blumenthal, president of the Bendix Corporation and a trustee of the Rockefeller Foundation, the Council on Foreign Relations, the Committee for Economic Development, and Princeton University. Carter had come to know Vance, Brzezinski, Brown, and Blumenthal in the preceding three years as fellow participants in the Trilateral Commission, the international policy discussion group founded in 1973 to think about a new world order for the 1980s. There soon followed the news that many Trilateral members—thirteen in all—were to become members of the new administration. Journalists began to debate whether the cabinet was more connected to the Council on Foreign Relations, Rockefeller Foundation, IBM, Trilateral Commission, Coca-Cola, or Wall Street.[65]

As with Carter, Reagan came to the Presidency with a promise to do something about all the problems that allegedly were being caused by the federal government. However, as a neoconservative he would accomplish this feat by removing the establishment figures who supposedly had caused them. Edward Meese III, who went on to serve as one of Reagan's most important White House advisers, told *Business Week* that "you will see people who have never served in Washington before and who can make a significant change in the course of government. It's like bringing a new management team to turn around a failing business."[66]

Nonetheless, Reagan's first secretary of state was a former army officer, Alexander Haig, who had served as an aide to the secretary of defense in the 1960s and to Henry Kissinger and then President Nixon in the 1970s. He was president of United Technologies, a director of Chase Manhattan Bank, Crown Cork & Seal, Texas Instruments, and Conagra as well as being a member of the Council on Foreign Relations when he was appointed.[67] Reagan's second appointment to that position, George Shultz, was president of the Bechtel Corporation, one of the largest construction firms in the world, and a director of Morgan Guaranty Trust. He also was a director of the Council on Foreign Relations, a former adviser to the Committee for Economic Development, and a former secretary of both labor and treasury in the Nixon administration.

The secretary of defense, Caspar Weinberger, was a corporate lawyer from San Francisco who had served in three different positions in Washington between 1970 and 1975. He was a vice-president and general counsel of the Bechtel Corporation, a director of Pepsico and Quaker Oats, and a member of the Trilateral Commission when chosen for the position. As for the secretary of treasury, Donald T. Regan, he was the chief executive officer of Merrill, Lynch, a trustee of the Committee for Economic Development, a member of the policy committee of the Business Roundtable, and a member of the Council on Foreign Relations.

The rest of the Reagan administration also consisted of members of the corporate community who had previous government experience or visibility in the policy-planning network. To the consternation of the John Birch Society, there were many other appointees who were members of the Council on Foreign Relations in addition to Haig, Shultz, and Regan. They included the director of the CIA, the secretary of commerce, the special trade adviser, the deputy secretary of defense, and eight top-level appointments at the State Department. According to one cataloguing of over 90 advisers, consultants, and members of the Reagan administration in early 1981, 31 were members of the Council on Foreign Relations, 25 were associated with the American Enterprise Institute, 13 were affiliated with the Center for Strategic and International Studies at Georgetown University, and 12 were participants in the Trilateral Commission.[68]

However, Reagan's equivalent to the Rockefeller Brothers' panels and the Trilateral Commission turned out to be the Committee on the Present Danger. This organization had been formed in 1976 at a luncheon in Washington's exclusive Metropolitan Club by hawkish members of the power elite. Its mission was to counter what its founders and supporters saw as a dangerously lax attitude toward the Soviet Union on the part of other members of the power elite as well as all too many people in the general population. Functioning as a lobbying and opinion-molding group in addition to holding meetings and discussions, it interpreted the vague and contradictory information that is available on such matters to claim that the Soviet Union was expanding its military capabilities at a rapid pace and was responsible for most of the unrest around the world. It opposed ratification of a new arms control treaty with the Soviets, and it called for large buildups in U.S. military forces.[69] By 1979, in the wake of the upheavals in Iran and the Soviet invasion of Afghanistan, most members of the power elite were in agreement with the proposals of the committee, and President Carter's foreign and defense policies began to change accordingly.

Just as Carter had been a member of the Trilateral Commission, so too had Reagan been a member of the Committee on the Present Danger, and so too did he appoint many of his fellow members, 32 in all, to government. Most of them were on advisory boards or in the Department of Defense, but they took control of disarmament negotiations with the Soviet Union as well. Unlike the staid Trilateral Commission, which shied away from publicity and did not seek to be an advocacy organization, the Committee on the Present Danger proudly mailed its list of members in the Reagan government to thousands of journalists and political commentators around the country.[70]

Scholarly studies of cabinet appointments demonstrate in a more systematic way that the corporate community is highly over-represented in government. However, those done by pluralists, though attesting to the presence of corporate officials in government, underestimate the actual extent of corporate involvement by placing lawyers in a separate category from businessmen even when their firms have major corporations as their clients.[71] Fortunately, the work of sociologist Beth Mintz and political scientist Philip Burch reveals the full extent of corporate involvements.

The study by Mintz focused on the 205 individuals who served in presidential cabinets between 1897 and 1972. Defining her indicators of the "social elite" to include the 105 social clubs listed in the front of the *Social Register*, in addition to the *Social Register* itself and the schools and clubs outlined in the first chapter of this book, she found that 60 percent of the cabinet members were members of the upper class. Defining the "business elite" broadly in terms of service on at least one board of directors in any business corporation, or as membership in any corporation-oriented law firm, she also found that 78 percent were members of the business community. About half the cabinet officers were members of both the social and business elites as defined in this study. There were no differences in the overall percentages for Democratic and Republican administrations, or for the years before and after 1933.[72]

The exhaustive three-volume study by Burch covers cabinet officers, diplomats, and Supreme Court justices for every administration from George Washington through Jimmy Carter. It uses a more restricted definition than the Mintz study of what Burch calls the "economic elite," but it comes to similar conclusions except in the case of the New Deal administration of Franklin D. Roosevelt.[73] For Burch, the economic elite are those who hold executive positions, directorships, or partnerships in a large corporation or law firm "at or around" the time of government appointment, or are from families with "considerable" wealth or top-level executive or director ties.[74] What is considered to be a large corporation or law firm varies from generation to generation with the growth of the economy.

For the years 1789 to 1861, Burch concludes that 96 percent of the cabinet and diplomatic appointees were members of the economic elite, with a great many landowners, lawyers, and merchants in the group. From 1861 to 1933, the figure was 84 percent, with an increasing number of financiers and corporate lawyers. The figures in this era varied from a low of 57 percent for the Wilson years to a high of 90 percent for the McKinley-Roosevelt-Taft era. The overall percentage fell to 64 percent for the years 1933 to 1980, with only 47 percent of the appointees during the New Deal coming from the largest of corporations and law firms. The percentages for the last three eras in the study were about the same—63 percent for the Kennedy-Johnson years, 69 percent for the Nixon-Ford years, and 65 percent for the Carter administration.[75]

The most dramatic change uncovered in Burch's study was in appointments to the Supreme Court. From 1789 to 1937, members of the Supreme Court were primarily upper-class lawyers, many of whom had little judicial experience before their appointments. However, between 1937 and 1943 Roosevelt made eight appointments to the court, none of whom were from the corporate community. Three were law school professors with extensive government experience, and the other five had served as senators, attorneys general, or solicitor general. President Harry S. Truman continued this pattern in all four of his appointments, three of whom were former senators and one a former attorney general. Between 1952 and 1980, 9 of the 14 appointees were once again corporate lawyers, but the nature of the court had been altered nonetheless. Only 4 of the 14 had upper-class backgrounds, most had had previous judicial or government experience, and there was a strong sentiment that a variety of groups deserved some representation on the court.[76]

One of our studies shows that corporate involvement in appointed positions in the executive branch also extends below the cabinet-level positions. Of 120 secretaries, under secretaries, and assistant secretaries in the Nixon administration, including those for the Army, Navy, and Air Force, 35 percent came from the corporate community, with another 20 percent coming from small business or small law firms. Only 28 percent had spent most of their occupational careers in government. The majority of those with government careers were serving as assistant secretaries for administration, accounting, or public relations, except in the case of the State Department, where members of the foreign service often attained significant positions.[77]

This study also demonstrated the close relationship between government and the corporate community in another way, by determining where appointed officials go when they leave their positions. Tracing the careers of the Nixon appointees to 1979, it was found that several of the small businesspeople and lawyers, along with 7 of the 16 career employees who left government service, took positions in the corporate community as vice-presidents, trade association executives, or lobbyists. Most of those originally from the corporate community who did not retire also returned to it.[78] The corporate community not only regained most of its members who had gone to government but was infused with new members who had gained what it thought to be valuable government experience that can be of use to the corporations in the future.

The general picture that emerges from this information on the overrepresentation of members of the corporate community and policy network in appointed governmental positions is that the highest levels of the executive branch, especially in the State, Defense, and Treasury departments, are interlocked constantly with the corporate community through the movement of executives and lawyers in and out of government. Although the same person is not in government and corporate positions at the same time, there is enough continuity for the relationship to be described as one of "revolving interlocks." Corporate leaders sever their numerous directorships to serve in government for two or three years, then return to the corporate community in a same or different capacity. This system gives corporate officials temporary independence from the narrow concerns of their own companies and allows them to perform the more general roles they have learned in the policy-planning groups. However, it does not give them the time or inclination to become fully independent of the corporate community or to develop a perspective that includes the interests of other classes and groups.[79]

THE STRUGGLE OVER POLICY ENACTMENT

In terms of access, expertise, and sheer number of appointments, corporate involvement in the shaping of government policy is extensive. However, the policy-making process within government is not without conflict. The struggle to enact policy in Washington involves three major groupings, two of them rooted in the power elite and corporate community.

The first and most important factor in policy making is the moderate cluster within the power elite, which is anchored by the Council on Foreign Relations and the Committee for Economic

Development. It is based in the very largest and most international of corporations, and it has the prestige and research backing of such organizations as the Rockefeller Foundation, the Carnegie foundations, and the Brookings Institution when it comes to policy suggestions. It has its greatest influence with the centrist or moderate politicians in both political parties. Its major governmental access is in the executive branch through numerous ties to the White House and cabinet officers under both Republican and Democratic administrations.

The second major grouping is led by the ultraconservative wing of the power elite, as exemplified by the Chamber of Commerce of the United States, the Hoover Institution, and the American Enterprise Institute. Its economic base is in highly conservative, often smaller, and often less international corporations. It is aided considerably by its close ties with the American Farm Bureau Federation, the American Medical Association, the American Bar Association, and the occupational associations of other upper-middle-class professionals. Its political influence is greatest among conservative Republicans and southern Democrats. Its major access to government is through Congress, where regional and small-city networks of businesspeople, big farmers, lawyers, and physicians give it considerable lobbying clout.[80]

The third grouping in the policy struggle is the more loose-knit and divided liberal-labor coalition that is rooted in trade unions, middle-income liberal groups, environmental and consumer groups, university communities, and the foundations and advocacy groups financed by a few rich mavericks. Its connections are to the liberal wing of the Democratic Party and to a few moderate foundations in the centrist wing of the power elite on specific issues such as civil rights. The liberal-labor coalition has no strong basis anywhere in the government.[81] And, as the earlier-cited survey of various leadership groups showed for 1971, the liberal groups are far more liberal on all issues than the average Democratic politicians. This is unlike the case at the other end of the liberal-conservative continuum, where the Republican politicians are just about as conservative as the leaders of the conservative action groups.[82]

Generally speaking, the leanings of the moderate conservatives determine the outcome of any policy struggle. If the CFR-CED wing of the power elite decides to move in the direction of policy change, it develops a plan of its own, or it modifies a plan advocated by liberals, as in the often-cited case of the Employment Act of 1946 that provided a little more government direction to the economy.[83] It then enlists the support of liberal Democrats, moderate Democrats, and moderate Republicans in the Congress, often with the aid of the liberal-labor coalition. However, if the CFR-CED wing does not wish to see policy changes, it remains silent while its ultraconservative brethren pressure Congress to defeat any programs suggested by liberals or labor.

There have been only a few occasions in the twentieth century when the conservative coalition in Congress, made up of most Republicans and most southern Democrats, did not have the means to block liberal initiatives in some way, either in open votes on the floor of the House or Senate, in committees and subcommittees, or through parliamentary maneuvers and filibusters. Therefore, when push comes to shove, the liberal-labor coalition has to hope that the moderate conservatives will be on its side, as they were on social security, medicare, civil rights legislation, and several other new policies long advocated by liberals and labor.[84] Such support for these liberal initiatives is most likely to be forthcoming during times of extreme social disruption, as in the 1930s and 1960s. This is because the moderate conservatives have preferred a policy of carrot and stick in dealing with unrest rather than the full-scale police repression and detention that looms behind the ultraconservative call for "law and order." In times of domestic tranquillity, however, the moderates join with the ultraconservatives in pushing for cutbacks in welfare programs.

Unlike the liberals, the ultraconservatives are a potent force even without the support of the moderates. Due to their strength in Congress, they are often able to delay or alter the proposals put forth by the moderates. The fighting between the two groups has been especially intense on certain foreign-policy issues. In the 1950s and 1960s, for example, when the moderates eagerly sought tariff reductions and had the support of liberals and labor, the conservatives were able to extract concessions for specific industries such as textiles and chemicals before the legislation was finally passed.[85]

No general analysis of this nature will fit each and every new bill that goes before Congress. However, it encompasses the findings of the classic pluralist case studies in the political science literature, and it explains most of the major issues of the twentieth century—foreign aid, tariffs, welfare spending, government reorganization, and some environmental policies. Indeed, of all the issues we have examined, there is only one that does not fit this model, and that is the passage of the National Labor Relations Act of 1935. This act, which established the National Labor Relations Board and gave the force of law to the process of collective bargaining between employers and unions, was vigorously opposed by almost all elements of the corporate community. And yet liberal politicians, supported by the leadership of an embattled trade union movement, were able to gain overwhelming congressional support for the act despite a massive lobbying effort coordinated from behind the scenes by moderate leaders in the corporate community.

The defeat suffered by the corporate community on the National Labor Relations Act demonstrates that it does not have total control within the policy-planning process on all issues. On the other hand, it was the first serious defeat it had suffered on a labor issue up until that point in American history, and subsequent major legislative victories on collective bargaining in 1947 (the Taft-Hartley Act) and 1977 (the Labor Law Reform Act) showed it was to be the only defeat it would suffer on the issue of labor relations in the first 80 years of the century.

There is, then, a genuine struggle over policy enactment within the federal government, and the power elite does not win on each and every issue. However, the weight of the evidence shows that the moderate conservatives and ultraconservatives within the power elite are the predominant influences on the ultimate outcomes of these conflicts.

BUT BUSINESSMEN FEEL POWERLESS

Despite these various kinds of objective evidence that the power elite has great power in relation to the federal government, many corporate leaders feel that they are relatively powerless in the face of government. To hear them tell it, the Congress is more responsive to organized labor, environmentalists, and consumers than it is to them. They also claim to be harassed by willful and arrogant bureaucrats who encroach upon the rightful preserves of the private sector, sapping them of their confidence and making them hesitant to invest their capital.

These feelings have been documented most vividly by David Vogel and Leonard Silk, one a political scientist, the other a business columnist for the *New York Times*. They were permitted to observe a series of meetings at the Conference Board in 1974 and 1975 in which the social responsibilities of business were being discussed. The men at these meetings were convinced that everybody but them was listened to by government. Government was seen as responsive to the immediate preferences of the majority of citizens. "The have-nots are gaining steadily more political power to distribute the wealth downward," complained one executive. "The masses have turned to a larger government."[86]

Some even wondered whether democracy and capitalism are compatible. "Can we still afford one man, one vote? We are tumbling on the brink," said one. "One man, one vote has undermined the power of business in all capitalist countries since World War II," announced another. "The loss of the rural vote weakens conservatives."[87] However, Silk and Vogel believe that businessmen in America are unlikely to go so far as to be fascists, even with their antidemocratic bias, because they are so antigovernment:

> Even with their elitist, anti-populist, and even anti-democratic bias, however, few American businessmen can fairly be regarded as "fascist," if by that term one means a believer in a policital system in which there is a combination of private ownership and a powerful, dictatorial government that imposes major restrictions on economic, political, social and religious freedoms. Basically, the anti-governmental mind set of the great majority of American businessmen has immunized them against the virus of fascism.[88]

The fear business leaders express of the democratic majority leads them to view recessions as a saving grace, for recessions help to keep the expectations of workers in check. Workers who fear for their jobs are less likely to demand higher wages or government social programs. For example, different corporate executives made the following comments:

> This recession will bring about the healthy respect for economic values that the Depression did.
>
> People need to recognize that a job is the most important thing they can have. We should use this recession to get the public to better understand how our economic system works. Social goals are OK, provided the public is aware of their costs.
>
> It would be better if the recession were allowed to weaken more than it will, so that we would have a sense of sobriety.[89]

The negative feelings these business leaders have toward government are not a new development in the corporate community, as some pluralists have claimed in blaming the New Deal and the social programs of the 1960s. A study of businessmen's views in the nineteenth century found that they believed political leaders to be "stupid" and "empty" people who went into politics only to earn a living. As for the ordinary voters, they were "brutal, selfish and ignorant."[90] A comment written by a businessman in 1886 could have been made at the Conference Board meeting in 1975: "In this good, democratic country where every man is allowed to vote, the intelligence and the property of the country is at the mercy of the ignorant, idle and vicious."[91]

The emotional expressions of businesspeople, or anyone else, about their power or lack of it, cannot be taken seriously as power indicators. To do so, as Mills wrote, is to "confuse psychological uneasiness with the facts of power and policy," which are in the realm of sociology, economics, and politics, not subjective feelings and verbal protestations.[92] But it is nonetheless interesting to try to understand why businessmen complain about a government they dominate. There are several intertwined aspects to the answer.

First of all, complaining about government is a useful political strategy. It puts government officials on the defensive and forces them to keep proving that they are friendly to business. McConnell makes the point as follows:

> Whether the issue is understood explicitly, intuitively, or not at all, denunciations serve to establish and maintain the subservience of government units to the business constituencies to which they are actually held responsible. Attacks upon government in general place continuing pressure on governmental officers to accommodate their activities to the groups from which support is most reliable.[93]

However, it still seems surprising that corporate leaders would feel the need to resort to this tactic. This is especially the case given the evidence that bureaucrats who in any way speak out or criticize their elected or appointed superiors are removed from their positions, left with no duties, or otherwise punished in a dramatic and public way that is a clear lesson to other civil servants.[94] Silk and Vogel suggest that part of the explanation might be found in the fact that so few civil servants are part of the upper class and corporate networks. They quote economist Edward S. Mason on the contrast between Western Europe and the United States on this point:

> It is clear to the most obtuse observer that there is a much more distant relationship between business and government in the United States than, say, in Britain, or France or the Netherlands. ... A British businessman can say, "Some of my best friends are civil servants," and really mean it. This would be rare in the United States.[95]

In Western Europe, the government officials whom American businessmen vilify with the hostile label "bureaucrats" are part of the same old-boy networks as the business leaders due to common class background and common schooling. But such is not the case in the United States, where the antigovernment ideology tends to restrain members of the upper class from government careers except in the State Department. Because middle-class people who are not part of the in-group network staff the bureaucracies, the different method of domination that McConnell describes is necessary. It means that "tough-talking" members of the corporate community have to come into government as top-level appointees in order to "ride herd" on the "bureaucrats" in Washington. In other words, lack of social contact in a situation of uncertainty explains much of the hostile feelings toward bureaucrats whose great power exists more in imagination than in reality.

There also seems to be an ideological level to the businessmen's attitude toward government. In a perceptive discussion of "why businessmen mistrust their state," Vogel explains their attitude in terms of their fear of the populist, democratic ideology that underlies American government. Since power is in theory in the hands of all the people, there always is the possibility that someday "the people," in the sense of the majority, will make the government into the pluralist democracy it is supposed to be.[96] In that sense, the great power of the ruling class is illegitimate, and the existence of such power is therefore vigorously denied. Another political scientist, James Prothro, studying businessmen's views during what are thought of as their halcyon days of the 1920s, nonetheless found the same mistrust of government. He reached conclusions similar to those of Vogel, conclusions that show that the hostility expressed by businessmen is not a response to "big government": "The conspicuous anti-governmental orientation of business organizations is itself an incident of the more basic fear that popular control will, through the device of universal suffrage, come to dominate the governmental process."[97]

The expressions of anguish from individual business leaders concerning their powerlessness also suggests an explanation in terms of the intersection of social psychology and sociology. It is the corporate community and the power elite that have power, not individuals apart from their institutional context. It is therefore not surprising that specific individuals might feel powerless. As individuals, they are not always listened to, and they have to convince their peers of the reasonableness of their arguments before anything begins to happen. Moreover, any policy that is adopted is a group decision, and it is sometimes hard for people to identify with group actions to the point where they feel personally powerful.

The power talked about in this book is the social power of an upper class and the institutions in which that class is based. It is a social trait of a collectivity. The feelings of corporate leaders as to their power or powerlessness are not an adequate indicator of this power, contrary to those scholars and journalists who unblushingly take their words at face value.

CONCLUSION

This chapter has demonstrated the power elite's wide-ranging access to government through the special-interest and policy-planning processes, as well as the ability of its members to influence the kind of people elected and appointed to government through their financial involvement in the candidate-selection process. When coupled with the several different kinds of power discussed in earlier chapters, this access and involvement add up to power elite domination of the federal government.

By *domination* social scientists mean the ability of a class or group to set the terms under which other classes or groups within a social system must operate. By this definition, domination does not mean control on each and every issue, and it does not rest upon government involvement alone. Involvement in government is only the final and most visible aspect of power elite domination, which has its roots in the class structure, the nature of the economy, and the functioning of the policy-planning and opinion-shaping networks. If government officials did not have to wait on corporate leaders to decide where and when they will invest, and if government officials were not further limited by the acquiescence of the large majority to the present economic arrangements, then power elite involvement in elections and government would count for a lot less than it does under present conditions.

Domination by the power elite does not negate the reality of continuing conflict over government policies. It has been a main purpose of this chapter to provide an analysis that can sort out and explain the political disagreements that persist in the United States. Most conflicts, it has been implied, do not involve challenges to the rules that create privileges for the upper class and domination by its leadership group. The numerous battles within the special-interest process, for example, are only over specific spoils and favors. Indeed, they often involve battles between competing business interests.

Similarly, conflicts within the policy-making process of government usually involve the long-standing differences between the moderate-conservative and the ultraconservative wings of the power elite. Sometimes they involve issues in which the needs of the corporate community as a whole come into conflict with the needs of specific industries, which is what happens to some extent on tariff policies and also on some environmental legislation. In neither case does the nature of the conflict call into question the domination of government by the power elite.

Some policy disagreements do spill over into the candidate-selection process and create candidates with opposing platforms. These electoral battles usually involve differences between moderate conservatives and ultraconservatives, especially within Republican primaries. However, conflicts between moderate conservatives and people who identify with labor or liberal causes also emerge as well, especially in Democratic primaries. But more often than not, the electoral contests, especially in general elections, boil down to image-building and name-calling contests between two ambitious people who are very eager to hold the same elected position. Moreover, the winner's views sometimes turn out to be other than what he or she told the electorate in order to win the necessary votes.

Nonetheless, enough room for maneuver exists within the three processes for opponents of the power elite to develop policies and candidates that bring a significant portion of the general population into conflict with a unified power elite. It is these types of conflicts, such as occurred on the National Labor Relations Act in 1935, which remind us that domination does not mean total control and does not go unchallenged.

There is more to government in the United States than the federal government in Washington, however. Any claims about domination would not be complete without considering other levels of government as well. In order to round out the picture of power in America, it is necessary to consider the literature on local government, the other level of government that has been studied with any intensity by social scientists. Such a consideration is especially necessary because the situation is somewhat different than has been described at the national level.

NOTES

1. Theodore J. Lowi, *American Government: Incomplete Conquest* (New York: Dryden, 1976), p. 265.
2. Seymour M. Lipset, *The First New Nation* (New York: Basic Books, 1963), p. 336.
3. Ibid. For the first full presentation of this argument in relation to the United States, see E. E. Schattschneider, *Party Government* (New York: Holt, 1942).
4. Richard Hofstader, *The Idea of a Party System* (Berkeley, Calif.: University of California Press, 1969).
5. Donald A. Wittman, "Parties as Utility Maximizers," *American Political Science Review,* June 1973, p. 491.
6. Nelson W. Polsby and Aaron B. Wildavsky, *Presidential Elections,* 2d ed. (New York: Scribner's, 1967), p. 269.
7. Ibid., pp. 273, 280.
8. Ibid., p. 274.
9. Richard Hamilton, *Class and Politics in the United States* (New York: Wiley, 1972), chapter 1, brings together the arguments and evidence against the unexamined assumptions of those who believe the two-party system is of necessity responsive to voter performance.

10. Horace Samuel Merrill, *Bourbon Democracy of the Middle West: 1865–1896* (Baton Rouge, La.: Louisiana State University Press, 1953); Wittman, "Parties as Utility Maximizers," p. 494.

11. Walter D. Burnham, "American Politics in the 1970s," in *The American Party Systems*, 2d ed., ed. William N. Chambers and Walter D. Burnham (New York: Oxford University Press, 1975), pp. 321–22.

12. Wittman, "Parties as Utility Maximizers," p. 498. Italics in the original.

13. Walter D. Burnham, "The 1980 Earthquake: Realignment, Reaction, or What?" in *The Hidden Election*, ed. Thomas Ferguson and Joel Rogers (New York: Pantheon, 1981).

14. Jules Witcover, *Marathon: The Pursuit of the Presidency, 1972–1976* (New York: Viking, 1977), p. 609.

15. Lipset, *The First New Nation;* Burnham, "The 1980 Earthquake."

16. Lowi, *American Government*, p. 299.

17. John S. Saloma III and Frederick H. Sontag, *Parties* (New York: Knopf, 1972), p. 295.

18. Burnham, "American Politics in the 1970s," p. 277.

19. Alexander Heard, *The Costs of Democracy* (New York: Doubleday, 1962), p. 34. Reprinted by permission of the University of North Carolina Press.

20. Herbert E. Alexander, *Financing Politics* (Washington, D.C.: Congressional Quarterly Press, 1976), p. 44.

21. Ibid., pp. 126–27; Herbert E. Alexander, "Political Action Committees and Their Corporate Sponsors in the 1980's," *Public Affairs Review* (1981).

22. Robert Sherrill, *The Accidental President* (New York: Grossman, 1967), pp. 145, 271.

23. Nicholas M. Horrock, "Reagan Resists Financial Disclosure," *New York Times*, August 13, 1976, p. A-10; "Ronald Reagan Up Close," *Newsweek*, July 21, 1980, p. 39.

24. Paul Hoffman, *Lions in the Street* (New York: Saturday Review Press, 1973), p. 156.

25. Sidney Hyman, *The Lives of William Benton* (Chicago: University of Chicago Press, 1969), pp. 262, 274, 512, 572; "Humphrey to Join Britannica Board of Directors," *New York Times*, January 9, 1969, p. 34.

26. Hoffman, *Lions in the Street*, p. 106.

27. "Scholarships for Politicians' Kids," *San Francisco Chronicle*, July 22, 1970, p. 2; "Lurie Tells of Scholarships," *San Francisco Chronicle*, July 23, 1970, p. 4.

28. Alexander, *Financing Politics*, pp. 85, 90–92.

29. Lester M. Salomon, *The Money Committees* (New York: Grossman, 1975), p. 53.

30. Alexander, *Financing Politics*, pp. 106–7.

31. "1980 Elections: $55 million," *New York Times*, August 4, 1981, p. 12.

32. Donald R. Matthews, *The Social Background of Political Decision-Makers* (New York: Doubleday, 1954); Suzanne Keller, *Beyond the Ruling Class* (New York: Random House, 1963), pp. 310ff.

33. Richard L. Zweigenhaft, "Who Represents America?" *Insurgent Sociologist*, Spring 1975.

34. "Outside Earnings Swell Wealth of Congress," *Congressional Quarterly*, September 1, 1979.

35. Ibid., p. 1823.

36. Zweigenhaft, "Who Represents America?"; Heinz Eulau and John D. Sprague, *Lawyers in Politics* (Indianapolis: Bobbs-Merrill, 1964), pp. 11–112.

37. Morgens D. Pederson, "Lawyers in Politics: The Danish Folketing and United States Legislatures," in *Comparative Legislative Behavior*, ed. Samuel C. Patterson and John C. Wahlke (New York: Wiley, 1972).

38. Eulau and Sprague, *Lawyers in Politics*, p. 44; James D. Barber, *The Lawmakers* (New Haven, Conn.: Yale University Press, 1965), pp. 68–69.

39. Drew Pearson and Jack Anderson, *The Case Against Congress* (New York: Simon & Schuster, 1968), chapter 4; Mark Green, *Who Runs Congress?* 3d ed. (New York: Bantam Books, 1979), pp. 166–68.

40. Joseph A. Schlesinger, *Ambition and Politics* (Chicago: Rand McNally, 1966) p. 5.

41. E.g., Robert Engler, *The Politics of Oil* (New York: MacMillan, 1961); Michael Parenti, *Democracy for the Few*, 2d ed. (New York: St. Martin's, 1977); Richard Harris, *The Real Voice* (New York: MacMillan, 1964); Morton Mintz and Jerry S. Cohen, *Power, Inc.* (New York: Viking, 1976); Joseph Goulden, *The Superlawyers* (New York: Weybright & Talley, 1971); James Deakin, *The Lobbyists* (Washington, D.C.: Public Affairs Press, 1966).

42. E.g., Robert Fellmeth, *The Interstate Commerce Commission* (New York: Grossman, 1970); James Turner, *The Chemical Feast* (New York: Grossman, 1970); Mark J. Green, ed., *The Monopoly Makers* (New York: Grossman, 1973).

43. Green, *Monopoly Makers*, p. 43.

44. Grant McConnell, *Private Power and American Democracy* (New York: Knopf, 1966), p. 21.

45. Ibid., p. 164.

46. Ibid., p. 339, but see also pp. 254 and 292 for similar conclusions.

47. Carl Marcy, *Presidential Commissions* (New York: King's Crown Press, 1945); Frank Popper, *The President's Commissions* (New York: Twentieth Century Fund, 1970).

48. Howard E. Shuman, "Behind the Scenes and under the Rug," *Washington Monthly*, July 1969.

49. Thomas R. Wolanin, *Presidential Advisory Commissions* (Madison, Wisc.: University of Wisconsin, 1975). For two informative case studies on specific commissions, see Morton H. Halperin, "The Gaither Commission and the Policy Process," *World Politics*, April 1961; Ushaa Mahanjani, "Kennedy and the Strategy of Aid: The Clay Report and After," *Western Political Quarterly*, September 1965.

50. Popper, *The President's Commissions*.

51. Craig Kubey, "Notes on a Meeting of the Business Council," *Insurgent Sociologist*, Spring 1973.

52. G. William Domhoff, "Social Clubs, Policy-Planning Groups and Corporations: A Network Study of Ruling-Class Cohesiveness," *Insurgent Sociologist*, Spring 1975, p. 178.

53. Kim McQuaid, "The Business Advisory Council of the Department of Commerce, 1933–1961: A Study of Corporate/Government Relations," in *Research in Economic History*, vol. 1, ed. Paul U. Selding (Greenwich, Conn.: JAI Press, 1976); idem, *Big Business and Presidential Power From FDR to Reagan* (New York: Morrow, 1982).

54. G. William Domhoff, *The Higher Circles* (New York: Random House, 1970), pp. 207–218; Daniel Nelson, *Unemployment Insurance* (Madison, Wisc.: University of Wisconsin Press, 1969), pp. 197, 208, 218.

55. "Business Roundtable: Big Corporation Bastion," *Congressional Quarterly*, November 23, 1974; Peter Slavin, "The Business Roundtable: New Lobbying Arm of Big Business," *Business and Society Review*, Winter 1975–76; Philip H. Burch, Jr., "The Business Roundtable: Its Make-up and External Ties," *Research in Political Economy*, vol. 14, 1981; Mark Green and Andrew Buchsbaum, *The Corporate Lobbies: Political Profiles of the Business Roundtable and the Chamber of Commerce* (Wasington, D.C.: Public Citizen, 1980); McQuaid, "The Business Advisory Council."

56. Richard L. Zweigenhaft, interview with Irving Shapiro, February 23, 1981.

57. "Business' Most Powerful Lobby in Washington," *Business Week*, December 20, 1976, p. 63; Eileen Shanahan, "Antitrust Bill Stopped by a Business Lobby," *New York Times*, November 16, 1975, p. 1.

58. Michael Useem, "Which Business Leaders Help Govern?" in *Power Structure Research*, ed. G. William Domhoff, Beverly Hills, Calif.: Sage Publications, 1980), p. 221.

59. Michael Useem, "Classwide Rationality in the Politics of Managers and Directors of Large Corporations in the United States and Great Britain," *Administrative Science Quarterly*, June 1982, p. 216.

60. Ibid.

61. Arthur M. Schlesinger, Jr., *A Thousand Days* (Boston: Houghton Mifflin, 1965), pp. 128–29.

62. David Halberstam, *The Best and the Brightest* (New York: Random House, 1972), p. 4.

63. Mark Johnson, "The Consensus Seekers: How the Power Elite Shape National Policy" (Masters thesis, University of California at Santa Barbara, 1978).

64. Robert Scheer, "Jimmy, We Hardly Know Y'All," *Playboy*, November 1976, p. 192.

65. E.g., W. E. Barnes, "Carter Had Links to Insiders All Along," *San Francisco Examiner*, December 12, 1976, p. 1; "Carter's Brain Trusts," *Time*, December 20, 1976, p. 19; William Greider, "Trilateralists to Abound in Carter's White House," *Washington Post*, January 16, 1977, p. 1; William Safire, "Carter's IBM Cabinet," *New York Times*, January 17, 1977, p. 25. For a full account of these connections, see Laurence H. Shoup, *The Carter Presidency and Beyond* (Palo Alto, Calif.: Ramparts Press, 1980).

66. "Putting His Philosophy to Work Fast," *Business Week*, November 17, 1980, p. 155.

67. Philip H. Burch, Jr., "Reagan's Top Appointees" (Paper, Bureau of Government Research, Rutgers University, 1981).

68. Holly Sklar and Robert Lawrence, *Who's Who in the Reagan Administration* (Boston: South End Press, 1981).

69. Alan Wolfe and Jerry Sanders, "Resurgent Cold War Ideology," in Richard R. Fagen, ed., *Capitalism and the State in U.S.–Latin American Relations* (Palo Alto, Calif.: Stanford University Press, 1979); Richard J. Barnet, "The Search for National Security," *New Yorker*, April 27, 1981.

70. David Schribman, "Group Goes from Exile to Influence," *New York Times*, November 23, 1981, p. A 20.

71. E.g., David T. Stanley, Dean E. Mann, and James W. Doig, *Men Who Govern* (Washington, D.C.: Brookings Institution, 1967); Kenneth Prewitt and William McAllister, "Changes in the American Executive Elite—1930–1970," in *Elite Recruitment in Democratic Politics*, ed. Heinz Eulan and Moshe M. Chaudnowski (New York: Halstead Press, 1976).

72. Beth Mintz, "The President's Cabinet, 1897–1972," *Insurgent Sociologist*, Spring 1975.

73. Philip H. Burch, Jr., *Elites in American History*, vols. 1–3 (New York: Holmes and Meier, 1980, 1981).

74. Ibid., vol. 3, p. 278.

75. Ibid., p. 383.

76. Ibid., p. 383 and appendix B.

77. Harold Salzman and G. William Domhoff, "The Corporate Community and Government: Do They Interlock?" in *Power Structure Research*, ed. G. William Domhoff (Beverly Hills, Calif.: Sage Publications, 1980).

78. Ibid., pp. 248–250.

79. Ibid., p. 251; Jonathan Neuman and Ted Gup, "The Revolving Door: Industry Plums Await Retired U.S. Officials," *Washington Post*, June 25, 1980, p. 1.

80. Wesley McCune, *Who's Behind Our Farm Policy?* (New York: Praeger, 1956); Donald R. Hall, *Cooperative Lobbying: The Power of Pressure* (Tucson, Ariz.: University of Arizona Press, 1969); Edward Malecki, "Union Efforts to Influence Non-Labor Policies" (Masters thesis, University of Illinois, 1963). For evidence that the American Bar Association supports this coalition except on court-related issues, see Albert P. Melone, *Lawyers, Public Policy and Interest Group Politics* (Washington, D.C.: University Press of America, 1977). For evidence that the New York Bar Association sometimes joins the moderate conservatives, see Ibid. and Hoffman, *Lions in the Street*, chapter 13.

81. G. William Domhoff, *Fat Cats and Democrats* (Englewood Cliffs, N.J.: Prentice-Hall, 1972), chapter 4.

82. Allan Barton, "Fault Lines in American Elite Consensus," *Daedalus*, Summer 1980.

83. Stephen Bailey, *Congress Makes a Law* (New York: Columbia University Press, 1950); David Eakins, "The Development of Corporate Liberal Policy Research in the United States, 1885–1965" (Ph.D. diss., University of Wisconsin, 1966), p. 393ff; Karl Schriftgiesser, *Business Comes of Age* (New York: Harper & Row, 1960), pp. 88–89; Robert M. Collins, *The Business Response to Keynes, 1929–1964* (New York: Columbia University Press, 1981). Bailey's classic study of this legislation is one of many case studies that pluralists cite as evidence for their view without understanding corporate involvement in the final outcome. The work of Eakins, Schriftgiesser, and Collins makes good this omission.

84. For an analysis of congressional voting patterns, see Aage R. Clausen, *How Congressmen Decide* (New York: St. Martin's, 1973).

85. Raymond A. Bauer, Ithiel de Sola Pool, and Lewis A. Dexter, *American Business and Public Policy* (New York: Atherton, 1963). For a critique of this favorite pluralist case study in terms of the overlooked role of moderates within the power elite, see Domhoff, *Higher Circles*, pp. 143–45.

86. Leonard Silk and David Vogel, *Ethics and Profits* (New York: Simon & Schuster, 1976), p. 50.

87. Ibid., p. 75.

88. Ibid., p. 197.

89. Ibid., p. 64.

90. Ibid., p. 193.

91. Ibid., p. 194. These findings on the attitudes of nineteenth-century businessmen undercut the claim by Silk and Vogel (p. 201) that business hostility toward government stems largely from the New Deal.

92. C. Wright Mills, *The Power Elite* (New York: Oxford University Press, 1956), p. 244.

93. McConnell, *Private Power and American Democracy*, p. 294.

94. For evidence that those who disagree with their appointed supervisors are dealt with summarily, see Ralph Nader, Peter J. Petkas, and Kate Blackwell, *Whistle Blowing* (New York: Grossman, 1972).

95. Silk and Vogel, *Ethics and Profits*, p. 199.

96. David Vogel, "Why Businessmen Mistrust Their State: The Political Consciousness of American Corporate Executives," *British Journal of Political Science*, December 1977.

97. James W. Prothro, *The Dollar Decade* (Baton Rouge, La.: Louisiana State University Press, 1954), as quoted in Silk and Vogel, *Ethics and Profits*, p. 194.

6

Community
Power Structures

INTRODUCTION

Not all power is wielded at the national level. To have a full picture of who rules in the United States, it is necessary to understand the power structures that exist at the local level and see how they relate to the national power elite described in previous chapters. It must be shown that leaders within a local area join together as a community power structure because they share a mutual interest in increasing the value of their land, buildings, and other real estate through intensifying land use and creating population growth.

Community power structures attempt to achieve their growth aims by attracting the capital investments of corporations, state and federal agencies, and universities and research institutes. This need for outside investors creates a basis for cooperation between local landed elites and the corporate community. However, the somewhat different concerns of these two groups, and the often-intense competition among local elites for growth opportunities, also provides the basis for considerable conflict and tension within the overall power system.

Only in the largest cities, where major corporations and a few extremely rich families are wealthy enough to capture the profits of both land use and production, does this distinction between land-based local elites and the capital-based national power elite tend to disappear. It may be that the corporatization of real estate profits is the wave of the future. But for now the distinction between two types of economic elites is useful in understanding the findings of social scientists concerning power structures at the local level, particularly in the small cities that usually were studied in the past.

THE COMMUNITY POWER LITERATURE

Systematic research on the structure of power in the United States actually began at the community level, where social scientists had the resources to observe and study the whole situation. At first such studies were merely a small part of investigations that encompassed all aspects of a community. This was the case, for example, in the path-breaking studies by sociologists Robert S. Lynd and Helen Merrill Lynd in "Middletown" (Muncie, Indiana) in the 1920s and 1930s. In their two books, the greatest emphasis was placed on earning a living, making a home, raising the young, and engaging in community activities. Thus, the observations and evidence on power were often extremely limited, although several generalizations made at different points in the accounts of these other concerns were widely reported in the community power textbooks without the qualifications with which the Lynds prefaced them.[1]

Mills, drawing on his own interviews in several middle-size cities of 25,000 to 100,000 in 1945, as well as on a synopsis prepared for him on power findings in 16 communities studied between 1929 and 1950, stated several conclusions about community power structures. He believed that they owned most of the commercial properties along "main street" in addition to the local newspaper and radio station, directed the local banks and the Chamber of Commerce, saw each other socially in such service clubs as the Rotary, and held "the keys" to local decisions. However, none of the studies he relied upon really provided a convincing picture of the internal workings of a local power structure nor an explanation of how it operated in relation to government.[2]

The first book on Muncie by the Lynds, for example, had only anecdotal comments concerning the influence of private groups on political decisions. The chapter on "the machinery of government" paid more attention to beliefs about government and the enforcement of moral prohibitions than it did to power or rule, words that do not appear in the index. In the second book, where they added a whole chapter on the wealthy family alleged to dominate the city, the Lynds relied almost exclusively on the testimony of a former community volunteer with many years of service in the business-supported organizations in the city. A long footnote at the end of this new chapter called it "necessarily impressionistic" and "but a pro-legomenon to a type of research too little attempted as yet by American social science."[3]

It was not until the early 1950s that the first systematic study appeared that was devoted to the analysis of a community power structure. It was undertaken by a former social worker from Atlanta, Floyd Hunter, who returned to that city to do a detailed study of how new policies were generated there as his doctoral dissertation in sociology. Hunter had a general idea of how things might work, for he had served under what he later called "second echelon" personnel of the power structure as head of a community welfare agency there. He also had learned something about power in Atlanta by being fired in 1948 for allowing a room in the agency's building to be used for an antisegregation speech by a former Vice-President, Henry A. Wallace, the presidential candidate of the Progressive Party in that year.[4] However, it was only after he had supplemented his past experience with dozens of systematic interviews that Hunter felt he understood the origin of new policies from within the power structure. Even then, he emphasized that he had but a sample of the people involved due to the limited time and money at his disposal: "No pretense is made that the group to be discussed represents the totality of power leaders in the community, but it is felt that a representative case sample is presented, and that the men described come well within the range of the center of power in the community."[5]

Hunter's study, which brought the term *power structure* into social science discourse for the first time, was recognized as a major and controversial contribution as soon as it was published in 1953. For one thing, its method, later called the reputational method, was new. Hunter began by asking a panel of 14 people highly knowledge-able about the city, essentially upper-middle-class professionals, to pick out the top ten leaders from the lists of organizational leaders he had collected from the Chamber of Commerce (business leaders), the League of Women Voters (government officials), the Community Council (civic leaders), and newspaper reporters and civic leaders ("society" leaders). From these lists containing 175 names he picked those 40 people who received the most votes, and then set out to interview as many of those people as he could. Among other things, he asked them who they thought were the most important leaders in the city, how well they knew the other people on the list, and what they thought were the two most important issues facing the com-munity at that time.

Hunter was able to interview 27 of the 40, and they over-whelmingly agreed that most of the top leaders in Atlanta were on the list. Only 5 people not on the list received four or more nominations from those already selected. To gain other perspectives, Hunter also interviewed 34 leaders from the black community and 14 planners and welfare workers who served as expert advisers in the city, asking them most of the same questions he had asked the top leaders. By interviewing everyone in the same way, he was able to develop rather precise information on the personal, economic, and policy relationships among the powerful.

Hunter's new method was not the only contribution of his book. His findings were also very striking. Most people who were interviewed believed that there were only a small number of power wielders in Atlanta and that most of them were major owners, top executives, and corporate lawyers for the biggest banks, department stores, and other businesses in the city. The leaders were found to live in the same neighborhood, belong to the same clubs, and sit on each other's boards of directors. They knew each other well and had definite opinions about which among them were the most powerful at the time, were about to become more powerful, or were on their way down in influence. A majority said that the most important leader in Atlanta was the centimillionaire chairman of Coca-Cola, but 21 of the 27 said that the best man to head a new policy committee would be the chairman of Georgia Power & Light. This was because the Coca-Cola chairman was so busy with state and national questions, including the presidential campaign of his friend Dwight D. Eisenhower, that he left most local matters to his company vice-presidents and his lawyers at King & Spaulding.[6]

Although a few men stood out as the foremost leaders, Hunter concluded that there was no single power hierarchy or power pyramid in Atlanta. Rather, there were overlapping cliques or crowds within the downtown business community, and different people took the lead on different policy issues. On one issue the banking crowd might take the initiative, on another issue it might be the utility crowd that carried the ball:

> Only a rudimentary "power pyramid" of Regional City will be presented. One may be content to do this because I doubt seriously that power forms a single pyramid with any nicety in a community the size of Atlanta. There are pyramids of power in this community which seem more important to the present discussion than *a* pyramid.[7]

As interesting as questions of power rankings and power pyramids may be, Hunter's primary concern remained the origins of policy initiatives. Consider the two sentences that open his book: "It has been evident to the writer for some years that policies on vital matters affecting community life seem to appear suddenly. They are

COMMUNITY POWER STRUCTURES

acted upon, but with no precise knowledge on the part of the majority of the citizenry as to how these policies originated or by whom they are really sponsored."[8] After his candid interviews with the top business leaders, Hunter felt he understood why most people had the same impression.

A new policy within the Atlanta power structure usually had its origin in informal discussions among friends at lunch or a social club. If the idea seemed plausible within that small group, it was checked out informally with people from other crowds and modified as necessary. If there was general agreement among those informally contacted, the idea might be brought up for discussion at the "49 club" or the "101 club," both of which were more formalized but highly private discussion groups involving a cross-section of community leaders. Such groups have been found since in other cities—the Committee of 25 in Los Angeles, for example, or the Monday Morning Group in Riverside, California. When Hunter returned to Atlanta for a second study in the early 1970s, he found that the older discussion groups had been superseded by one including both black and white leaders. Called the Atlanta Forum, it was described by *Business Week* in 1973 as "the informal power center of the city."[9]

If the idea still seemed sound after consideration by the 49 club or 101 club, a committee might be formed and discussion would turn to more specific questions, such as which organizations and bureaucracies at the middle levels might be brought into the picture. Preliminary discussions of which people should be out front as members of formal public committees would also begin. In addition, one or two people might go to the newspaper for the purpose of planting a background story suggesting that a new proposal may be afloat. Since nothing had been made public in a formal way, it was possible for the idea to be dropped at this point, and Hunter notes that new initiatives were often dropped if it seemed they would generate resistance within middle-level voluntary associations or the general public.

Only when everything seemed to be firmly in place did a policy suddenly become a matter for formal public discussion, often officially proposed by the Chamber of Commerce or a civic organization. From that point on, the problem became a matter of execution, the carrying out of the policy. But the policy—defined as "a set course of action" by Hunter—had already been formulated in the complex process that involves both informal and formal discussions within the power structure. Hunter's tight summary of his findings remains a minor gem:

> The top group of the power hierarchy has been isolated and defined as comprised of policy-makers. These men are drawn largely from the

businessmen's class in Atlanta. They form cliques, or crowds, as the term is more often used in the community, which formulate policy. Committees for formulation of policy are commonplace, and on community-wide issues policy is channeled by a "fluid committee structure" down to institutional, associational groups through a lower-level bureaucracy which executes policy.[10]

Given the ease with which the new method could be utilized and the striking nature of the results, several social scientists greeted Hunter's study with great interest and proceeded to apply the reputational method with very similar results, often making innovations in the method and presenting new findings on "submerged" and "symbolic" leaders in the process. Hunter went on to show that the method yielded similar findings in the northern city of Salem, Massachusetts, and utilized it with equally informative results at the national level, isolating the same clubs, policy groups, and corporate leaders that were discussed in earlier chapters.[11]

However, the pluralists within the social-science fraternity reacted to the Atlanta study with great dismay. Most of all, they criticized the method for the possible bias that might be introduced by the way in which the first set of knowledgeable informants are selected to go through the leadership lists, by the wording of the questions that are asked in the interviews, and by the alleged lack of concern with whether or not a reputation generated from newspaper publicity or success on a single community issue actually reveals anything about leadership in general. The reputational method aside, pluralists felt Hunter's portrait of power in Atlanta was inaccurate because he had spent no time studying the workings of government on issues of general significance within the community. Without such studies of specific issues, they said with almost one voice, it would be impossible to ascertain the distribution of power in an American community.[12]

The kind of study Hunter's critics called for was some time in coming, but it was worth the wait in terms of the impact it had. Published in 1961, *Who Governs?* included a detailed study of decision making in three different issue areas in New Haven, Connecticut, a city of about 150,000 people that is best known as the home of Yale University. Written by Robert A. Dahl, later to be voted the most influential political scientist of the 1960s by his colleagues, the book won the Woodrow Wilson Foundation prize for that year as the outstanding book in political science, providing what the foundation termed "a dynamic, pluralist theory of local power structure" that would become "a classic reference for those seeking an understanding of political behavior in modern urban environments under democratic regimes."[13]

Dahl began his study by providing indicators for identifying what he called social notables and economic notables, members of the local upper class and local business community, respectively. The social notables were 231 families that had attended the local debutante ball at the New Haven Lawn Club in either 1951, 1958, or 1959. The economic notables, who numbered 238, included all those people in the following categories:

1. The president or chairman of the board or corporation with property in New Haven assessed in any of the five years 1953–1957 at a value placing it among the fifty highest assessments in the city.
2. Any individual or group of individuals with property in the city assessed in the years 1953–57 at a value of $250,000 or more.
3. Any individual who was a director of three or more of the following: a firm with an assessed valuation of $250,000 or more; a manufacturing firm with fifty employees or more; a retailing firm with twenty-five employees or more; a bank.
4. All directors of New Haven banks.[14]

Dahl then compared the two groups of notables and found only 24 people who were in both categories, an overlap that is much smaller than what has been found in the studies of larger cities that were reported in the third chapter of this book. He concludes that the most important businesspeople in New Haven are not part of the local social elite.

However, the most crucial aspect of Dahl's study was to determine the degree to which people in either of his two categories involved themselves in one or more of three different issue areas— nominations for office in both political parties, public education, and urban renewal. Dahl chose those particular issue areas for their visibility, diversity, and apparent importance within the city as a whole. The area of political nominations was chosen because "nominations determine which persons will hold office," and he found that leaders within the two parties determine mayoral candidates without the help of either social or economic notables.[15]

Dahl chose to study the school system in good part because it was the largest item in the city budget, accounting for between a quarter and a third of all city expenditures. Moreover, the schools play a large role in the lives of most citizens at one time or another.[16] Isolating eight different decisions that occurred between 1953 and 1959, including an eye-testing program, a program to deal with juvenile delinquency, new procedures for teacher promotions, and proposals to increase appropriations for school libraries, he found that in all but a few instances the successful participants in these decisions were "officially and publicly involved in the school system."[17] The mayor and his appointees on the Board of Education were the most important of these officials. No economic notables had any role, and only a handful of social notables took part.

The third issue studied by Dahl was urban renewal, the term for a program financed primarily at the federal and state levels, which makes it possible for cities to buy and clear what they define as slum land and then resell it to developers. The issue was chosen because of the great amount of money involved and its potential interest to the business community. Although he found that the number of social and economic notables involved was 27 times greater than would be expected by chance, particularly as members of a government committee that was supposed to be an important advisory group for the program, Dahl does not attach much weight to this evidence for two reasons. First, the number of notables involved was only 10 percent of all participants even though they were proportionally overrepresented. Second, he believed the committee on which many of them served was a passive body that did the mayor's bidding; it was primarily a rubber-stamp committee with a symbolic function.[18]

Dahl's conclusion from his inquiries in these three issue areas is that neither type of notable is significantly involved in the decision-making process in New Haven, and that a variety of groups take part. His negative conclusions about the role of the economic notables also express his general findings:

> To reconstruct these decisions is to leave little room for doubt that the Economic Notables, far from being a ruling group, are simply one of the many groups out of which individuals sporadically emerge to influence the policies and acts of city officials. Almost anything one might say about the influence of the Economic Notables could be said with equal justice about a half dozen other groups in the New Haven community.[19]

The finding in the issue area of urban renewal was especially surprising, for it is an area in which businessmen could be expected to be intensely active. However, according to Dahl, New Haven's very large urban renewal program, which received nationwide attention in the 1950s, was made possible by the efforts of the Democratic mayor who took office in 1954 when the program was at a standstill:

> Few aspects of local policy could be more salient to the Notables than efforts to save downtown New Haven, yet the Economic Notables were able neither to agree on nor put through a program of urban redevelopment even under a Republican mayor anxious to retain their support. When redevelopment came to New Haven the leadership for it came less from the Notables than from a Democratic mayor, whom most of them originally opposed and who as mayor had to wheedle, cajole, recruit, organize, plan, negotiate, bargain, threaten, reward, and ma-

neuver endlessly to get the support needed from the Notables, the small businessmen, the developers (who came principally from outside New Haven), the federal authorities, and the electorate.[20]

Even the largest and most prestigious institution in the city, Yale University, was found to be relatively powerless as compared with the mayor and the city government. Yale had been in New Haven since the eighteenth century, was the largest landowner in the city, had one of the two or three largest payrolls in the community, and provided a significant portion of the consumer spending in the downtown area through both employees and well-to-do students. Many of the local business leaders, and almost all the partners in leading law firms, were graduates of Yale, and the mayor had been the university's public relations man for ten years before becoming mayor. But Yale was seen by Dahl as separate from the local business community and at the mercy of the mayor's wishes. This relative powerlessness was due to several factors:

> Although the university is sometimes regarded by suspicious citizens of New Haven as an obscurely powerful force in local politics, in fact it is in a weak political position. Like academic people everywhere, Yale faculty members are politically heterogeneous and jealous of their individual autonomy; they can be counted on to raise a cry for academic freedom at the first suggestion from an incautious university administration that they are expected to have a single political line on anything. Certainly no administration in recent years has even hinted at the existence of a Yale party line. Although a few individual faculty members are involved in New Haven politics—the last three Democratic aldermen from the First Ward have been young Yale faculty members—most Yale people are much less interested in the politics of New Haven than in the politics of Yale, their professional associations, the nation, or the international arena. And more of Yale's faculty and other employees live outside New Haven than in the city. Finally, although the university is one of the biggest property owners in New Haven, it also happens to be far and away the largest owner of tax-free property; hence Yale officials are highly sensitive to community hostility and fearful of any action that might embroil the university in local controversy.[21]

In Dahl's view of New Haven, then, the local upper class is not based in the business community, the business community is passive and not very influential, and Yale is on the periphery of local politics. The business community can often block proposals it does not like that directly affect its economic interests, but it seldom takes an initiatory role. When it comes to power, the most important arena in New Haven is the political one. It is the mayor and his aides who initiate new programs and forge new coalitions, selling their programs to the business community, Yale, and the general populace.

Although no one social class or interest group is able to dominate the political sector on a variety of issues, there are inequalities in New Haven. However, they are "dispersed inequalities," meaning that no one group has all of the different types of resources, such as social standing, legitimacy, wealth, knowledge, and public office, that can be utilized to exercise power. Moreover, it is relatively easy to become involved in the "political stratum," defined as the small number of citizens who are highly active in politics. The result of dispersed inequalities and the permeability of the political stratum is a pluralistic distribution of power.

There have been several community power studies since those by Hunter and Dahl, but their work on Atlanta and New Haven has remained the only major focus of debate within the social science community. Despite the new studies, textbooks in urban sociology and urban politics often begin and end their discussions of local power by noting that Hunter, using his reputational method, found a relatively cohesive and business-dominated power structure in Atlanta, whereas Dahl, using what is called the decisional method of studying power, discovered a loose-knit and middle-class pattern of power with government officials at the center. It is then noted that the matter remains unsettled, perhaps with the additional comment that the concentration of power probably varies from city to city in any event. Faced with this impasse, interest in the study of community power structures waned considerably in the 1960s and 1970s.

Such a state of affairs is clearly unsatisfactory. A new start is needed. The remainder of this chapter, then, will suggest a framework for understanding the dynamics of community power structures and their relationships to national levels of power. As part of this effort, it will present evidence that the Atlanta power structure does involve itself in local government decisions, and it will use new data uncovered in the archives of Yale University, the New Haven Chamber of Commerce, and the local Redevelopment Agency to suggest that Dahl was fundamentally mistaken about the nature of the power structure in that city, especially when it comes to urban renewal.

POWER STRUCTURES AS GROWTH MACHINES

A theoretical framework for encompassing the diverse and seemingly contradictory findings on power at the local level has been suggested by urban sociologist Harvey Molotch. Surveying the separate literatures on city development and community power structures, Molotch concludes that a community power structure is at bottom an aggregate of land-based interests that profit from increasingly intensive use of land. It is a set of property owners who see their futures as linked because of a common desire to increase the value of their individual parcels. Wishing to avoid any land uses on adjacent parcels that might decrease the value of their properties, they come to believe that working together is to the benefit of each of them: "One sees that one's future is bound to the future of the larger area, that the future enjoyment of financial benefit flowing from a given parcel will derive from the general future of the proximate aggregate of parcels," Molotch writes. "When this occurs," he continues, "there is that 'we feeling' which bespeaks of community."[22]

The most typical way of intensifying land use is growth, and this growth usually expresses itself in a constantly rising population. A successful local elite is one that is able to attract the corporate plants and offices, the defense contracts, the federal and state agencies, or the educational and research establishments that lead to an expanded work force, and then in turn to an expansion of retail and other commercial activity, extensive land and housing development, and increased financial security. It is because this chain of events is at the core of any developed locality that Molotch calls the city and its local elite a "growth machine."

The most important activity of a community power structure in this view is to provide the right conditions for outside investment—in Molotch's phrase, to prepare the ground for capital. However, this preparation involves far more than providing level and plentiful acreage with a stream running through it. It also involves all those factors that make up what is called a "good business climate," such as low business taxes, a good infrastructure of municipal services, vigorous law enforcement, an eager and docile labor force, and a minimum of business regulations. Molotch stresses that the local "rentiers" expend considerable effort in keeping up with the changing place needs of corporate capital:

> To better understand the needs of capital, and hence to better prepare the ground for them, sophisticated rentiers may take business school courses, read relevant trade journals, make use of their social ties with local capitalists, foster studies at the local university, governmental, or planning agency, or, as is most common, use their own "good business sense." The point is that they maintain an attitude of constant alert to the needs of this dominant class.[23]

Although the growth machine is based in land ownership, it includes all those interests that profit from the intensification of land use. Thus, executives from the local bank, the savings and loan, the telephone company, the gas and electric company, and the local department store are often quite prominent as well. As in the case of the corporate community, the underlying unity within the growth machine is most visibly expressed in the intertwining boards of directors among local companies. And, once again, the central meeting points are most often the banks, where executives from the utilities companies and the department stores meet with the largest landlords and developers.

There is one other important component of the local growth machine, and that is the newspaper. The newspaper is deeply committed to local growth so that its circulation and, even more important, its pages of advertising, will continue to rise. No better expression of this commitment can be found than a statement by the publisher of the *San Jose Mercury News* in the 1950s. When asked why he had consistently favored development on beautiful orchard lands that turned San Jose into one of the largest cities in California within a period of two decades, he replied, "Trees do not read newspapers."[24]

However, the unique feature of the newspaper is that it is not committed to growth on any particular piece of land or in any one area of the city, so it often attains the role of "growth statesman" among any competing interests within the growth machine. Its publisher or editor is deferred to as a voice of reason.

> Competing interests often regard the publisher or editor as a general community leader, as an ombudsman and arbiter of internal bickering, and at times, as an enlightened third party who can restrain the short-term profiteers in the interest of a more stable, long-term, and properly planned growth. The paper becomes the reformist influence, the "voice of the community," restraining the competing subunits, especially the small-scale arriviste "fast-buck artists" among them.[25]

The local growth machine sometimes includes a useful junior partner—the building trade unions. These unions see their fate tied to growth in the belief that growth creates jobs. They often are highly visible on the side of the growth machine in battles against environmentalists and neighborhood groups. Although Molotch shows that local growth does not create new jobs in the economy as a whole, which is a function of corporate and governmental decisions beyond the province of any single community, it does determine where the new jobs will be located. For that reason it is in the interest of unions to help their local growth machine in its competition with other localities.

Those who make up the local growth machine are able to have it both ways. At the state and national levels they support those politicians who oppose, in the name of fiscal and monetary responsibility, the kinds of government policies that might create more jobs, whereas at the local level they talk in terms of their attempts to create more jobs. Their goal is never profits, but only jobs:

> Perhaps the key ideological prop for the growth machine, especially in terms of sustaining support from the working-class majority, is the claim that growth "makes jobs." This claim is aggressively promulgated by developers, builders, and chambers of commerce; it becomes part of the statesman talk of editorialists and political officials. Such people do not speak of growth as useful to profits—rather, they speak of it as necessary for making jobs.[26]

The concern with growth, said by Molotch to be the activating force of a community power structure, was one of the most striking findings in Hunter's study of Atlanta. When he asked the question "What are the two major issues or projects before the community today?" 23 of 26 gave the plan for growth created by the Central Atlanta Improvement Association as one of their choices. Second, with 9 votes, was a plan developed by the business community's Traffic and Safety Council to move traffic in and out of the city more quickly by means of new highways. No other issue received even 5 mentions. Twenty years later, in 1970, when Hunter returned for the second study and asked the same question, he received the same answer. The number-one interest was in physical improvements related to growth, but this time it was a rapid transit system, a new airport, and a downtown sports and convention center. "In the interviews, they could speak of nothing else," reported Hunter.[27]

By way of comparison, Hunter found very different emphases in other parts of the community. The 14 professional workers he asked the same question in 1950 gave as many votes (4) to housing and slum improvement as they did to the plan of development, and 3 of the 14 also mentioned improved race relations. The contrast with black leaders was even more striking; blacks thought that improved schools and better housing were the main issues, and they placed better housing and higher employment as their top concerns in 1970.[28]

Although a concern with growth in general is hypothesized by Molotch to be at the basis of each local elite, every city enters into the competition with a different set of priorities and strategies for achieving it. Calculations have to be made about what investment possibilities are the most desirable and possible based upon such factors as the availability of natural resources; the nature of the climate; the proximity of oceans, lakes, and rivers; the skills of the work force; and the past history of successes and failure in growth competition. Rather obviously, there is a clear preference for clean industries that require highly paid skilled workers over dirty industries that use unskilled workers, but dirty industries will be accepted if other locales win the clean ones. Attractive beach-front towns are not as likely to seek out just any type of industry, as are inland cities; their property can bring in more money as sites for tourist resorts and convention centers. When an area has little or nothing to offer, as in the case of most of Nevada, it settles for gambling and prostitution to create a Las Vegas. Then, too, growth strategies can change over time; when Atlantic City lost out as a "nice" resort, it adopted the Nevada strategy and turned to legalized gambling.

Historical factors also enter into growth strategies. If one locale gets there first with a once-in-a-generation opportunity, such as a stockyard or a railroad, over which competition was very fierce in the nineteenth century, then nearby communities have to settle for lesser opportunities even though they have very similar natural conditions. On the other hand, earlier successes may lock an area into relationships and obligations that make it very difficult for it to take advantage of new opportunities. The rise of Sunbelt cities is not only due to cheaper labor costs, the availability of land, and good weather but also to the previous lack of heavy industry that made them more alert to the possibilities in electronics and information processing.[29]

The way in which differing resources create different growth strategies can be seen in the case of Muncie, a sleepy county seat that existed primarily to serve nearby farms until the discovery of natural gas under the land in 1886. With that discovery Muncie suddenly became a boom town with something unique to offer to industries such as glass, iron, steel, and metal production that had high heat requirements. Local land owners and the promoters who were attracted to the area began to send telegrams and advertisements to industrialists all over the East and Midwest, offering them cheap fuel, cheap land, and even help in building a new factory if they would relocate in Muncie. The local newspaper wrote of the trainloads of capitalists who came to see the city from such important centers as New York, Buffalo, and Cincinnati, and over 40 new factories were brought to the city in a three-year period.[30]

Among those industrialists who received such a telegram was Frank C. Ball, a manufacturer of Mason jars in Bowling Green, Ohio. Enticed by an offer of seven acres of land, a gas well, and $5,000 for plant development, Ball and his brothers moved their operation to Muncie and within a generation built one of the several hundred largest corporations in America. It was this Ball Corporation and its owning family that were said to dominate Muncie by the time the Lynds returned in the mid-1930s for their second study. A few of the other industries that came grew to a large size as well, and Muncie was transformed from a county seat to a manufacturing center.

Within a very few years, the natural gas was used up. Many industries then picked up and left. However, the Ball family stayed, as did several others, and factories in the new automobile industry came in to take advantage of the industrial labor force and the good business climate. As the Lynds report, "the gas boom had provided a solid enough industrial base for the city to continue to develop." The new Muncie had survived its first crisis.[31]

Unlike many industrialists, the Balls developed roots in the community rather than moving themselves and their headquarters to a larger city. They became part of the landed elite by making large property investments, and they prospered as landlords and developers as well as industrialists. If the Balls did dominate the city, and there are reasons to doubt that claim, it was not merely as industrialists but as a strategic part of the growth machine.

Perhaps the most critical land decision made by the Balls, although no one could realize it at the time, was the donation in 1917 of 64 acres and two buildings to a struggling state normal school. The Indiana State Normal School, Eastern Division, was slowly transformed into Ball State Teachers College and then Ball State University, with the Balls developing adjacent land at a handsome profit. From a campus of 1,000 students in 1944, Ball State burgeoned to over 20,000 students in the 1970s. As factories began to move south after World War II, the university became the most important spur to the growth machine. The industrial city became an education and research city. In 1969 it was estimated that each 1,000 students generated 413 local jobs, increased local retail trade by $101,000, and created $20,000 in added city revenue through taxes.[32]

The Muncie story is not without its parallels as a changing growth machine. The growth of large universities saved several dying industrial cities after World War II, and the creation of entire new campuses in other small cities was their economic godsend. One of the cities saved by the presence of its university, as will be shown shortly, was New Haven.

The growth machine hypothesis leads to certain expectations about the relationship between power structures and local government. Rather obviously, the primary role of government is to promote growth according to this view. "It is not the only function of government," writes Molotch, "but it is the key one and ironically the one most ignored."[33] Local government promotes growth in several ways, the most visible of which are the construction of the necessary streets, sewers, and other public improvements and the provision of the proper municipal services. However, government funds for the boosterism that gives the city name recognition and an image of togetherness are also considered important by the growth machine in attracting industry. Sometimes the money for boosterism is given directly to the Chamber of Commerce. In some places, it is given to an Industrial Development Commission or a Convention and Visitors Bureau that is jointly funded by government and private enterprise. Then, too, government officials are expected to be the growth machine's ambassadors to outside investors, traveling to meet with them in their home cities or showing them the local community and answering their questions when they come to inspect it for possible investment.

Since so many specific government decisions can affect land values and growth potentialities, leaders of the growth machine are prime participants in local government. Their involvement is even greater than that of corporate capitalists at the national level, where the power elite can rely to some extent on such "signals" as stock prices, interest rates, and the level of new investments to tell government officials what they think of current policies. The growth machine is the most overrepresented group on local city councils, as numerous studies show, and it also is well represented on planning commissions, zoning boards, water boards, and parking authorities, the decision-making bodies of greatest importance to it. However, this direct involvement in government is usually not the first or only contact with government for members of the growth machine. They often have previous service on the local Chamber of Commerce's committees and commissions that are concerned with growth, planning, roadways, and off-street parking.[34]

For all their participation on city councils, boards of finance, and planning commissions, community power structures have not dominated local government without challenge. They have faced two major oppositional thrusts at different times in the twentieth century—from machine Democrats and the Socialist Party in the early years of the century and from middle-class environmentalists, neighborhood groups, and college students in the 1960s and 1970s. Not all local power structures had to face both of these challenges, and the strength of the opposition has varied greatly from city to city, but there is a considerable commonality in their experience.

So typical were the problems with working-class voters early in the century, for example, that leaders from various cities joined together as the National Municipal League. Aided by foundation money and university experts, the National Municipal League perfected a program of "good government" reforms, such as nonpartisan elections, at-large elections, and adoption of the council–city manager form of government, which effectively limited local opposition in all but the larger cities in the Midwest and Northeast, where the reforms were defeated.[35] In the 1970s and early 1980s there were even a few victories over local growth machines, usually in such beautiful residential towns as Palo Alto, California, where well-to-do residents wanted to protect their amenities, or in such university towns as Santa Cruz, California, where the growth machine suddenly and unexpectedly found itself with a Trojan horse inside its walls due to passage of the 26th Amendment permitting the 18-year-old vote in 1971.

The idea that the heart of a community power structure is provided by those businesses concerned with local real estate values explains what has been considered a perplexing issue in community power studies: the relative absence of industrial executives as top leaders within the city. Industrial corporations provide finance support and leadership that are often important within the Chamber of Commerce. Their executives are active in community service organizations if the company is one in which such activity is considered part of good citizenship. But in most cases such corporations and their executives are not central figures at the local level. Some studies conclude that this lack of involvement is even greater when the local executives are only branch managers for corporations with headquarters in other cities.[36]

The growth machine hypothesis suggests that the basic issue is not one of "local" versus "absentee" ownership but the fact that manufacturers are not concerned with land values. Their focus is on making profits through the sale of products in regional, national, and international markets. For an industrialist, any given locality is merely a site for production that can be abandoned with a fair amount of ease if it becomes too costly, as the great concern with plant closings attests. Their power is not in their involvement in local government but in their ability to move, which makes the local growth machine eager to satisfy their requests and creates an underlying tension between the two sets of interests.[37]

URBAN RENEWAL AND THE GROWTH MACHINE

The most significant policy undertaken by a wide range of cities since World War II was that of urban renewal. Since 1954 urban renewal programs have changed the face of many downtown areas and displaced millions of low-income citizens. The programs have led to lawsuits, demonstrations, and sit-ins by liberals, university students, blacks, and senior citizens. If there is anything to the growth machine hypothesis, the origins of this program at the national level, and the implementation of it in different cities, should reveal the guiding influence of the growth machine, for what these programs do is to clear downtown land of low-income housing and small buildings so that central business districts and such major institutions as universities and hospitals can be expanded and enhanced.

The urban renewal program had its shaky origins in the Housing Act of 1949, but it did not get under way in a serious fashion until 1954, when the Eisenhower administration made several changes in the law. Our analysis of the events leading up to this legislation and the subsequent amendments reveals a conflict between two contending forces, one of which was rooted in local growth machines. The other was the liberal-labor coalition.[38]

The liberal-labor coalition was concerned with creating more housing for the poor. This concern manifested itself in terms of programs for public housing, subsidized housing, and the rehabilitation of slums. The coalition was opposed by downtown business interests, who were concerned with protecting real estate values and creating more space for the expansion of businesses and other large institutions. There was some overlap in the two camps, created by the many liberal planners who also shared some of the business perspective and the few farsighted businesspeople who were willing to grant the need for some housing programs within an overall urban renewal program. But at their cores the two groups were fundamentally opposed. The prohousing group saw the business interests as "the reactionary real estate lobby," which was embodied in the U.S. Savings and Loan League, the Mortgage Bankers Association, the National Association of Real Estate Boards, and the real estate committees of the Chamber of Commerce of the United States. Those in the real estate lobby called the public housing advocates "the housers" and often claimed their programs were socialistic or communistic.[39]

The first federal legislation related to this conflict, the Housing Act of 1937, was a redevelopment program for low-income housing that provided federal aid to municipal housing authorities. While modest in size, there were 200,000 people living in these federally aided projects by 1941, and there was vigorous opposition to this liberal initiative from the real estate interests. Not only did it ignore their interest in downtown expansion, but it posed a mild threat to real estate values because the administrator of the housing authority preferred to build public housing on vacant land. By building outside of slum areas, the liberal director of the United States Housing Authority, a wealthy real estate owner from New York who knew the business well, was trying to deflate land values. As he later wrote:

It would indeed have been a betrayal of a public trust to allow the USHA program to become a means of bailing out owners of slums at "values" of three, five, or ten dollars a square foot when such fictitious values arose out of use of property in a manner which was dangerous to the health of tenants and detrimental to the well-being of the community. The USHA program accordingly was planned to enable local authorities to build some of their projects on low-cost land outside of slum areas.[40]

It was about this time that downtown business interests and real estate developers, with the aid of economists and planners, began to develop their own plans for the inner city, partly to counteract the liberal housing program but also to find a way to clear expensive land for their own growth plans. As urban analyst Jeanne Lowe writes in her colorful history of urban renewal, which sometimes becomes an encomium to the pioneers in urban renewal:

Business interests, particularly downtown property owners and realtors, wanted a clearance and rebuilding program that would be on a more "economic" basis—that would allow private entrepreneurs to participate as developers; permit reuses other than public housing, especially in centrally located slum areas; and let cities reap the higher tax returns which private developers promised. Equally important, these interests had come to accept the fact that in order to assemble land for feasible rebuilding, local government's power of eminent domain would be required to eliminate hold-out prices.[41]

Even with the power of eminent domain, however, it was likely that the high cost of slum land would make it too expensive for those who wanted to renew and expand downtown areas. The answer to this financial problem was provided in the early 1940s by two economists, Alvin Hansen and Guy Greer. Their work was part of the large-scale postwar planning already under way in 1940–1942 under the auspices of three national-level policy-planning organizations, the Council on Foreign Relations, the Committee for Economic Development, and the smaller and more liberal National Planning Association. From the point of view of these organizations, urban renewal was one of several spending programs that might be utilized if economic depression returned after the war.[42]

The general Greer-Hansen proposal for redeveloping the cities was very similar to one developed at the national level by planners at the Urban Land Institute, the national-level policy-planning organization of the real estates interests, but with one major difference. Hansen and Greer suggested that the federal government might have to pay much of the cost for buying and clearing the land instead of merely granting long-term loans, as in the Urban Land Institute plan. Local government was to pay the remainder of the cost, which was set at one-third when the act was passed several years later. The land would then be leased (under the Hansen-Greer plan) or either leased or sold (under the Urban Land Institute plan) to private developers at a lower price than the government had paid, a lower price that supposedly reflected the true earning power of the land when redeveloped. In other words, small property holders, mortgage holders, and slumlords would be bought out at a handsome price by the government, and the bigger real estate interests would be able to obtain the land at a reduced price that supposedly was necessary if they were to make a reasonable profit with nonslum structures. The difference was to be absorbed by the ordinary taxpayer.

Greer and Hansen realized that the new plan might be viewed by some as "a bail-out of the owners of slum properties and the lending institutions that held the mortgages." They therefore argued that "the social and economic mess" that had been left by "past generations" was something for which "society as a whole can be held mainly to blame."[43] This rather general argument was not appreciated by such liberals as the U.S. Housing Authority administrator already quoted:

> The high profits obtained from slum properties, the dogged insistence of slum-owners on their right to maintain housing which flagrantly violates human decencies, the high returns derived from this method of operation, and the high capitalized value placed on the properties—these are typical conditions throughout the country. In view of the facts, the thesis that society is to blame for slum conditions and that there is moral justification for using the taxpayer's funds to bail out owners of the slums is hardly tenable.[44]

The conservative real estate interests had different reservations about the program, but they were tempted by it. They were opposed in principle to federal interference, and they feared the guidelines that might be tied to any federal handouts, but they decided they could live with the basic proposal if certain changes could be made and the emphasis on housing kept to a minimum.

The Hansen-Greer proposal was included in new legislation introduced into the Senate in 1943, and a slightly different bill was introduced later in the same year by the Urban Land Institute. Hearings on the ideas contained in the two bills were first held in 1944–1945 before the Special Subcommittee on Post-War Economic Policy and Planning. In the legislative struggle that ensued, the prohousing interests were able to place a great emphasis on housing construction by introducing the requirement that residential areas that were cleared had to be returned to predominantly residential uses, with *predominantly* being eventually defined as over 50 percent. This requirement was vehemently opposed by the real estate lobby, but it was unable to have it removed. The lobby thus worked to block passage of the bill and was successful in doing so until 1949.

The bill as finally passed contained two important concessions to the real estate interests. They were introduced as amendments early in 1948 by a moderate Republican, Senator Ralph Flanders of Vermont, a major industrialist who was also one of the top leaders in the Committee for Economic Development. The first change mandated that federal money be given to the local community in one lump sum, which made it more difficult for federal agencies to monitor the local program in any detail. The second change allowed city-cleared land to be sold as well as leased to private developers.[45] This concession, which had been part of the original Urban Land Institute proposal, was essential to leaders of the growth machine because it made it possible for private entrepreneurs, rather than the city, to realize the gains from long-term increases in land values. Liberals and moderates, fearing fiscal crisis for the cities, wanted to give them a more secure financial basis by letting them share in the profits of ownership, but the conservatives wanted no part of such a plan. They wanted all the profits, and they wanted city officials dependent on them.

Because the final bill still contained the strong emphasis on housing, the defeated real estate lobby moved to block its implementation through its strong influence with the Appropriations Committee in the House. It also suggested to local leaders that they lobby for passage of state legislation that would allow them to set up local redevelopment agencies that could compete with local housing authorities for federal grants. This plan by the Urban Land Institute, created in the mid-1940s, had been developed in anticipation of a possible defeat at the hands of the liberals at the national level.[46]

The outbreak of the Korean War also contributed to the delay in starting the program, diverting money and attention away from the program. Then, too, developers were very leery that protests might flare up over programs that were going to tear down people's houses with no guarantee of where and when new ones would be completed. The result, as Lowe recounts, is that very few urban renewal programs of any consequences were in process by 1954. Put in this national context, Dahl's emphasis on local leadership in explaining delays in the New Haven program up to that point is muted considerably. "Redevelopment proved doggedly slow in getting started," Lowe writes, "in spite of the apparently attractive opportunity that Title I [of the Housing Act] presented to private enterprise and the cities

themselves. ... The pertinent fact here is that by 1954, few munici-
palities had been able to take a redevelopment project beyond its
initial planning stage."[47]

The advent of the Eisenhower administration in 1952 raised the
possibility that the real estate interests could change the law to their
liking, and their opposition to the program began to soften. The first
step in this process was the creation of a presidential commission in
1953 that was dominated by bankers, savings and loan officials, and
real estate and development leaders. When their suggestions, in the
form of a commission report, were brought to Congress, there was
little or no protest from any business groups, although conservative
southern congressmen continued to register their disagreement.

The key change suggested by the commission was to create an
exception to the rule that residential areas had to be restored to
predominantly residential usages. The new provision allowed another
10 percent of urban renewal grant monies for a given project to be
used for nonresidential uses. The commission also proposed that the
program should encompass slum prevention as well as slum clearance. In practical terms, this made it possible for a plan to encompass
areas that were not run down by claiming they would become slums if
they were not part of the redevelopment program.

The combination of these two provisions freed local growth
machines to move ahead with their plans. Requests for money
burgeoned, and numerous programs got under way. The gradual
enlargement of the exception rule made the program even more
attractive. It was increased to 20 percent in 1959, to 30 percent in
1961, and to 35 percent in 1967. The real estate lobby had won a
complete victory over the housers even though it took them a long
time to do so. As urban sociologist Scott Greer succinctly summarized the legislative struggle between 1937 and the early 1960s,
"the slum clearance provisions of the Housing Act of 1937 have been
slowly transformed into a large-scale program to redevelop the
central city."[48]

As one part of its report to President Eisenhower, the Commission on Urban Renewal and Housing also suggested that implementation of the urban renewal program should be aided by "the formation
outside of government of a broadly representative national organization to help promote and lead this dynamic program for renewal of
the towns and cities in America."[49] This new group was formed in
November 1954 as ACTION, the American Council to Improve Our
Neighborhoods, and it included bankers, corporate executives, and
real estate developers as well as urban planners and housing experts
from major cities across the country. Its ambitious program included

a research division that would amass all available information on how to carry out a good program, a national advertising campaign that would "arouse individual action against the threat of home and neighborhood decay," and a technical assistance program that would provide trained personnel to both citizens and governmental groups.[50]

Four days after the founding of ACTION, the Advertising Council announced a new national campaign to be called "Action on Slums." The aim of the campaign was to "stimulate the rehabilitation or rebuilding of depressed areas."[51] At the same time, various real estate and home-building associations were conducting their own campaigns under such slogans as "Build America Better," "New Face for America," and "Better America, Inc."

As one small aspect of the ACTION program, in an attempt to give people the feeling that something was happening and that they should become involved, the organization hired writer Jeanne Lowe in 1957 to be its public information officer. This work took her to various cities. It was not long before she had visited New Haven and written an article for the October 1957 *Harper's Magazine* entitled "Lee of New Haven and His Political Jackpot." As might be expected, it was an enthusiastic endorsement of what was happening in New Haven, proof that there was no political danger in creating an urban renewal program. There was great emphasis on Mayor Richard C. Lee's leadership qualities. It began:

> Richard C. Lee of New Haven is the first city Mayor in the country to make urban renewal the cornerstone of his political career. Today, as a result, this twice-defeated candidate for a once semi-ceremonial job in a second-rate city is apparently assured of re-election next month for his third term. ... Mayor Lee has struck political paydirt in an unpromising issue.[52]

Five paragraphs later, Lowe notes that "what redevelopment needed was an example like New Haven's, which other cities have watched with envy and which Housing Administrator Cole has called 'spectacular, imaginative, exciting, comprehensive—a model for urban renewal in the cities of America.'"[53] ACTION made a movie about the New Haven story and adopted the city as its ideal example of an urban renewal program.

The legislative successes and image-building efforts of local growth machines, then, were not without outside help. Leaders within the national corporate community had given their considerable support through the opinion-forming process. But their interest in New Haven as a model city remains something of a mystery as yet.

URBAN RENEWAL AT THE LOCAL LEVEL

Several different studies of urban renewal programs in specific cities reveal the predominant role of local business interests. Social scientists Timothy K. Barnekov and Daniel Rich, through questionnaires and interviews in 33 cities, found that downtown associations, chambers of commerce, and small committees of top business leaders have been highly active in the urban renewal programs in most of these cities. They conclude that "these data suggest that it is inaccurate to conclude that businessmen have been hostile or indifferent to urban renewal, or that they lack the sustained organization to promote redevelopment."[54]

Case studies of urban renewal programs in such major cities as Pittsburgh, Philadelphia, Chicago, San Francisco, and Atlanta shed light on how local growth machines dominate local programs even though there are wide differences in how this is accomplished. In Pittsburgh, one of the first cities to undertake urban renewal, it was one family, the Mellons, that spearheaded the program through a coalition known as the Allegheny Conference. Founded in 1943, the Allegheny Conference developed a close working relationship with local government and the Democratic Party that was considered the basis for its success. Because of the great wealth and influence of the Mellons, urban renewal was possible in Pittsburgh even before federal monies were available. Although few cities could emulate Pittsburgh in this regard, the Allegheny Conference nevertheless became the model for Philadelphia, Baltimore, Syracuse, Saint Louis, and other cities in the "formation of public-private partnership."[55]

Philadelphia became a case worthy of study because it created a strong urban renewal program despite the absence of a super-wealthy family. It therefore had to develop a deeper and more broad-based leadership coalition that spent most of the 1940s drawing plans and changing the structure of local government. One of the key steps in this process was the formation in 1948 of an organization called the Greater Philadelphia Movement. It was composed primarily of downtown business leaders, but there were minority group representatives and a labor official among its 35 members who were considered essential symbolic representatives. Not least among its efforts was support for the election of a reform Democratic mayor who was more responsive to the program than his conservative Republican predecessor had been. The Philadelphia model was one that New Haven specifically tried to emulate in its programs.[56]

A detailed study of Chicago's first urban renewal project is of interest because it showed the central role that can be played by a major university—in this case, the University of Chicago—when it has direct ties to both the downtown business community and the Democratic political machine. In Chicago, the university provided aid to various planning and citizens' groups in the formative years between 1949 and 1953 and became even more open in its participation after that time. Utilizing its trustees' connections to city government, it lobbied vigorously for the first city project to be located in the area surrounding the university. In 1959 trustees and administrators from the University of Chicago convinced the Eisenhower administration to amend the urban renewal legislation so that new university construction could be counted as part of the city's one-third contribution to the project costs.[57]

Urban renewal in San Francisco also showed strong downtown business involvement, but there was a different relationship with government. The process began with a group of business leaders who started meeting regularly in 1945 to plan the revitalization of the city and then formalized themselves as the Bay Area Council and the San Francisco Program for Urban Renewal in 1948. However, the plans were carried out by a strong redevelopment administrator who was often at odds with the city council and received minimal support from the mayor's office. Instead of a coalition between downtown business and the mayor, as in many cities, there was a coalition between business and the Redevelopment Agency.[58]

The best and most detailed case study of an urban renewal program concerns the city of Atlanta between 1950 and 1970. Written by political scientist Clarence Stone, it is of special interest because it was designed with the controversy between Hunter and Dahl clearly in mind. It redresses Hunter's lack of detail on government decision making by showing how city officials functioned to aid cohesion in business groups and to discourage and fragment neighborhood groups.

In the course of his study, Stone arrived independently at a position similar to that expressed by Molotch. Land values and growth are the key issue in community politics, and urban renewal is "part of a general struggle over the control of land."[59] Stone came to this conclusion because he found that urban renewal in Atlanta was based on the desire to expand the central business district into the land occupied by low-income black neighborhoods that were also in the process of expanding.

The growth machine's concern for urban renewal was expressed through the Central Atlanta Improvement Association. Members of this group involved themselves with government through membership on the City Housing Authority and a Citizen's Action Committee on Urban Renewal that was jointly financed by business and government, and through informal contacts with the mayor, who was himself a former downtown businessman. Responsibility for specific government plans was lodged in an Urban Renewal Planning Committee composed of commissioners from the Housing Authority and elected officials from the city council's Committee on Urban Renewal. The mayor stayed in the background as much as possible, and responsibility for the program was insulated from him so that he would not become the center of any political controversies over it.

In tracing the history of the program, Stone finds immediate contrasts with New Haven. Whereas neighborhood resistance to the New Haven program did not appear until the 1960s, after Dahl had completed his study, it appeared almost immediately in Atlanta. A tentative plan floated in 1950 was protested by residents in the white neighborhood that would be most affected, and a black newspaper editorialized that there was a danger of urban renewal becoming "Negro removal," a phrase that was to be made famous in the 1960s by the fiery speeches of Malcolm X.[60]

Atlanta also suffered delays in getting its program under way when the Georgia Supreme Court in 1954 ruled that the state's enabling legislation on urban renewal was unconstitutional. The legislation had to be rewritten and was not passed until 1957. Such legal challenges, which were often initiated by ultraconservatives concerned with the implications of the program for the rights of private property, were not uncommon in other cities and states, but only cities in California suffered these delays into the 1960s.

Stone studied several specific decisions from both the formative years of the program, 1954–1962, and the more protest-laden years of 1962–1969. He found that the downtown business community was overwhelmingly successful in achieving its major objectives during the first phase. Its only setback was a partial one of little direct interest to it: Sites for low-income housing that it had agreed to as the price for black leadership support were blocked by a middle-income white neighborhood.[61]

In the second phase the downtown business interests were successful in obtaining land for a stadium, a civic center, and the expansion of a downtown university while quietly vetoing the repeated requests of specific neighborhoods for public housing. This second phase was highlighted by black demonstrations and protests, actions that should have met with great success, Stone notes, if pluralistic theorists are right that "the prizes go to the interested and active."[62] For a time, it did look as if they were going to be successful. In early 1966 a neighborhood group was able to save one-half of its area from plans for urban renewal clearance. The outbreak of relatively mild civil disorder in two other black neighborhoods in September 1966 galvanized the city into promises for larger recreational and fix-up programs for neighborhoods. In November 1966 the mayor announced a goal of 17,000 new units of low- and moderate-income housing, with 9,800 of those units to be completed within two years. By the end of 1966, Stone reports, the program seemed to be changed rather dramatically:

> The change had come abruptly. As late as the 1965 Declaration of Policy in the city's Workable Program document, Atlanta's urban renewal program was explained primarily in terms of the "encouragement of economic expansion," physical planning and development, and "the overall economic ability of the City to support ... urban development and renewal activities." By the close of 1966 the urban renewal program was completely recast; neighborhood improvements, grass-roots participation, and expanded supply of standard housing for low- and moderate-income families appeared to be central elements in a new renewal policy.[63]

However, the policies did not change after all. As protest receded, the promises went unfulfilled. City officials stalled and delayed as they fought with neighborhood groups and as the groups within neighborhoods began to argue with one another. Only a few thousand of the 17,000 promised housing units were built. City officials blamed neighborhood opposition for this failure. Stone suggests that lack of business support was even more important, for the business leaders had made it clear that they preferred low-income housing to be built outside the city limits.[64] Also left unmentioned by city officials was the opposition of real estate interests to any government involvement in the construction and management of housing.

Stone sees these results as a direct contradiction to the general theory of pluralist politics that Dahl derived from New Haven. Poor citizens do not have what Dahl called the "slack," or extra resources, to invest in politics when they feel their interests are threatened enough to make politics worthwhile. Despite sustained protests and other efforts, blacks in Atlanta were not able to induce politicians and government officials to forward their interests. Instead, the link between the business community and city hall, based upon common values, organizational ties, and campaign finance, proved more durable. Between 1956 and 1966 one-seventh of the people in Atlanta were moved out of their homes to make way for expressways, urban renewal, and a downtown building boom that drew nationwide attention throughout the 1970s.[65]

On the basis of the studies on Atlanta and other cities, it would seem that Dahl's findings in New Haven represent a unique case. However, there were also problems with the adequacy of Dahl's analysis. The comparative studies raise three basic questions about it. First, the fact that businessmen and university officials were active in most cities makes it doubtful that those in New Haven would be the only ones who would be hesitant about the possibilities of the program. Second, the fact that most of the programs picked up steam only after changes were made in the urban renewal law in 1954 makes it less likely that the election of a new Democratic mayor in New Haven in November 1953 was the key to the local program. Third, the fact that many cities developed large urban renewal programs without an energetic mayor leading the way suggests that other factors may be more basic in the competition for urban renewal funds.

It is clearly time to reconsider the New Haven study, for it is the most credible challenge that has been offered to the idea that downtown business leaders are the most powerful people in their communities. More generally, it is one of the few systematic, empirical investigations concerned with overall power at either the local or national level that ever has been made by a pluralist. If it could be shown that there are serious defects in what is generally considered to be the best pluralist study to date, it would suggest that careful scrutiny of the more casual instances and anecdotes pointed to by pluralists to support their position might reveal similar problems of method and findings.

Who Really Governs In New Haven?

The pluralistic findings on this coastal city 80 miles east of New York and 47 miles south of Hartford are in striking contrast to what has been found in other studies of local communities, not only on the urban renewal program, but on the overlap of social and business elites as well. However, our detailed restudy of New Haven completed in 1978 provided new empirical evidence that the case for pluralism in that city is also extremely weak.[66]

Our analysis of interlocking directorships among all businesses in New Haven in 1959 with $1 million or more in assets and all corporate law firms showed that there was a well-knit downtown business community. It included 54 of the 60 million-dollar firms and all 5 law firms with four or more partners. The 10 most interconnected firms were all financial institutions and public utilities, with the exception of one law firm. The largest bank in the city, with half of all commercial bank assets, had 26 connections with 7 of the other 9 central firms and 52 connections to 28 organizations overall through its 25-person board of directors.[67] Yale was found to be connected to this network through corporate law firms, most of whose partners were graduates of Yale, and bank directorships. For example, the assistant to the president of Yale was on the board of the largest bank.

Then, too, the two most prestigious law firms shared Yale as one of their most important clients.

The directors of the central firms in this business network were very likely to be members of the local social elite as defined by their membership in one or more of three social clubs that were shown to be reliable indicators of upper-class standing in the New Haven area. Twenty-four of the 25 directors of the largest bank were in one of the three clubs, for example, and 13 were in two of the three. Of the 319 local directors and law partners encompassed by the entire network, 56 percent were in one or more clubs.[68] Similarly, individuals with two or more directorships, the inner group of the local business community, were very likely to be in the social elite. Of the 91 New Haven residents on two or more boards, 80 percent were in at least one of the clubs, and 40 percent were in two. The overlap was even greater for those who sat on several boards. Of the 25 men who sat on three boards, 76 percent were in at least one club; of the 15 who sat on four or more boards, 90 percent were in one of the clubs.[69] These findings are similar to those for larger cities and the national level in general.

The restudy also showed that the people who attended the debutante ball, thereby satisfying Dahl's sole indicator of upper-class standing, were in good measure members of the three clubs. Of the 198 couples or individuals who attended the ball in 1958 and 1959, the years for which club membership lists were available, 70 percent were in at least one of the three clubs and 29 percent were in two or more.[70] A similar picture emerges from a comparison of Dahl's list of economic notables with the club membership lists. Of the 236 people on his list, 43 percent were in one or more of the three clubs. Of the 139 local businesspeople who were both on his list and in our business network, 70 percent were in one of the clubs. Virtually none of the smaller businesspeople and small property owners on his list were in any of the three clubs.[71]

A reconsideration of the three different issue-areas studied by Dahl suggested that two of them, political nominations and public education, did not have any relevance to the local business community. In the case of political nominations, there is no evidence that it makes any difference whether one person or another is nominated, especially when there is evidence that the business community had access to the mayors studied by Dahl through campaign finance and personal contact. Moreover, as sociologist Robert Alford argues, nominations are not in and of themselves a substantive policy area in the way that public education and urban renewal are. It therefore must be demonstrated that nominations affect policy outcomes:

But this is an issue-area quite different from the others; it is a procedural device to determine which particular individuals will hold particular positions, and is not at all the same as a struggle over which policies shall be carried out, except insofar as individuals represent different policy positions and different interest groups, and this aspect Dahl doesn't really consider. The electoral struggle is not a "policy" at all, and should not be seen as in the same theoretical plane.[72]

This issue-area also turned out to have a formal bias against participation by economic and social notables. It was a rule of both parties that leaders had to live in the city, but most notables lived in the suburbs and were not eligible for party office.

In the case of the school system and the decisions within it that were studied, there is no evidence that these issues were of any concern to the New Haven power structure. Indeed, as already noted, most of the economic and social notables lived in the suburbs, where they had access to better school systems. Those who did live in New Haven often sent their children to private schools. As Dahl wrote: "Most social notables and many economic notables living in New Haven send their children to private schools; as a consequence, their interest in public schools is ordinarily rather slight."[73] Thus, as Dahl also notes, the main concern of the local business leaders vis-à-vis the school system was the control of its expenditures. That function was taken care of by the Board of Finance, which is also appointed by the mayor.[74] The Board of Finance has two main functions that are relevant to the school system. It recommends a tax rate that the elected Board of Aldermen can raise but not lower and prepares budget estimates for departments that the aldermen can cut but not increase.[75] Members of the Board of Finance were overwhelmingly from the business community.

However, when it comes to the issue of urban renewal, there is agreement on all sides that it was indeed a crucial issue for the power structure. Certainly it was the kind of issue that interested the leaders of Atlanta, as the interviews by Hunter and the decisional study by Stone made clear. It is also an issue that is of obvious theoretical significance from the growth machine perspective.

Our analysis of records in various archives in New Haven, supplemented by personal and telephone interviews with many of the participants in the urban renewal program between 1940 and 1957, revealed that the local business community did have a very great involvement in the urban renewal program, with officers and directors from many of the most central organizations in the business network playing prominant roles. The records of the Chamber of Commerce and the Redevelopment Agency show that its leaders had a long-standing interest in urban renewal and had been developing plans for it since the early 1940s. Chamber documents show that it was one of the first organizations in the city to argue for the creation of a Redevelopment Agency, and the minutes of Agency meetings demonstrate that the only group to concern itself with the Agency's activities was the Chamber and related organizations. The correspondence files of the Agency's outside consultant show that he was in constant contact with the Chamber leaders as he developed his plans. Far from being unconcerned with the program, business leaders agonized over the delays it was suffering. The flavor of their concerns is captured in the Chamber's minutes for November 9, 1953, after a meeting with the city planner, Norris Andrews. The minutes also reveal some of the problems the program faced:

> Mr. Giese, Mr. Thompson, Mr. Costello, and Mr. Johnson met with Mr. Andrews to see if they could determine what pressure could be brought on the State Highway Commissioner to make decisions regarding U.S. Route 1 and the Oak Street Extension. Mr. Andrews said there were many roadblocks. One of them is a Supreme Court decision regarding the constitutionality of the Urban Redevelopment Act. To obtain a decision, a friendly suit has been brought by the advocates of urban redevelopment against the City of Hartford.
> Mr. Andrews indicated that the Urban Redevelopment Agency had full knowledge of the exact location of the Oak Street Extension. However, it was his impression that the Federal Government would not give full approval to proceeding with Number Three Project until it is determined whether the City or the State will pay for developing the Oak Street Extension.[76]

The eagerness of the business leaders is also seen in their reaction to the election of the new mayor. Contrary to Dahl, who in fact received much of the information he relied upon the most from interviews with Mayor Lee and his aides, the mayor did not have to sell them the program. In fact, they worried that they might have to sell it to him. On November 10, seven days after he was elected, Chamber leaders decided to ask for a meeting with him at which "the entire program would be explained to him and he would be urged to get action started on the program." The November 19 meeting, held over lunch at the New Haven Lawn Club, included Lee and five Chamber officers. The minutes report that "the entire program was explained to Mr. Lee" and that "Mr. Lee said he was in entire agreement with a program for action." The final words in the minutes, which certainly were not written for the benefit of future researchers, also reveal the Chamber's eagerness: "In bringing the meeting to a close, Mr. Giese promised Mr. Lee the full cooperation of all those present and assured him the Chamber is willing to do anything possible to get action started and to get a steamshovel starting work on the redevelopment program."[77]

Evidence such as this does not prove that the Chamber caused the program to happen. However, it does show that its leaders were anything but hesitant about it, which is a central claim of Dahl's account. Other evidence, including transcripts of Dahl's original interviews, demonstrates the Chamber's role in the initiation of the program. For one example among several, a top business leader in the city, whom Dahl obviously did not take very seriously, had this interchange with Dahl:

> *Dahl:*   You suggested this to the city, did you?
>
> *Business Leader:*   Yes, we [the Chamber of Commerce] had our own ten-point program which was incorporated in this phase of it. Finally, we got approval of the plan by the city and Mayor Lee took the ball and has been throwing it ever since.[78]

Even more surprising, given Dahl's strong claims about the supine position of Yale University in New Haven politics, it was in fact Yale that made possible the large urban renewal program. It was Yale's presence that provided the city with the legal and planning talent to develop plans in a relatively short period of time. It was the prestige of Yale that attracted top-level redevelopment administrators to the city, including one who had graduated from Yale and married the daughter of one of its highest administrative officials. Then, too, Yale's eagerness to protect its elite image and expand its campus boundaries made it willing to purchase land and lend money to projects, thereby ensuring the feasibility of the first two projects. An interest in helping Yale on the part of thousands of its graduates working in the corporate community and the elite media created a sympathetic national climate for New Haven's efforts. It was a wealthy Yale trustee serving in the Senate who opened the doors in Washington for New Haven officials. After 1959, when university construction counted toward a city's share of the cost, Yale's growth provided the credits that made more projects possible. Finally, it was Yale's own growth that energized the growth machine. Since these claims are so contrary to Dahl's accounts, they deserve more detailed documentation.

Planning for urban renewal in New Haven, which began in the early 1940s, paralleled developments on the national level. However, it began in a context of serious decline rather than potential expansion, for New Haven had stopped growing in 1920. Its industrial base was collapsing or moving away. This was particularly the case with its once-illustrious carriage manufacturers, hopelessly lost in the face of the automobile. But New Haven also had been bypassed as a port city when the railroads became ascendant, and only later did the port become important again as an oil depot. Not only was industry declining, but the middle classes, aided by the automobile, were moving to the suburbs and the surrounding countryside, which meant that many downtown retail businesses were losing customers to suburban shopping centers.

There was one overriding issue that faced the power structure in New Haven and its city planners: how to revive the lagging growth machine. And there was only one bright spot in the picture, Yale University. Although Yale had been in New Haven since 1716, it was not highly significant economically until it began to grow in the late 1920s, coincidentally taking up some of the slack from the decline in industry. Its expansion in the 1930s was especially crucial to the economy. During that decade it accounted for 51 percent of all local construction, with no other organization or sector accounting for more than a few percent of the remaining 49 percent.[79]

By the early 1940s, it was clear to city planners that Yale was the primary engine to the new growth machine. It was Yale's construction plans, Yale's yearly budget and payroll, and the consumer spending by Yale students that would underpin the economy henceforth. Yale's ability to attract government research institutes, medical facilities, and similar organizations would be critical. The past and future of New Haven were spelled out in 1938 in a prescient book called *New Haven's Problems* by Yale graduate Arnold Dana, who had returned to the city after many years as a business reporter for several different newspapers:

> The 40-year comparison for the years 1936 and 1897 confirms the belief that this city is actually undergoing radical transformation in many respects. Half a century ago, as already noted, there was here an exceptionally flourishing manufacturing and commercial shipping town, with Yale College highly important but not the greatest of the city's establishments. Today New Haven is rapidly becoming an institutional, professional, technical, and garment-making center with shipping an almost negligible issue and manufacturing interests slowly decreasing in importance as a source of income to the city.[80]

Every planning study that was done in the 1940s accepted this type of analysis and made three or four basic points. First, it would be necessary to provide better highways so suburban shoppers could come to the downtown business district. Second, the remaining industry should be moved to cheaper land on the outskirts of the city. Third, the port facilities should be improved. Fourth, land for the growth of Yale and related research institutions must be provided. In keeping with these recommendations, a 1943 plan commissioned by the city from a visiting planning professor at Yale, Maurice Rotival, suggested that a slum neighborhood between Yale and the medical school-hospital complex be "allocated to future development of an institutional nature."[81] A 1944 report on housing by a prominent local architect who numbered Yale, its medical school, the hospital, and the telephone company among his clients, came to the same conclusion. Housing should be eliminated from what was called the Oak Street Area. Emphasizing that land adjacent to the downtown, the hospital, and the university was too valuable to be used for housing, he recommended for the Oak Street Area that (1) part of it be put in the central business district; (2) part of it be utilized for highways into the central business district; (3) part of it be used for professional buildings near the hospital; and (4) the northern part of it be used for housing professional persons and graduate students from the hospital, medical school, and university. Ten years later, this is exactly what was done in the first urban renewal project, but Dahl considers such planning just so much talk because nothing happened until 1954.[82]

Planning in the late 1940s and early 1950s took place in the context of Yale's own widely publicized growth plans. In 1947 the trustees appointed a top-level committee to explore in great detail the university's future needs. The committee was headed by investment banker Prescott Bush, a partner in Brown Brothers, Harriman of New York, who had been a member of Yale's board of trustees since 1944. Bush's ties to the university were many and varied. He had graduated from Yale in 1917. One of his banking partners was a trustee before him, and his brother-in-law was to be a fellow trustee in the 1950s. His niece was married to the university's secretary, the second most important campus administrator after the president. Finally, one of his former banking partners was treasurer of the university at the time as well as a director of the largest commercial bank in the city. Nearly 30 years later, in 1978, his son, future Vice-President George Bush, was to co-chair a $370-million fund-raising drive for the university.

The committee's report, *Yale and Her Needs*, was released on January 4, 1950. Calling for a ten-year growth program that would require $80 million in gifts, including $20 million for new buildings, it was the answer to any local growth machine's prayers, especially one that was experiencing no growth. Most of the projected buildings were to be placed within the existing framework of the campus or on available adjacent land. However, there also was a desire for housing for students in the medical and other professional schools. The report said:

> Because of the shortage of all kinds of housing in the community, the students at the university's professional schools have to put up with some demoralizing makeshifts. This is particularly true of medical students, often housed far from the hospital where they might have night duty. Other housing is also needed for student nurses, married

divinity students and their families, and members of the student bodies of the Schools of Fine Arts and Music.[83]

In 1951, when planner Maurice Rotival returned to New Haven to update his earlier plans at the request of the Redevelopment Agency, he proposed that the Oak Street Area between the hospital and the University be considered for the first project. He suggested a mixture of institutional uses and high-rise apartments for students. Representatives of the Agency then met with top Yale officials in October 1951, and a process of cooperation was set into motion. Among other things, the president asked the head of the campus publicity office, Richard C. Lee, to help the Agency on a housing survey it needed.[84]

The interest expressed by Yale in the program was absolutely essential from the point of view of the Redevelopment Agency because local urban renewal agencies could not make applications to the federal government for assistance unless they could show that there was some private institution willing and able to purchase the reclaimed land. Without Yale or some other private organization, the city could not move ahead. A high Yale official later explained this point as follows in a candid interview with Dahl:

> The Mayor and [one of his aides] both testified publicly again and again at the Citizens Action Commission meetings and at luncheons and elsewhere that if it hadn't been for Yale's willingness to step up as original bidders on that property the whole Oak Street project would have died aborning ... you know the rules, the laws, the policies in Washington that require a firm bid from some private agency in the community before contracts of this kind could be signed and the way cleared for the financing of the whole project. Well, anyhow, this is what we did. Now here again ... this was not sheer altruism on Yale's part. It was a case of, I think, truly enlightened self-interest. We were hard pressed, as we still are, for housing.[85]

The interest Yale showed in the housing project did not lead immediately to an administrative committee within the university. Instead, the president appointed one of his closest friends and confidants, Morris Tyler, a New Haven corporate lawyer who had graduated from Yale and Yale Law School, to serve as a liaison between the Redevelopment Agency and the university. The role that Tyler played in the urban renewal program throughout the 1950s makes it very important to establish in detail his central place in the New Haven power structure, for it is Tyler who provided Yale with a tie to the Redevelopment Agency and the very heart of the downtown power structure.

Tyler was one of four senior partners in Gumbert, Corbin, Tyler, and Cooper, the only law firm among the ten most central firms in the business network. The firm represented several of the major banks and businesses in New Haven as well as doing some work for Yale. One of Tyler's partners was a director of the largest commercial bank, the largest savings bank, and four other local corporations. Another partner was on the board of the third largest commercial bank, the second largest savings bank, and two other local corporations. Yet another partner was on several other boards. As for Tyler, he was on the board of the second largest commercial bank.

The importance of Tyler becomes even more apparent when it is added that he and his law firm became counsel to the city on redevelopment matters in 1954 and that he was appointed to the Citizen's Action Commission that oversaw the program. When I asked about the importance of Tyler to the program, the former chief aide to the mayor replied very simply, "He was my lawyer."[86]

Two major points contradictory to the standard history of New Haven urban renewal are established by the October 1951 meeting between redevelopment officials and Yale administrators, and the subsequent efforts by Tyler for Yale. First, the contact between Yale and the city preceded the election of Lee as mayor by two years, contrary to almost all accounts of New Haven's urban renewal history. Second, Yale was connected to the downtown redevelopment efforts at its highest levels, the absence of interest in New Haven on the part of 98 percent of the Yale faculty notwithstanding.

The very great importance of Yale to the program was increased even more in 1952, with the election of trustee Prescott Bush to the U.S. Senate as a Republican from Connecticut. Bush was appointed to the Senate Banking and Currency Committee, which was chaired by his good friend and fellow Yale trustee, Robert H. Taft. The committee had oversight responsibilities on the urban renewal program, and Bush immediately began to take an interest in the program. He was one of the sponsors on the 1954 legislation that made the program more attractive to real estate interests, and he brought representatives of the Housing and Home Finance Agency to explain the new law to Connecticut's mayors shortly after it was passed. As he told a Columbia University oral historian: "I remained on the Banking and Currency Committee for ten years, and in the course of that had a good deal to do with promoting the so-called urban redevelopment programs, in the state of Connecticut, under the law."[87]

Bush's claim that he did everything he could for urban renewal in all of Connecticut receives empirical support from the calculations I did on per capita commitments by state based on data through 1972. Connecticut was at the top of the list with $175 per person. Even without New Haven included in its total, Connecticut was second at

$132 per person, surpassed only by sparsely populated Alaska's $166, and still well ahead off such nearby and similar states as Massachusetts ($110), Pennsylvania ($95), New Jersey ($72), and New York ($70). Clearly, then, it is Connecticut that did well, and not just New Haven. Unless Mayor Lee had some kind of contagion effect, this fact argues more in favor of some statewide influence on urban renewal in Connecticut cities than it does for the extraordinary powers of one local mayor.

Although Bush was new to the Senate, his power was enhanced by two factors. First, there was a Republican in the White House for the first time since 1932, which meant that the top appointees to the Housing and Home Finance Agency were Republicans. Second, the Republicans also held control of both houses of Congress in 1953–54, which meant that the bureaucracy was likely to be even more responsive to requests from a Republican Senator on a committee that had so much influence on the fate of the agency.

Bush's role in gaining approval for the first two New Haven projects was very crucial, as is quickly acknowledged in most accounts of the topic before they go on to praise Mayor Lee. The only thing not fully understood by these authors is Bush's intimate knowledge of and concern with Yale's growth plans. The following excerpt from one of Dahl's interviews with a local urban renewal official shows both the importance of Bush and Dahl's lack of information on his previous involvement in Yale's growth plans. The dialogue is in relation to the second and largest of New Haven's projects, called the Church Street project, which covered a significant area of the downtown:

Informant: What we're doing is a land use concept. We had a helluva time. We had to put pressure on Bush, who was most helpful in getting it out.

Dahl: This is one thing I didn't question [other informant] about last night and should have. I don't really understand why it is that Bush has been helpful on this.

Informant: Bush's connections, I've never asked [other informant] directly why, but my own interest from what I know goes back to the fact that Yale was to be the developer on the Oak Street Liner. [Here he is referring to Yale's tentative agreement to buy property for apartment housing in the first renewal area, Oak Street.] Bush is on the Yale Corporation and there is an. ... [Here there is a blank in the transcript due to difficulties in understanding the tape.] Also Bush is on the Banking and Currency Committee, which handles redevelopment legislation. So that he has a logical interest. Also taking advantage of the Yale connection, Logue and Lee, whenever Bush comes to town, dealing with the Yale Corporation, manage to have lunch with him at Mory's. And I've

> gone to some of those luncheons. The preparations when we're putting on a show for Bush, preparation for this one man, is quite intensive. We put out publications limited to him.

Dahl: Is that so?

Informant: Explaining what the program was, what the answers were, answers to the problems, and where he could help in getting those answers.[88]

Bush also was essential in gaining federal approval of the first project in 1955. Indeed, he pressed hard to gain project approval in time to give a boost to the reelection campaign of Mayor Lee. Lowe writes that Lee was receiving bad press because of the possibility Yale might purchase land in the project, but approval of the project overwhelmed any criticism:

> But a week before election day, with an assist from Republican Senator Prescott Bush, federal approval of the $7,650,000 loan and grant for Oak Street came through; the announcement by Lee and Bush in a joint press conference from the Mayor's office made eight-column headlines. Lee was re-elected by a margin of 20,000—the largest ever achieved by a Connecticut Mayor—and the voters also gave him a 31–2 Democratic Board of Aldermen.[89]

In his Columbia oral history, Bush acknowledges his efforts on the part of New Haven and other Connecticut cities. He also points out that even though the projects were large in terms of New Haven's small population, they were not large in dollar amounts, which made it a little easier to obtain approval: "Fortunately, the size of the money that we required didn't compare with what Detroit needed or New York and so forth, so that we were pretty lucky in getting our projects approved and getting them underway, do you see?"[90]

Bush's role weakens Dahl's emphasis on the importance of Lee's aides in working with the complex federal bureaucracy. Instead, the main connection was between Bush and Lee, a fact that is stated by Bush in his oral history and confirmed by Lee's former aides in interviews conducted as part of the restudy. They were no doubt very intelligent, and they clearly had a great deal of energy and enthusiasm, but it was Republican Bush who opened the doors for them at the Housing and Home Finance Agency.

The Bush connection is of general theoretical interest as well. The fact that New Haven received generous amounts of urban renewal money is an instance of a phenomenon widely commented upon by political scientists and journalists, namely, the garnering of favors for major constituents by those who are on congressional committees with plums to pass out. Just as those on defense-related committees see to it that large defense contracts go to companies in their states and those on public works committees direct big federal projects to their states, so too do senators and representatives with seats on committees related to urban renewal make sure that their constituents are well treated.

As Dahl rightly emphasizes, there are two questions of theoretical interest about urban renewal in New Haven. First, why did the program suddenly take off in 1954 and 1955 after many delays? Second, why was the New Haven program so large—indeed, by 1972 the largest in the nation in its per-capita grants, receiving $1,018 for each of its citizens while its nearest competitors, Newark and Boston, were averaging only $453 and $409 per person, respectively? For Dahl, the answer to both questions is to be found in the special skills of Mayor Lee and his aides. They organized the coalition in New Haven and they convinced the federal bureaucracy in Washington to give them the money.

In contrast to this typical pluralist interpretation, which puts its emphasis on the actions and abilities of individuals operating in the political arena on a decision-by-decision basis, my restudy of the program suggests very different answers to both questions. First, the program moved into full gear when it did because of legislative, legal, and administrative decisions at the national and state levels. The program did not advance in New Haven or anywhere else until the federal law was changed by Republicans in 1954, and it could not go forward in New Haven until (1) the Connecticut Supreme Court of Errors ruled on the constitutionality of urban renewal and (2) the state highway commission agreed to pay for the large highway that New Haven was demanding without offering to pay any of the cost.[91] As to the second question, the large amount of money that New Haven attracted, the answer is to be found in Yale's needs, prestige, and nationwide corporate and class connections, all of which became embodied in a wealthy upper-class trustee, Senator Prescott Bush.

Although Dahl is quite wrong about the eagerness of the business community, the reasons for the program's emergence in 1954–1955, and the reasons for its large per-capita size, the restudy does support his view that it was Lee and his aides who played a very important role in carrying out the program. Indeed, as difficulties with specific projects developed, serious weaknesses in the local business community were exposed. Its leaders were unable to bring businessmen together in such a way that they could keep a few dissidents from hampering the work of the outside developers. Most of the top business leaders ended up sitting on the sidelines while Bush, Tyler, Lee, and his aides did the essential coordinating work with the federal government.[92] By the time Dahl began his study in 1957, the program was almost completely in the hands of the

Democratic mayor and his appointees, who of course gave little credit to the work that had been done by business leaders and Republicans a few years before. In the 1960s, the program was to move even further from the business community, becoming for a short time the province of a strong and relatively well insulated Redevelopment Agency.[93]

The later years of the New Haven case therefore suggest that a well-organized and highly skilled government administration may be in some cases the final necessary ingredient for obtaining outside monies. But such an administration is by no means the sufficient condition implied by Dahl. In the relationship between local power structures and city administrations, it is more likely that the power structures can find and support those with political skills than that politicians can create power structures to support them. Only the presence of Yale University in the little and declining city of New Haven gave Mayor Lee and his aides, who were very close to Yale to begin with, the basis from which they could compete for urban renewal funds at the national level.

CONCLUSION

The community power structure literature includes far more than Atlanta and New Haven. It also concerns Chicago, Syracuse, Wichita, and Bennington, Vermont—where pluralistic power arrangements were found from the study of specific decisions—as well as Seattle, El Paso, and Salem, Massachusetts—where more concentrated business-oriented power structures were found using the reputational method.[94] It includes excellent studies of Dallas, Oakland, and Saint Louis—where a variety of methods, including the decisional, pointed to tight-knit power structures rooted in the largest local businesses.[95] There also is a very fine study of how business elites in San Francisco and Los Angeles dealt with a variety of transportation initiatives in their cities and in California in general in the decades after World War II.[96] There is even a cursory study of Lorain, Ohio, where labor unions were said to be almost as important as the business community in the 1950s, and there are studies where unions were found to be unimportant, as in Lansing, Michigan.[97] Like it or not, however, Atlanta and New Haven became the laboratories for understanding community power, and it is power in those cities that needs to be explained by any comprehensive theory of power in America.

The idea that local power structures are at bottom growth machines with an interest in the intensification of land use provides a theoretical basis for understanding similarities and differences in community power structures. The idea that they seek to accomplish

their goals by preparing the land for investment by major corporations, universities, and federal agencies provides a basis for understanding both cooperation and conflict between local and national
elites. Most important, as this chapter shows, the growth machine
framework seems to fit Atlanta and New Haven quite well, especially
on the overriding issue of urban renewal.

The differentiation between a national corporate community
based in production and local growth machines based in land use,
provides a more subtle, less monolithic picture of power in America.
At the same time, it shows once again that the politics of America, at
whatever level, is mostly business in one form or another.

But what will the critics say about all this?

NOTES

1. Robert S. Lynd and Helen M. Lynd, *Middletown* (New York: Harcourt,
   Brace, 1929); idem, *Middletown in Transition* (New York: Harcourt, Brace,
   1937).
2. C. Wright Mills, *The Power Elite* (New York: Oxford University Press,
   1956), pp. 30ff; idem, "The Middle Classes in Middle-Sized Cities," in
   Power, Politics, and People: The Collected Essays of C. Wright Mills, ed.
   Irving L. Horowitz, (New York: Balantine, 1963), pp. 281–82.

   In a famous and vitriolic attack on the community power structure
   literature, Nelson W. Polsby (*Community Power and Political Theory* [New
   Haven, Conn.: Yale University Press, 1963]) claimed that the Lynds and
   several other sociologists made "five assertions in common about power
   in American communities" (p. 8): (1) The upper class rules in local
   community life; (2) political and civic leaders are subordinate to the
   upper class; (3) a single power elite rules in the community; (4) the upper-
   class power elite rules in its own interests; and (5) social conflict takes
   place between the upper and lower classes.

   In fact, as Allan Rosenbaum showed in a careful checking of the
   books cited by Polsby, none of them held to more than three of the tenets,
   and most held to only two ("Community Power and Political Theory: A
   Case of Misperception," *Berkeley Journal of Sociology,* 12 [Summer 1967]).
   As far as their work was concerned, Polsby had created and then attacked
   a straw man in classic polemical fashion.

   However, there was at least one person who held to all five tenets—
   C. Wright Mills. It is too bad that Polsby did not aim his charges at Mills,
   who at the time Polsby wrote was the most active and visible social
   scientist holding such views.
3. Lynd and Lynd, *Middletown in Transition,* p. 100. For the fascinating story
   of the Lynds' major informant on the Ball family, see Howard M. Bahr,
   "The Perrigo Connection: A Significant Local Influence upon *Middletown
   in Transition*" (Middletown III Project, Paper no. 29, 1979).
4. For the story of Hunter's principled conflict with Atlanta leaders, see
   Curtis MacDougal, *Gideon's Army,* vol. 3 (New York: Marzani & Munsell,
   1965), pp. 703–4.

5. Floyd Hunter, *Community Power Structure* (Chapel Hill, N.C.: University of North Carolina Press, 1953), p. 61.

6. Ibid., pp. 62–64.

7. Ibid., p. 62. His italics.

8. Ibid., p. 1.

9. Floyd Hunter, *Community Power Succession* (Chapel Hill, N.C.: University of North Carolina Press, 1980), pp. 79–80; "Integrating Atlanta's Power Elite," *Business Week*, November 24, 1973.

10. Hunter, *Community Power Structure*, p. 113.

11. Charles M. Bonjean and Miehael D. Grimes, "Community Power: Issues and Findings," in *Social Stratification*, Joseph Lopreato and Lionel S. Lewis (New York: Harper & Row, 1974); Delbert C. Miller, *International Community Power Structure* (Bloomington, Ind.: Indiana University Press, 1970); Floyd Hunter, Ruth C. Schaffer, and Cecil G. Sheps, *Community Organization: Action and Inaction* (Chapel Hill, N.C.: University of North Carolina Press, 1959).

12. Raymond Wolfinger, "Reputation and Reality in the Study of Community Power," *American Sociological Review*, October 1960; Robert Dahl, "A Critique of the Ruling Elite Model," *American Political Science Review*, June 1958; Nelson Polsby, *Community Power and Political Theory* (New Haven, Conn.: Yale University Press, 1963).

13. Robert A. Dahl, *Who Governs?* (New Haven, Conn.: Yale University Press, 1961). The quote appears on the back cover of the paperback edition.

14. Ibid., pp. 64, 67–68.

15. Ibid., p. 64.

16. Ibid., pp. 64, 142–43.

17. Ibid., p. 151.

18. Ibid., pp. 64–65, 69–71.

19. Ibid., p. 72.

20. Ibid., p. 79.

21. Ibid., p. 138.

22. Harvey Molotch, "The City as a Growth Machine," *American Journal of Sociology*, September, 1976, p. 311.

23. Harvey Molotch, "Capital and Neighborhood," *Urban Affairs Quarterly*, March, 1979, p. 295.

24. Leonard Downie, Jr., *Mortgage on America* (New York: Praeger, 1974), p. 112.

25. Molotch, "The City as a Growth Machine," p. 316.

26. Ibid., p. 320.

27. Hunter, *Community Power Structure*, pp. 214–15; idem, *Community Power Succession*, pp. 150–52.

28. Ibid.

29. Harvey Molotch, "Capital and Neighborhood in the United States."

30. Lynd and Lynd, *Middletown*, pp. 12–15; Sandra W. Marsh and Joseph D. Brown, *Sketches of the Changing Muncie Economy* (Muncie Economic Development Reports, no. 12, Bureau of Business Research, Ball State University, 1975), pp. 1–2.

31. Lynd and Lynd, *Middletown,* p. 16.

32. Marsh and Brown, *Sketches,* pp. 11–16. For evidence that the Ball family did not dominate Muncie on three salient issues of the 1930s, see Carrolyle M. Frank, "Who Governs Middletown? Community Power in Muncie, Indiana, in the 1930s," *Indiana Magazine of History* 75 (December 1979); idem, "Middletown Revisited: Reappraising the Lynd's Classic Study of Muncie, Indiana," *Indiana Social Studies Quarterly* 30 (Spring 1977).

33. Molotch, "The City As a Growth Machine," p. 313.

34. Ibid., Robert T. Daland, *Dixie City: A Portrait of Political Leadership* (Birmingham, Ala.: University of Alabama Bureau of Public Administration, 1956); Gladys M. Kemmerer et al., *The Urban Political Community* (Boston: Houghton Mifflin, 1963); Donald H. Bouma, "Analysis of the Social Power Position of a Real Estate Board," *Social Problems,* Fall 1962; Richie P. Lowry, "Leadership Interaction in Group Consciousness and Social Change," *Pacific Sociological Review,* Spring 1964.

35. James Weinstein, "Organized Business and the Commission and Manager Movements," *Journal of Southern History,* May 1962; idem, *The Corporate Ideal in the Liberal State* (Boston: Beacon Press, 1968), chapter 4; Samuel P. Hayes, "The Politics of Reform in Municipal Government in the Progressive Era," *Pacific Northwest Quarterly,* October 1964; Robert R. Alford and Eugene C. Lee, "Voting Turnout in American Cities," *American Political Science Review,* September 1968; Raymond Wolfinger, *The Politics of Progress* (Englewood Cliffs, N.J.: Prentice-Hall, 1974), chapter 11.

36. E.g., Robert O. Schultz, "The Bifurcation of Power in a Satellite City," in *Community Political Systems,* ed. Morris Janowitz (Glencoe, Ill.: Free Press, 1961); Donald A. Clelland aand William H. Form, "Economic Dominants and Community Power: A Comparative Analysis," *American Journal of Sociology,* March 1964.

37. Molotch, "Capital and Neighborhood."

38. See G. William Domhoff, *Who Really Rules? New Haven and Community Power Re-Examined.* (New Brunswick, N.J.: Transaction Books, 1978), chapter 3, for a complete account of this legislative conflict.

39. Ibid., p. 50.

40. Nathan Straus, *The Seven Myths of Housing.* (New York Knopf, 1944), pp. 59–60.

41. Jeanne Lowe, *Cities in a Race with Time* (New York: Random House, 1967), p. 28.

42. Laurence H. Shoup and William Minter, *Imperial Brain Trust* (New York: Monthly Review Press, 1977), chapter 4; Karl Schriftgiesser, *Business Comes of Age* (New York: Harper & Row, 1960).

43. Guy Greer and Alvin Hansen, *Urban Redevelopment and Housing,* Planning Pamphlet no. 10 (Washington, D.C.: National Planning Association, 1941).

44. Straus, *Seven Myths,* p. 81.

45. Ashley A. Foard and Hilbert Fefferman, "Federal Urban Renewal Legislation," in *Urban Renewal: The Record and the Controversy,* ed. James Q. Wilson (Cambridge, Mass.: MIT Press, 1966).

46. Domhoff, *Who Really Rules?* pp. 60, 116 (footnote 51).

47. Lowe, *Cities in a Race with Time*, p. 34.

48. Scott Greer, *Urban Renewal and American Cities* (Indianapolis: Bobbs-Merrill, 1965), p. 32.

49. *The President's Advisory Commission on Government Housing Policies and Programs*, December 1953, p. 2.

50. "ACTION to Fight Slums and Neighborhood Blight," *American City*, December 1954, p. 23.

51. "Action on Slums," *New York Times*, November 19, 1954, p. 39.

52. Jeanne Lowe, "Lee of New Haven and His Political Jackpot," *Harper's Magazine*, October 1957, p. 36.

53. Ibid.

54. Timothy K. Barnekov and Daniel Rich, "Privatism and Urban Development: An Analysis of the Organized Influence of Local Business Elites," *Urban Affairs Quarterly* 12 (no. 4, June 1977): 434.

55. Lowe, *Cities in a Race with Time*, p. 442; Roy C. Lubove, *Twentieth-Century Pittsburgh* (New York: 1969).

56. Lowe, *Cities in a Race with Time*, chapter 8.

57. Peter H. Rossi and Robert A. Dentler, *The Politics of Urban Renewal* (New York: Free Press, 1961).

58. Chester Hartman, *Yerba Beuna: Land Grab and Community Resistance in San Francisco* (San Francisco: Glide Publications, 1974); Frederick M. Wirt, *Power in the City* (Berkeley, Calif.: University of California Press, 1974).

59. Clarence Stone, *Economic Growth and Neighborhood Discontent* (Chapel Hill, N.C.: University of North Caroliina Press, 1976), p. 45.

60. Ibid., pp. 59, 62–63.

61. Ibid., pp. 82–83.

62. Ibid., p. 90.

63. Ibid., pp. 128–29.

64. Ibid., p. 150.

65. Ibid., pp. 3, 227.

66. Domhoff, *Who Really Rules?*, chapters 2–3, presents a detailed account of this new empirical evidence.

67. Domhoff, *Who Really Rules?* pp. 20–22.

68. Ibid., pp. 30–31. The figure in this book is 2 percent lower than the overall overlap reported on page 30 because those five people who only attended the debutante ball have not been included this time.

69. Ibid., p. 31.

70. Ibid., p. 16.

71. Ibid., p. 31. The percentage of economic notables on Dahl's list who were also in one of the three clubs does not appear on page 31 but comes from our unpublished findings.

72. Robert R. Alford, "New Haven: A Test of Stratification Theory?" (Manuscript, University of California at Santa Cruz, n.d.), p. 44.

73. Dahl, "A Critique," pp. 70, 144–45.

74. Ibid., p. 53.

75. Wolfinger, "Reputation and Reality," pp. 218–20.

76. Domhoff, *Who Really Rules?*, p. 94.

77. Ibid., pp. 94–95.

78. Ibid., p. 49.

79. *Go to School, Learn to Rule* (New Haven, Conn.: American Independence Movement, 1970), p. 6.

80. Arnold G. Dana, *New Haven's Problems* (1937), as quoted in John Whitehead, "The Problem of Tax Exemption: A Resume of Yale's Physical Relation to New Haven, 1745–1969" (Paper, Yale University, 1970), p. 6.

81. Domhoff, *Who Really Rules?* p. 70.

82. Ibid., pp. 71–72.

83. *Yale and Her Needs* (Prepublication draft, Office of University Development, Yale University), p. 20.

84. Domhoff, *Who Really Rules?* p. 82.

85. Ibid., pp. 82–83.

86. Personal interview with Edward Logue, New York City, June 26, 1981.

87. *Prescott Bush Oral History* (Oral History Research Office, Butler Library, Columbia University), p. 88.

88. Domhoff, *Who Really Rules?* pp. 46–47. In a telephone interview I conducted with this planner in June 1981, he confirmed to me directly how important Bush was to the program.

89. Lowe, *Cities in a Race with Time*, pp. 424–25.

90. *Bush Oral History*, p. 151. New Haven nonetheless received a great amount of money in absolute terms: $142.5 million, by 1972. Only ten cities, starting with New York at $474.5 million and working down to Pittsburgh at $158.3 million, had received more committed funds by 1972, and no other city under 300,000 in population was close.

91. Domhoff, *Who Really Rules?*, pp. 86–96.

92. Ibid., pp. 107–12; Lowe, *Cities in a Race with Time*, pp. 436–63; Wolfinger, "Reputation and Reality," chapter 10.

93. Phillip A. Singerman, "Politics, Bureaucracy and Public Policy: The Case of Urban Renewal in New Haven" (Ph.D. diss., Yale University, 1980).

94. Edward C. Banfield, *Political Influence* (Glencoe, Ill.: Free Press, 1961); Linton C. Freeman, *Patterns of Local Community Leadership* (Indianapolis: Bobbs-Merrill, 1968); Donald O. Cowgill, "Power as Process in an Urban Community," in *Approaches to the Study of Urbanization*, ed. Richard Stauber (Lawrence, Kan.: Governmental Research Center Series, no. 27, 1964); Harry Scoble, "Leadership Hierarchies and Political Issues in a New England Town," in *Community Political Systems*, ed. Morris Janowitz (Glencoe, Ill.: Free Press, 1961); Delbert C. Miller, "Decision-Making Cliques in Community Power Structures; A Comparative Study of an American and an English City," American Journal of Sociology, November 1958; William V. D'Antonio and William H. Form, Influentials in Two Border Cities (South Bend, Ind.: University of Notre Dame, 1965); Floyd Hunter, Ruth C. Schaffer, and Cecil G. Sheps, Community Organization: Action an Inaction (Chapel Hill, N.C.: University of North Carolina Press, 1956).

95. Carol Estes Thometz, *The Decision-Makers: The Power Structure of Dallas* (Dallas: Southern Methodist University Press, 1963); Theodore Hayes, *Power Structure and Urban Policy: Who Rules in Oakland?* (New York:

McGraw-Hill, 1972); Richard Ratcliff, M. B. Gallagher, and K. S. Ratcliff, "The Civic Involvement of Bankers: An Analysis of Economic Power and Social Prominence in the Command of Civic Policy Positions," *Social Problems* 26 (1979).

96. J. Allen Whitt, *Urban Elites and Mass Transportation: The Dialectics of Power* (Princeton, N.J.: Princeton University Press, 1982).

97. James B. McKee, "Status and Power in the Industrial Community: A Comment on Drucker's Thesis," *American Journal of Sociology*, January 1953; William H. Form, "Organized Labor's Place in the Community Power Structure," *Industrial and Labor Relations Review*, July 1959; William H. Form and Delbert C. Miller, *Industry, Labor and Community* (New York: Harper and Brothers, 1960).

7

But What Will
The Critics Say?

INTRODUCTION

Now that readers have been introduced to my full argument concerning power in America, along with the best of the evidence for it, it may be helpful to comment on the questions and criticisms that are likely to be raised by those who are not entirely convinced. Such criticisms are easily anticipated because the discussion over the structure and distribution of power in the United States has been going on for a long time.

PLURALIST OBJECTIONS

The first and primary objection from the pluralists will concern the validity of "who benefits" and "who governs" as power indicators. In the case of "who benefits," a likely response can be found in Dahl's extended theoretical discussion of power and democracy, which reflects his lifetime of thinking on the subject. Dahl begins by noting that power or control is not "equivalent" to "benefits" and then claims that some writers are "unclear" on how power and benefits are related:

> To begin with, control is not equivalent to benefits. The distinction needs to be emphasized, since some writers propose to identify power

with benefits: if Alpha derives benefits from Beta's actions, then Alpha must have power over Beta. It is sometimes unclear whether benefits are meant to be identical with power or whether instead benefits are simply meant to be a surrogate for power, an operational indicator employed on the assumption that power and benefits are always strictly correlated.[1]

After casting aspersions on the conceptual clarity of his opponents, Dahl then provides what he thinks is a telling example against the use of benefits as an operational indicator of power:

> In either case, to stipulate that power and benefits are equivalent can prove seriously misleading: American wheat farmers can benefit from a decision of Soviet leaders to buy American grain, but they can hardly be said to control the Soviet leaders in their decision to buy American grain.[2]

In terms of my discussion of concepts and their measurement in the first chapter, the problems with Dahl's comments are several. First, no one who talks about "benefits" claims that they are "equivalent" to "power." Power is the concept, benefits are one of the indicators. Second, there is no claim that a concept and its indicators are "strictly" correlated; as Lazarsfeld emphasized, there is a probabilistic relation between a concept and its indicators.[3] Finally, the "who benefits" indicator has to do with the distribution of values within a given society, not with the outcomes of specific decisions of the type Dahl mentions. Indeed, the absurdity of Dahl's example is of course obvious to everyone, and he no doubt chose it to make this indicator of power seem absurd.

Polsby presents four reasons for his claim that "knowing value distributions is insufficient and perhaps misleading in discovering who rules."[4] They are:

1. That no explicit decision-making took place at all, and that beneficiaries, far from actually governing, are simply reaping windfall benefits (e.g. largely powerless Black Panthers, who oppose gun control, are beneficiaries of the fact that there are no gun control laws).

2. That beneficiaries are receiving benefits from decisions made outside the community and over which they have no control (e.g. shopkeepers in a community prosper from a decision made in a far-off corporate headquarters to operate a local plant on overtime).

3. That beneficiaries are the unintended recipients of benefits resulting from decisions made by others within the community (e.g. apolitical, absentee, or deceased owners of adjacent real estate prosper because of decisions made in the bureaucracy to site a public facility).

4. That the powerful are intentionally conferring benefits on the non-powerful (e.g. in at least some welfare systems.)[5]

None of these objections amounts to a very great problem. When Polsby says that value distributions can occur without explicit decisions taking place, he is equating "power" with "decision-making," and thus limiting the more general conception of power. When he notes that some people may be unintended beneficiaries of decisions, he is raising an objection that might be relevant in isolated cases but not for the general value distributions of a society or a community. When he argues that the powerful may intentionally distribute values to the nonpowerful, he is suggesting a posssibility that is not likely to be a regular occurrence of any magnitude, and which in any case would only serve to decrease an estimate of the degree of the power differences, not to eliminate differences altogether. As to his point that value distributions within a community may be affected by decisions outside the community, that is the same kind of argument used by Dahl in his example of Soviet decision-makers and American wheat farmers, and it is as irrelevant on the local level as it is on the national one. But even if there were some substance to each of Polsby's arguments, it would merely suggest that there were irrelevant components in the indicators, as there are in any indicators. It would not invalidate the indicators, but would only mean that they have to be interpreted with caution in some cases.

The objections put forth by Dahl and Polsby are strictly hypothetical. That is, there may be certain problems with some "who benefits" measures. But what about the specific cases of the wealth and income distributions, which are the ones most frequently utilized? Are the highly stable and highly skewed wealth and income distributions mainly the products of decisions in other countries, such as the Soviet Union? Could it be that they occur without a whole series of decisions and actions by highly interested people? Is the irrationality that creeps into all human activities, including decision making, leading to wealth and income distributions that therefore tell us nothing about the distribution of power in the society? Merely to ask these rhetorical questions demonstrates how trivial these seemingly profound objections really are.

Despite the inability of most pluralists to comprehend the straightforward argument about the wealth and income distributions as indicators of power, there are occasional signs that their general hostility to it is crumbling. In 1969, for example, political scientist William C. Mitchell came out in favor of "who benefits" indicators:

> Let us try defining power not as one who makes decisions but as who gets how much from the system. Those who acquire the largest share of the goods, services, and opportunities are those who have the most power.[6]

After making this large concession, however, Mitchell saved the day for pluralism by citing a narrowly conceived study that suggested that poor people receive more from the government than they put in, whereas the rich pay more to government than they receive back. Aside from the fact that Mitchell ignores the general value distributions of the society, his focus on this particular value distribution is highly questionable because it ignores all the subsidies that go to the corporate community in a variety of programs. Nevertheless, Mitchell concluded that a power elite does not dominate government, and he did so with sarcasm: "One might additionally speculate that it is an interesting political situation when the 'power elites' permit the lower income groups to have more favorable or net balances with the government, while they incur deficits."[7]

After denying that the wealth and income distributors can be used as power indicators, pluralists will say that they are instead "power resources." That is, they can be used to exercise power in specific situations, just as status, time, expertise, and many other qualities and possessions can be utilized as power resources. There is nothing wrong with this pluralist claim. It is a very obvious and acceptable assertion. What the pluralists cannot seem to grasp is that it is possible for wealth and income to be both power indicators and power resources. It all depends on what question is being asked.

Pluralists, then, are almost sure to dismiss the information on the wealth and income distributions as irrelevant. Since there are two other indicators that point to the same conclusion, this would not be a very big problem if they did not tend to dispute the "who governs" indicator as well. First they will say that a group or class need not hold office in order to be powerful. An example of this argument can be found in the work of political scientist Donald Matthews. After bringing together evidence that shows that the upper social levels are highly overrepresented in government and the lower social levels extremely underrepresented, Matthews explains away his findings as follows:

> It is misleading to assume that a group must literally be represented among the political decision-makers to have influence or political power. The unrepresentative nature of America's political decision-makers no doubt has its consequences, but it does not free them from their ultimate accountability to the electorate at large. Thus the frequency with which members of certain groups are found among decision-makers should not be considered an infallible index of the distribution of power in a society. In America at least, lower-status groups have political power far in excess of their number in Congress, the Cabinet, and so on.[8]

The problem with Matthews' argument is that the utilization of indicators does not imply that a group or class "must literally be represented" in order to have power. That is a causal statement not implied by the logic of indicators. Instead, the rationale that underlies the use of indicators is something to this effect: If a group or class is in fact powerful, one manifestation of that power might be a disproportionate number of office holders coming from that group or class. While Matthews is quite certain that overrepresentation is "not an infallible index" and that lower-status groups have political power "far in excess of their number" in government, he does not go on to provide his evidence for this claim about lower-class power. ·

A second pluralist objection to this indicator is that there may not be a strong correlation between social background and political behavior. A typical example can be found in the work of political scientist Ezra Suleiman. Suleiman begins by agreeing that "no one will deny that social background data are extremely important in elite studies, if only because they permit an appraisal of the relative representation of a society's groups and classes in its elites." This conceded, he then goes on to say that "it is all too easy, as numerous elite studies have demonstrated, to regard social background as the master key that unlocks all doors." The mistakes he perceives, which is attributed to me in particular, is the alleged assumption that "there exists a clear correlation between a particular socioeconomic background and a particular mode of thought and behavior."[9]

But no one is trying to predict political behavior from a power indicator. This objection is in reality an entirely different issue. It turns the indicator of overrepresentation into a causal statement about what people will do when confronted with specific decisions while in government office. This confusion is especially surprising because my analysis does contain a separate argument that shows the way in which foundations, policy-discussion groups, and think tanks shape the political thinking of those corporate leaders and policy experts likely to be involved in policy matters outside the corporate community. Suleiman professes a great interest in explaining the political behavior of elites, but he nonetheless ignores the entire discussion of how leadership is selected and socialized within the power elite.

Given the difficulties they think they see with the first two indicators, pluralists are almost certain to focus most of their attention on the question of who initiates and who vetoes on specific decisions. In so doing, they will bring forth examples of influential actions by members of other groups and classes. This pluralist emphasis on specific issues is useful in its place, but it is blown out of all proportion to its overall value, ignoring the very great problems that exist in using this indicator. For example, Raymond Bauer, who was involved in a decisional study of tariffs in the 1960s, came to believe the method was less than perfect because it does not make much sense to study decisions in isolation from an overall context:

> However, we have treated the process involving the formation of a particular decision as a closed system which can for practical purposes be isolated for analysis. Regrettably this cannot be done. The parties involved in any policy issues have other responsibilities and obligations. They also have a past and a future. One of the fallacies of treating the policy process as decision making is that it assumes that someone is aware of the problem, that he can devote full time and attention to it, and that the issue has a clear-cut beginning and end. In practice, other events compete for his resources, including time, attention, and energy. Other issues raise the question of other interests and values involved in the policy issue that somehow has captured our attention. I have coined the phrase "the envelope of events and issues" to refer to those events and issues which must be considered as the context within which to analyze a given policy problem.[10]

Bauer's point can be generalized to say that a social framework is necessary for the proper interpretation of people's roles in specific issues. By focusing only on individuals who are involved at the point of decision, many powerful people and institutions are lost from sight. No better example of this problem can be found than in the great emphasis placed on the role of experts by pluralists who study specific issues. To hear them tell it, America is ruled by planners, congressional aides, and professors. Consider this finding reported by Polsby on who initiates new policies: "innovators are typically professors or interest group experts."[11]

Now Polsby's claim probably has a great deal of truth, but it is devoid of context. In fact, the experts and professors almost always work within the framework of the policy-planning network, which provides the agenda and sets limits on the range of alternatives that will be entertained. Experts and professors who are "too far out" will not be approved for foundation research grants. They will not be asked to spend a visiting year at the Brookings Institution or Resources for the Future. Nor will they be invited to present their ideas to study groups of the Committee for Economic Development or Council on Foreign Relations.

None of this would seem relevant to Polsby. What he sees is the great diversity among the people who talk at these places, and what he hears is that the new ideas are generated by experts after much reading, listening, and thinking. He cannot see the forest (the class system) for the trees (individuals).

Power indicators aside, the other major criticism that will be made by pluralists is that the inequalities in power are not so great as to merit the term *domination*. They will accept many of the specific findings as interesting, but they will add that the power situation is more permeable and fluid than my terminology implies. This type of reaction by pluralists usually involves a comparison with other countries, particularly nondemocratic countries. The implication is that the United States is a pretty wonderful place compared with most nations, and everyone should be grateful for what power they do have. Though I too believe it is a very great blessing to live in a democratic country, even after acknowledging the mistreatment of minorities, women, and pro-union workers, that does not resolve the question of whether or not there is a ruling class and a power elite in the United States. Pluralists seem to take the fact of political democracy as all the proof that is needed against the idea of class domination. But social reality, which includes social classes and economics and expertise as well as free speech and voting, is more complex than their focus on political procedures allows.

This pluralist criticism is manifested in disputes over terminology. Dahl, for example, recoils from the use of the term *domination*. He sees it as a simple and crude concept that has no business being used in a democratic country:

> If the military dictatorship in Chile is not significantly more powerful and less "democratic" than Allende and his predecessors, if Portugal and Spain today are not importantly different from what they were under authoritarian regimes, then domination and subjection will do. But if regimes make a difference, do we not need theoretical concepts more sensitive than the simple crudities of domination and subjection?[12]

In a later discussion Dahl states that the terms *domination* and *subjection* are ones that "carry extremely harsh overtones."[13] He believes they lead to thinking about power in all-or-nothing terms rather than in terms of varying magnitudes. This claim about the harshness of *domination* is not surprising, for he defines it as total control: "Alpha dominates Beta if Alpha's control (a.) is strictly unilateral, (b.) persists over a relatively long period of time, (c.) extends over a range of actions of great importance to Beta, and (d.) compels Beta to act in ways that on balance are costly to her."[14] Following this extreme definition of domination, he proposes to use the term *mutual control* to discuss power in most situations, even though he quickly adds that mutual control does not necessarily mean equality, fairness, or democracy.[15] His preference for this term is due to the fact that it emphasizes the possibility of developing some political autonomy even in situations of domination:

> Views of domination like those found in standard Marxism and Italian elite theory are surely correct in emphasizing the strength and universality of tendencies toward domination. Where these views go wrong is in underestimating the strength of tendencies toward political autonomy and mutual control.[16]

Dahl goes on to give examples of what he means by mutual control. It involves the development of independent organizations and the breaking of complete control by rulers through raising the costs of domination. The rise of trade unions is one specific case: "In the nineteenth and early twentieth centuries, workers combined their meager resources in trade unions and successfully overthrew the unilateral domination of employers over wages, hours, and working conditions."[17] But the trade unions are only one example:

> One could endlessly multiply historical examples showing how members of a weaker group have combined their resources, raised the costs of control, overcome domination on certain matters important to them, and acquired some measure of political autonomy. Often what results is a system of mutual controls.[18]

In terms of the substance of Dahl's discussion, I have no strong disagreement. That is because the situation he describes as the one most people find themselves in is what I mean by domination. This argument over words is an argument over whether the glass of water should be described as half empty or half full, but it reveals differences in emphasis and values. Dahl thinks *domination* sounds too harsh for an admittedly unequal reality because things could be a lot worse. I think *mutual control* sounds too benign for a power situation that is much more unequal than Dahl allows even though there is freedom of religion, freedom of expression, the right to vote, and the possibility of influence on some specific issues.

I agree with Dahl and other pluralists that power is a matter of degree. It is not all or nothing, and it even varies from capitalist democracy to capitalist democracy to some extent. In my view, however, the degree of wealth and income inequality in the United States, the degree to which members of the power elite are overrepresented in government, and the degree to which the power elite exerts influence on specific issues still requires us to speak in terms of domination even though the country is pluralist in the formal sense of having independent organizations and associations that cannot be eliminated by all-powerful rulers. Pluralists, in my view, see only part of social reality, the political part. They miss the social reality of classes and the class system.

MARXIST OBJECTIONS

Marxists will have their own objections to the argument of this book even though it puts almost as much emphasis on domination and class conflict as they do. Many Marxists will first of all object that the account is somehow too personalistic and individualistic. They will say that the tracing of people and their social connections seems superficial, not related to the laws of motion that underlie the development of capitalism. These Marxists will say, as three of them did in an article that caused great bitterness among power structure researchers when it appeared in 1975, that such research "rests almost entirely at the very personal level of showing the social connections between individuals who occupy positions of economic power."[19]

Contrary to this misguided claim, the research in a book such as this is inherently based on both the personal and institutional levels simultaneously, on what sociologist Ronald Breiger calls "the duality of persons and groups."[20] Following Breiger, the underlying basis of power structure research can be seen as a form of sociometry called *membership network analysis*. It can be visualized as a matrix in which individuals are listed down the vertical axis and institutions across the horizontal axis. The cells formed by the intersection of a person and an institution are filled with various kinds of information on the relationships that connect the two. Most typically, this information concerns such matters as membership or ownership, but it also can include various kinds of financial relationships—donor, debtor, or recipient of grants or loans.

This people-by-institutions matrix, which is the first step of power structure research, incorporates the two social ties that are considered basic to sociological theorizing—individual social relations and group membership. Therefore, both the personal and institutional levels can be derived from this single matrix, making it possible to describe friendship circles and social cliques on the one level and interconnecteed social institutions on the other. In Marxist terms, it is possible to abstract from the people-by-institutions matrix to either the personal level or the impersonal level. It is really not different from an often-quoted passage in Marx that says individuals are relevant to his analysis only to the extent that they are "bearers" or embodiments of the system.[21] From the level of societal principles, capitalists are but the "personifications" of capital, to use a favorite Marxist term. In terms of our research operations, however, there is no such thing as a strictly personal level any more than there is a strictly institutional level. Both are always present.

Moreover, Marxists actually have to do exactly what other power structure researchers do when they conduct their own investigations, as they sometimes must to deal with the objections to their views raised by those who do not accept the idea that there is a ruling capitalist class. I have demonstrated this point elsewhere by analyzing the research operations of the major Marxist books and articles on class and power. All of them first define a "capitalist class" and then attempt to establish its existence through describing the activities of actual capitalists. They then turn to two indicators to demonstrate the power of this class—its great wealth and income, particularly in the form of stock and dividends, and the disproportionate number of capitalists who hold positions of power inside and outside of government.[22]

The claim that Marxists do the same things, methodologically speaking, as other students of power structures does not hold true for those Marxist theoretical works that take the idea of a ruling class for granted. In theoretical books by Marxists the only "indicator" of the power of this class is in effect the persistence of capitalism. Capitalists rule as long as there is capitalism, by definition, just as the working class is not fully class conscious, no matter what its members say and do, until it has come to agree with Marxists that capitalism is inherently exploitative of the working class and must be replaced by socialism. But such claims are much too abstract for anyone not already convinced of basic Marxist assumptions through some other means. This is not meant as a criticism of Marxist theoretical work, but it is meant as a criticism of those Marxists who have created an either-or relationship in the minds of students between books such as this one, which ask one kind of question, and the theoretical texts of Marxism, which explore other questions.

A second possible objection by Marxists will come as a surprise to those readers who have accepted the pluralist claim that the concept of domination understates the power and independence of the lower classes. To the contrary, some Marxists will object that the book does not emphasize enough that there is class struggle, that is, independent political action by organizations of the working class. They will note, along with Dahl, that there have been victories for the working class, such as collective bargaining, social security, and health insurance. I can only agree that these can be seen as victories, or at least partial victories. But I do think that some Marxists, like pluralists, overstate the extent of working-class success. Bigger changes may be in store in the future, but they are not here yet, as the various power indicators attest. In the meantime, the emphasis should be on the reality of the current situation, not on hopes for the future. I agree with one-time Marxist David Horowitz in his criticism

BUT WHAT WILL THE CRITICS SAY?   **213**

of those Marxists who allow their need for an optimistic interpretation to lead them to exaggerate the role of the working class in understanding the functioning of the present system:

> That Marx's sociological model has been subject to widespread misunderstanding can be seen at a glance in the fact that the Marxian concept of class is almost exclusively discussed in terms of the proletariat and its revolutionary potential, whereas the operative group in terms of the *functioning* and *development* of the capitalist system (the subject of Marx's major work) is not the proletariat at all, but the *capitalist ruling class.*[23]

The third major objection that will be raised by Marxists concerns the fact that there has been little general discussion of what Marxists call "the state" and "state apparatus," which mean about the same things as "nation" and "government" in pluralist language. They will want to know if the state apparatus is merely a committee for managing the common affairs of the whole bourgeoisie (Marx and Engels); a repressive apparatus for protecting private property (Lenin); a "condensation of class forces," as in the theorizing of French Marxist Nicos Poulantzas; or even an "arena of class struggle," as in the version by neo-Marxists Gösta Esping-Anderson, Roger Friedland, and Erik Wright.

In my view, an analysis of Marxist books and articles on the nature of the state demonstrates that the Marxist view does not differ greatly in practice from that of non-Marxist social scientists.[24] Marxists emphasize that the capitalist class dominates the state in one way or another, and they believe that the state apparatus has a strong bias in favor of the capitalist system. But once they concede that the ruling class is divided into "segments" or "fractions," that the state apparatus is often "autonomous" or "relatively autonomous," that other classes can control pieces of the state or at least have great influence in them, and that the ruling class does not always get exactly what it wants, then the differences become ones of degree and emphasis.

For the pluralists, there are several "interest groups" that clash over state policy. For the Marxists, there are two basic "interest groups" underlying the many interest groups that pluralists emphasize. One is the capitalist class, in all its segments, and the other is the working class, which is admitted by Marxists to be "multi-layered" and internally divided politically. In the pluralist view, interest groups form coalitions. For the Marxists, coalitions are primarily class segments coming together on issues basic to capitalism. In the pluralistic view, every interest group has some influence and often can block the legislation it dislikes the most. In the Marxist view, the capitalists almost always have their way, whether through their own efforts or through the efforts of far-seeing state managers who are independent of capitalist influence but act in capitalist interests because of the nature of the overall social system.

In the pluralist view, the government is an independent and class-neutral institution that plays a coordinating role and tries to compromise the disputes among contending interest groups. For Marxists, the state apparatus is far from independent in theory, but it is "relatively autonomous" at the very least, with some Marxists stressing that it has to be independent of the short-run interests of the capitalist class in order to ensure the smooth functioning of the capitalist system. The state is no mere coordinator and compromiser in the general Marxian conception, but it does end up doing things for the working class in some situations, especially when it is pressured by the working class. Considerations such as these show that the differences between the Marxists and pluralists are matters of degree even though the initial concepts are different. Marxists, then, start out with definitions that sound very different from those of pluralists, but they end up saying that the state apparatus does what pluralists say it does.

It might be objected that Marxists claim that the state is ultimately based on force, but so do many of the pluralist followers of Max Weber. Moreover, many Marxists now agree that consent or legitimacy, even if it is not deserved, is an important basis for the state, precisely the other factor emphasized by pluralist theorists in other language. The question that remains is the weight to be given to each of the two factors, but there exists considerable variation on this issue among both pluralists and Marxists.

I believe the similarities between Marxists and non-Marxists concerning the general nature of the state apparatus are masked by their extreme political differences. Where Marxists really differ from all other theorists is in their fervent belief that the capitalist economic system is inherently exploitative of working people and therefore unjust and dehumanizing, in their great skepticism that significant changes could be brought about in the class system solely through the processes of representative democracy, and in their strong desire to see capitalism replaced with their vision of a democratic socialism. These strong beliefs, I am asserting, lead Marxists to exaggerate their theoretical differences with their opponents over the general nature of government.

Politics aside, I do not think the primary theoretical concern of Marxists themselves is with the nature of the state apparatus, but with social classes. When they discuss government, they do so in terms of classes and class domination. The issue is class power. Poulantzas, whose work shaped the Marxist debate in Europe over these questions in the 1970s, put the matter in this way:

> Power is not a quantifiable substance held by the State that must be taken out of its hands, but rather a series of relations among the various social classes. In its ideal form, power is concentrated in the State, which is thus itself the condensation of a particular class relationship of forces. The State is neither a thing-instrument that may be taken away, nor a fortress that may be penetrated by means of a wooden horse, nor yet a safe that may be cracked by burglary: it is the heart of the exercise of political power.[25]

Ralph Miliband, who emerged as the major critic of Poulantzas as well as the leading Marxist theoretician on the state in English-speaking countries, also emphasizes the importance of class power. He begins by noting that there is a distinction between "class power" and "state power," which "it is important not to blur."[26] Class power is the more important concept because there is far more to ruling-class domination than domination of the state:

> Class power is the general and pervasive power which a dominant class (assuming for the purpose of exposition that there is only one) exercises in order to maintain and defend its predominance in "civil society." This class power is exercised through many institutions and agencies.[27]

Miliband goes on to note that the state apparatus is "in *all* respects the ultimate sanctioning agency of class power." But the emphasis remains on class power: "The important point, however, is that the class power of the dominant class is not exercised, in some important respects, by state action but by class action, at least in 'bourgeois democratic' regimes, and in a number of other forms of capitalist regimes as well."[28]

Finally, there is the testimony of Maurice Zeitlin, whose class-domination theory has been influenced by a careful reading of all strands of Marxism. He comes to a very similar view independently of Poulantzas and Miliband: "In the broadest sense, then, *the 'state' is a concept for the concentrated and organized means of legitimate class domination*, whether or not these are explicitly *recognized* as political in any given historical society."[29]

Marxists will have other objections at a more general or philosophical level than is the concern of this book, for Marxism includes a theory of history, an explanation of capitalist economics, a moral critique of capitalist society, and a body of political tradition, as well as a sociological theory of class domination. These objections can be summarized by saying that Marxists will recognize that the book shares only one concept with the overall Marxian theory, that of class domination. Marxists will lament the absence of their other concerns, or say that the class theory cannot stand without the larger Marxian framework, but I am unable to agree with them in these claims. A new theory of class domination will have to rest on a broader base than the Marxists' ultimate economic determinism and the overly narrow focus on class that lead to distortions in their analyses. The flexible Marxism of a Miliband comes very close to what is needed when it acknowledges the failure of Marxism to comprehend nationalism and admits that factors other than economic ones play a very great role in social systems. But my starting point remains that of Bertrand Russell, as stated in the first chapter of this book. Power has many forms; none of these forms is subordinate to any other; and there is no basic form, economic or otherwise, from which the others are derivable.

ELITIST CRITICS

There is a third view of power in America that has its disagreements with both the pluralists and the Marxists. In this view, called institutional elitism, power is much more concentrated than the pluralists contend, but this power is not rooted in the class structure. Instead, power is exercised by those who manage the major institutional structures in the society.

The first American social scientist to articulate this view in a systematic way was the radical sociologist C. Wright Mills. In a book that generated a heated debate when it appeared in the 1950s, Mills claimed that America was ruled by a power elite that was based in what he thought were the three most important hierarchies in the country—the corporations, the executive branch of the federal government, and the military. Although Mills noted that common social backgrounds were one factor in the cohesiveness of this power elite, he put greater emphasis upon the institutional careers of its members in understanding its overall operations. Most of Mills's critical comments were reserved for the work of the pluralists, which he claimed was at best a description of what happens at the middle levels of power, overlooking the existence of a small power elite at the top and a largely powerless mass on the bottom. However, Mills also criticized the Marxist perspective because it did not allow enough "autonomy to the political order and its agents, and it says nothing about the military as such." He dismissed the idea of a ruling class as a "badly loaded phrase."[30]

Although the institution elite perspective was first put forth by a radical sociologist, its major proponents since the 1960s have been two conservative political scientists, Andrew Hacker and Thomas R. Dye. In Hacker's case, there is perhaps some influence from the work of Mills, but in Dye's there is a separate path to a similar position.

Because of their focus on institutions, both Hacker and Dye will say that the book puts too much emphasis on social class. Hacker's views are clearly stated in a 1964 essay in a volume in memory of C. Wright Mills. After expressing his belief that the corporate rich are even more important within the power elite than Mills allowed, Hacker goes on to say that he does not think "the corporate elite" is a class. He dismisses the idea of a ruling class because members of the corporate elite come from "at least every stratum of the middle class," because "birth and breeding are of negligible importance," and because the corporate roles "have the power rather than their occupants."[31] In a reaction to my book on the Bohemian Grove, he makes his institutional position even more clear:

> Domhoff makes corporate executives the central members of his ruling class. I have been following his and other arguments to this effect for some time, and I still cannot see the point of giving them that label. Mills called them an "elite," a term referring to people whose power accompanies their occupancy of certain offices—bishops, generals, judges, salaried managers of public and private enterprises. Most have little in the way of property and their influence lasts only so long as they sit in a particular desk. Members of this elite are easily replaceable; in many cases it is impossible to distinguish an officeholder from his predecessor or successor. Ruling classes, in contrast, have traditionally consisted of persons who can be named and remembered. Since both individual and family property play a much smaller part in our own leading institutions, it is misleading to keep on speaking of a ruling class. ... We do indeed have classes; but their arrangement reflects the corporate structure.[32]

Similar views are expressed by Dye: "It is our contention, then, that great power is institutionalized, that it derives from roles in social organizations, and that individuals who occupy top institutional positions possess power whether they act directly to influence particular decisions or not."[33] The secondary role he assigns to social class can be seen in his discussion of social clubs and the implications of membership in them:

> It is our judgment, however, that club membership is a result of top position-holding in the institutional structure of society rather than an important independent source of power. An individual is selected for club membership *after* he has acquired an important position in society; he seldom acquires position and power because of his club memberships.[34]

It is my belief that Mills, Hacker, and Dye overstate the role of institutions, just as Marxists overstate the role of class. The major thrust of this book has been to show that both concepts are necessary to understand power in America. The ruling class could not exist without the institutions, but the institutions are infused with class values.

My answer to Hacker and Dye is embodied in the fact that I have used the concept of a "power elite" as well as that of a "ruling class." I have adapted Mills's term to mean the leadership group of the ruling class, and I have shown empirically that the people he called the power elite are disproportionately members of the upper class except in the case of military officers.[35]

I do not think the institutional view can account for the fact that the corporate community remains so single-mindedly profit-oriented. If the institutional view were correct, managers would be acting in the less-capitalist way that theorists began saying they would back in the 1940s and 1950s. But none of these predictions have come true. Class values continue to prevail in the corporate community.

By focusing only on the corporate elite, Hacker and Dye in effect dismiss the idea of the upper class as a reference group that embodies and perpetuates the values that shape both the functioning of institutions and the behavior of upwardly mobile members of society. Put another way, their view does not explain the class-oriented behavior of people both inside and outside the upper class. Clubs, prep schools, and exclusive social activities are not mere social froth. Nor do they merely "pass on values." They are goals in and of themselves that upwardly mobile, status-oriented institutional and political leaders seek to achieve. In their desire to become part of these clubs and groups, they make themselves acceptable to members by becoming like the members themselves. In the process they take on the values of the upper class, the most important of which is the concern with the corporate profits that make a privileged life possible.

Why is it fairly unusual for social scientists to think in terms of both class and institutions? I think the answer is in part political. To Marxists, the idea of institutional elitism seems inherently conservative. In the hands of some theorists, the concept has been used to claim that elites are inevitable, which is not something Marxists like to hear. To many non-Marxists, on the other hand, the concept of a class system seems inherently radical; it is too closely linked with Marxism, and its history of dictatorial Communist parties and doctrinaire sects. Moreover, the concept seems to imply that there are injustices in the system, which some institutional elitists (but not Hacker and Dye) think the society has transcended now that salaries are allegedly handed out in terms of a person's contribution to the functioning of the system.[36]

But these political connotations are not part of the ideas themselves. There are institutional elitists who are political radicals. Indeed, Mills expressly rejected the claim by several Marxist critics that his view had any "latent ideological bias" against "radical values."[37] Conversely, there are class-oriented theorists who are non-Marxist in their politics and overall framework. Such theorists agree that members of the working class are at the mercy of capitalists for their livelihood because they have no other means of gaining an income. However, they do not choose to label this relationship as "exploitative," as Marxists do, for they do not believe that all value is created by workers with no contribution from the capitalists. They also believe that capitalists have their risks and vulnerabilities in trying to make a profit. As Mills wrote about the Marxian concept of exploitation to characterize the class relationship: "it is a moral judgment, disguised as an economic statement."[38]

Non-Marxists who accept the idea that there is a class system but do not advocate revolutionary change have another concern as well. They think it is better to try to attenuate the injustices of a class-based capitalism through labor legislation and social welfare programs rather than risk the loss of freedom—to vote, to express opinions, even to change jobs—that might come with a socialist system if state bureaucracies ended up running everything. This is not an abstract fear, even if the totalitarian regimes in the Soviet Union, China, and other present-day socialist countries are explained away by some Marxists as unusual cases due to their undemocratic histories and low levels of economic development before their revolutions. It is once again Mills who makes the point very clearly:

> To nationalize property does not necessarily eliminate "the powers of property." It may in fact increase the actual exploitation of men by men in all social spheres; it may be more difficult to oppose exploitation or to do away with it. Marx generally assumed that, with the abolition of propertied classes, democratic mechanisms would accompany the collectivization. For us today, this must, to say the least, be taken as an open question.[39]

Whatever the merits of these political arguments and concerns, the idea that there is a complex interplay between classes and institutions should not be dismissed in the future because one concept is allegedly radical and the other allegedly conservative. Corporate America is an institutionalized America, but it continues to have a class system.

DOES ANYBODY RULE?

A final objection to the idea that there is a ruling class in the United States is based in vague feelings about the alleged inadequacies of modern-day human beings. This objection is put forth by those reporters, academics, and government aides who have seen the big boys up close and found to their dismay that they are ordinary mortals, often moved by egotistical and self-serving concerns, and sometimes stupid.

These observers came into contact with the powerful harboring great expectations. Forgetting that sociological studies of class and power like this one are not concerned with the psychological motives and foibles of the leaders in the social system, but with actions and their social effects, they expected to meet up with high-minded and intelligent people who knew how to exercise power like real members of a ruling class should. But all they found were other struggling human beings like themselves. Such mundane people could not be part of a ruling class, so there must not be a ruling class after all. These critics then complain that books such as this are "one-dimensional" or that they are not attuned to the "psychological nuances" and "complex motives" that animate the powerful.

There used to be a ruling class according to these critics, but that was before authority gave way to manipulation and people became narcissists, or whatever it is that the disappointed romantic thinks they have become. The decade in which the ruling class died varies somewhat with the theorist, of course, but as a rule it died just before the commentator in question reached his or her middle adulthood. Thus, we have had the death of the ruling class in every generation for at least the past 75 years, with a special emphasis on the time of the New Deal because so many famous public scolds came of age in the 1950s.

Historian Christopher Lasch provides an interesting example of this genre. He has gone so far as to say that explicit class leadership died with President McKinley. The evidence for this assertion, says Lasch, is everywhere about us. It can be seen in the general "crisis" of authority, in the "exhaustion" of ruling class ideologies, and in the "resort to psychological manipulation in place of ideological coercion." Moreover, there has been a "retreat from confrontation over principles." As for the American belief in individualism, free enterprise, and competition, Lasch claims that it "long ago gave way to a therapeutic, permissive style of leadership that dispenses with appeals to authority, sides sentimentally with the underdog and the outcast, and seeks to co-opt dissension through programs of affirmative action and 'innovative' social change."[40]

All this leads Lasch to the grandest of ironies: "the United States today presents the curious spectacle of a capitalist society in which the capitalist class plays an altogether negligible role."[41] Perhaps Lasch has some deep insight that leads him to know that the keys to power in America are in psychoanalytic consulting rooms, public relations firms, and the editorial offices of little magazines and journals that feature crisis, anxiety, and ennui. But with business leaders sitting in just about every seat of authority in the executive branch of government, not to mention their directorships in all other areas of American institutional life, this is indeed a rather astonishing perspective.

The ruminations of Lasch and other secular Jeremiahs have the timeless quality of the "back when men were real men" fantasy. There used to be people of dignity and responsibility and principle, but now there are only ordinary people. Indeed, it is the repetitiveness of the observation from era to era and epoch to epoch that suggests such theorizing should be explained in terms of the individual life cycle rather than any historical change. Things just never seem to be like they supposedly were when we were children, impressed by authority figures in a world that seemed timeless.

One thing is certain. No advocate of any psychological theory of the way people "used to be" has ever presented any empirical evidence that people today are more or less narcissistic, alienated, confused, manipulated, or unheroic than they were in the past.

CONCLUSION

After all these arguments and counterarguments, what are readers to think? How can they decide what to make of all this disputation? There are many ways in which they might make their own assessments. They could explore the underlying assumptions of each viewpoint further, for example, or they could examine some power question of interest to them to see how well the different perspectives assimilate their findings. In the end, however, I think it comes down to what people think about power indicators and what philosophy of science they find most reasonable.

If wealth and income statistics are accepted as valid indicators of power that reveal the outcomes of ongoing power struggles, then the case for the upper class as a ruling class will be considered a strong one, for those indicators have been very stable throughout the twentieth century in the United States even while income and related inequalities have declined in countries with strong labor unions and cohesive social democratic and socialist parties. However, if these outcomes are seen as a result of general societal structures or various irrational decisions, with only an indirect relation at best to the underlying concept of power, then readers will be less persuaded.

If overrepresentation in corporate, foundation, and government positions is seen as a useful indicator of institutional power, then the argument will be considered fairly strong. But if readers are unimpressed with this indicator because they believe that real power may lie behind the throne of the formal offices, or that government position holders are constrained to follow the will of the majority by a fear of not being reelected, then the evidence will be downgraded.

If influence on specific decisions in a wide range of issue-areas is seen as the only valid indicator of power, as pluralists have insisted, then support for the hypothesis will be viewed as less impressive. Hopefully, though, it will be seen as greatly improved since the 1960s due to the demonstration of a policy-planning network and the articulation of how the special-interest, policy-planning, and candidate-selection processes bring the power elite into direct and very often successful involvement in government.

Beyond the evidence of any one type of indicator, the strength of the argument will be determined by the philosophy of science to which the reader holds. If it is believed that concepts should be studied in terms of multiple indicators, as has been stressed in this book, the evidence for the hypothesis will be seen as very strong, for three very different types of indicators have pointed to the upper class as a ruling class. However, if an approach based upon intervening variables and social traits is rejected in favor of the single-indicator operational definitions advocated by a strict form of scientific positivism, then the case will be seen as less impressive. This is especially so if that single operation consists of adding up influence scores on a wide variety of issues that are picked by pluralists without any regard for the surveyed interests of contending power groups.

Weaknesses in the evidence remain. More work needs to be done on the relationship between the upper class and the corporate community; in particular, little is known in detail about the social and career patterns of the children of upwardly mobile corporate executives. Then, too, more studies need to be done on a wider range of issues within the framework of the policy-planning network, and further information must be developed on if and how the liberal-labor coalition gains concessions from the moderates in the struggle to enact general social legislation.

But if the question is asked once again, who rules America? then on the basis of available evidence the best answer still seems to be that dominant power in the United States is exercised by a power elite that is the leadership group of a property-based ruling class. Despite all the turmoil of the 1960s and 1970s, and the constant chatter about economic crisis that is ever with us, there continues to be a small upper class that owns 20 to 25 percent of all privately held wealth and 45 to 50 percent of all privately held corporate stock, sits in seats of formal power from the corporate community to the federal government, and wins much more often than it loses on issues ranging from the nature of the tax structure to the stifling of reform in such vital areas as consumer protection, environmental protection, and labor law. This conclusion is not the be-all and end-all of political sociology, as the gatekeepers of the intellectual world will quickly reassure us, but it must be the starting point for any social inquiry or political analysis that wishes to avoid hopeless irrelevance and embarrassing superficiality from its very outset.

NOTES

1. Robert A. Dahl, *Dilemmas of Pluralist Democracy* (New Haven, Conn.: Yale University Press, 1982), p. 17.
2. Ibid.
3. Paul Lazarsfeld, "Concept Formation and Measurement," in Gordon J. DiRenzo, ed., *Concepts, Theory, and Explanation in the Behavioral Sciences* (New York: Random House, 1966).
4. Nelson W. Polsby, *Community Power and Political Theory*, 2d ed. (New Haven, Conn.: Yale University Press, 1980), p. 132.
5. Ibid., p. 207.
6. William C. Mitchell, "The Shape of Political Theory to Come: From Political Sociology to Political Economy," in *Politics and the Social Science*, ed. Seymour M. Lipset (New York: Oxford University Press, 1969), p. 114.
7. Ibid., p. 119.
8. Donald Matthews, *The Social Background of Political Decision-Makers* (New York: Random House, 1954), p. 32.
9. Ezra Suleiman, *Politics, Power and Bureaucracy in France* (Princeton, N.J.: Princeton University Press, 1974), pp. 100–1.
10. Raymond Bauer, "Social Psychology and the Study of Policy Formation," *American Psychologist*, October 1966, p. 937.
11. Nelson W. Polsby, "Policy Initiation in the American Political System," in *The Use and Abuse of Social Science*, ed. Irving L. Horowitz, (New Brunswick, N.J.: Transaction Books, 1971), p. 303.
12. Robert A. Dahl, "Who Really Rules?" *Social Science Quarterly*, June 1979, p. 150.
13. Dahl, *Dilemmas of Pluralist Democracy*, p. 23.
14. Ibid., p. 32.
15. Ibid., p. 33.
16. Ibid.

17. Ibid., p. 35.

18. Ibid.

19. David A. Gold, Clarence Y. H. Lo, and Erik Olin Wright, "Recent Developments in Marxist Theories of the Capitalist State," *Monthly Review*, October 1975, p. 33. One of these authors, Clarence Lo, has since written that the article was inaccurate in some of the labels it attached to some theoretical positions. See his "Theories of the State and Business Opposition to Increases in Military Spending," *Social Problems*, April 1982.

20. Ronald Breiger, "The Duality of Persons and Groups," *Social Forces*, December 1974.

21. Nicos Poulantzas, "The Problem of the Capitalist State," *New Left Review*, November–December 1969, p. 70.

22. G. William Domhoff, "Do Marxists Do Differently?" in *Who Really Rules? New Haven and Community Power Reexamined* (New Brunswick, N.J.: Transaction Books, 1978), pp. 140–45.

23. David Horowitz, "A Note on Marx's Theory of Class," in *The Fate of Midas and Other Essays, ed. idem* (Palo Alto, Calif.: Rampart Press, 1973), p. 105. The italics are in the original.

24. My understanding of the Marxist view of the state is based on the following sources: Ralph Miliband, *The State in Capitalist Society* (New York: Basic Books, 1969); idem, *Marxism and Politics* (New York: Oxford University Press, 1977), idem, "Poulantzas and the Capitalist State," *New Left Review*, November–December 1973; Nicos Poulantzas, "The Capitalist State—A Reply to Miliband and Laclau," *New Left Review*, January–February 1976; idem, *State, Power, Socialism* (London: NLB, 1978; V. I. Lenin, *The State* (Peking: Foreign Language Press, 1970); Claus Offe, "Structural Problems of the Capitalist State," in *German Political Studies*, ed. Klaus von Beyme (Beverly Hills, Calif.: Sage Publications, 1974); Gosta Esping-Anderson, Roger Friedland, and Erik Olin Wright, "Class Struggle and the Capitalist State," *Kapitalist State*, no. 4 (1975); Maurice Zeitlin, "On Classes, Class Conflict, and the State: An Introductory Note," in *Classes, Class Conflict, and the State*, ed. idem (Cambridge, Mass.: Winthrop Publishers, 1980); and Gold, Lo, and Wright, "Recent Developments."

25. Nicos Poulantzas, "Toward a Democratic Socialism," *New Left Review*, May–June 1978, p. 81.

26. Miliband, *Marxism and Politics*, p. 54.

27. Ibid., pp. 54–55.

28. Ibid, p. 55.

29. Zeitlin, "On Classes," p. 15.

30. C. Wright Mills, *The Power Elite*. (New York: Oxford University Press, 1956), p. 277.

31. Andrew Hacker, "Power To Do What." In Irving L. Horowitz, ed. *The New Sociology*. (New York: Oxford University Press, 1964), pp. 141–142.

32. Andrew Hacker, "What Rules America?" *New York Review*, May 1, 1975, p. 10.

33. Thomas R. Dye, *Who's Running America?* (Englewood Cliffs, N.J.: Prentice-Hall, Inc., 1976), p. 8.

34. Ibid., p. 163. Italics in the original.
35. My criticism of Mills's empirical claims have been published in several different places. In *Who Rules America*, chap-5, I present evidence against his view that the military is as important as the corporate rich within the power elite. In particular, I believe that he misunderstood the role of the military in the defense reconversion process at the end of World War II. Since the reconversion issue was highly important to his claims about the military, I should add that work by historian Barton Bernstein also is contrary to his interpretation. See Bernstein's "The Removal of War Production Board Controls on Business, 1944-11946," *Business History Review*, Summer, 1965; and "The Debate on Industrial Reconversion," *American Journal of Economics and Sociology*, April, 1967. Then too, Samuel P. Huntington, *The Common Defense*. (New York: Columbia University Press, 1961), presents several decisional studies which show that the military had a subordinate role even on important defense decisions in the 1940's and 1950's.

   In *The Higher Circles*, chapter 3, I present evidence that Mills was incorrect in claiming that the world of celebrity had been cut off from the upper class. High society or the jet set remains the upper class at play, even if it includes people who are there to entertain.

   More generally, I commented on each aspect of Mills' power elite thesis in "The Power Elite and Its Critics," in G. William Domhoff and Hoyt B. Ballard, eds., *C. Wright Mills and The Power Elite*. (Boston: Beacon Press, 1968).
36. See Zeitlin, "On Classes," p. 9, for a critique of theories of "bureaucratic functionalism" because "class domination" is replaced by a differentiated occupational order, which is intrinsically related to merit: "Rewards" are distributed by "society" according to ability, or the scarcity of the skill involved and the occupation's "functional importance."
37. C. Wright Mills, "Comment on Criticism," in Domhoff and Ballard, *C. Wright Mills and The Power Elite*, p. 247.
38. C. Wright Mills, *The Marxists* (New York: Dell, 1962), p. 109.
39. Ibid., p. 118.
40. Christopher Lasch, "Review of Books: The Powers That Be," *American Historical Review*, April 1982, p. 483.
41. Ibid.

Index

227

Lowi, Theodore, 117
Lubell, Samuel, 102
Lundberg, Ferdinand, 43
Lurie, Louis, 124
Lynd, Helen Merrill, 158–59, 170, 171
Lynd, Robert S., 158–59, 170, 171

McCarthy, Eugene, 119–20
McConnell, Grant, 130–31, 148
Mace, Myles, 67
McGovern, George, 120, 124
McNamara, Robert, 138
Marriage, upper class, 34–36
Marx, Karl, 211, 213
Marxists, 6, 9, 211–19
Mason, Edward S., 148
Massachusetts Institute of Technology, 95
Mass media, public opinion and, 107–9
Matthews, Donald, 206–7
Means, Gardner, 57
Meese, Edward, III, 139
Mellon family, 61–62, 180
Membership network analysis, 211
Metropolitan Life Insurance Company, 134
Milband, Ralph, 215
Mills, C. Wright, 27, 37, 43, 59, 77, 148, 158, 216–19
Mintz, Beth, 141
Mitchell, William C., 205–6
Mobil Oil Corporation, 70
Mobil Oil Foundation, 87
Molotch, Harvey, 166–69, 171, 181
Morgan Guaranty Trust Company, 69, 86, 134
Mortgage Bankers Association, 174
Mutual control, 209–10
Myer, Gustavus, 43

Nader, Ralph, 130
National Association of Manufacturers, 90, 136
National Association of Real Estate Boards, 174
National Audubon Society, 96
National Bureau of Economic Research, 95
National Civic Federation, 85
National Labor Relations Act of 1935, 145–46, 151
National Labor Relations Board, 145
National Municipal League, 172
National Planning Association, 175
National Wildlife Federation, 96
Nature Conservancy, 96
Nixon, Richard M., 124, 126, 142–43

Occupations, upper class, 37–39

O'Connor, James, 111
Organized labor, 2, 11, 125, 210
Ostrander, Susan, 5, 33, 34, 38–39

Pacific Gas and Electric Company, 70
Palmer, Robert R., 3, 4, 7
Parliamentary systems, 117–18
Peck, Morton, 98
Pew Memorial Trust, 94
Phipps family, 61
Pierson, Mary Rockefeller, 23
Pluralist theory of power, 1, 2, 203–10
Policy-discussion groups, 82, 84, 85–92
Policy-making process, 116, 131–43
Policy-planning network, 82–98
    foundations, 82, 84–85, 92–95
    policy-discussion groups, 82, 84, 85–92
    think tanks, 82, 84, 85, 95–98
    university research institute, 82, 84, 85, 95–98
Political Action Committees (PACs), 123, 125
Political parties, 117–22, 128, 129, 144
Politics, 2, 116–56
    candidate-selection process, 116, 117–29
    policy enactment, struggle over, 143–46
    policy-making process, 116, 131–43
    special-interest process, 116, 129–31
Polsby, Nelson W., 119, 204–5, 208
Poor's Register of Corporations, Directors, and Executives, 69, 86
Population Council, The, 96
Poulantzas, Nicos, 213, 214–15
Power:
    defined, 8–9
    indicators of concept, 10–13
    in revolutionary America, 7–8
Power elite (*see* Upper class)
Presidential commissions, 132–33
Private property, 2
Professionals, 2
Prothro, James, 149
Public opinion, 82–83, 98–109
    advertising and, 105–7
    economics and, 103–5
    foreign policy and, 100–3
    mass media and, 107–9

RAND Corporation, 95
Ratcliff, Richard, 62
Rayburn, Sam, 129
Reagan, Ronald, 48, 120, 123–24, 126, 137, 139–41
Regan, Donald T., 140
Resorts, 18
Resources for the Future, 95, 96

Revolutionary America, 3–4, 7–8
Rhodes, John J., 127–28
Rich, Daniel, 180
Rockefeller Brothers Fund, 93, 138
Rockefeller family, 61
Rockefeller Foundation, 85, 87, 93, 96, 144
Roosevelt, Franklin D., 126, 142
Roosevelt, Theodore, 126
Rostow, Eugene V., 98
Rotival, Maurice, 189, 191
Rupert, Anton E., 63
Rusk, Dean, 138
Russell, Bertrand, 9, 78, 216
Russell Sage Foundation, 93

Safeway Corporation, 70
Sallach, David, 104
Scaife, Richard Mellon, 94n
Schlesinger, Arthur M., Jr., 137–38
Schlesinger, Joseph A., 129
Schools, 18–20, 24–28, 44–46, 48
Schwartz, Charles, 61, 64, 97
Sears, Roebuck and Company, 70
Shapiro, Irving S., 135
Shoup, Laurence, 101
Shultz, George, 139–40
Silk, Leonard, 146–48
Slavery, 4
Sloan Foundation, 93
Smith, James D., 58
Smith Richardson Foundation, 94
Social class:
  defined, 5–6
  in revolutionary America, 3–4
  (see also Upper Class)
Social clubs, 18–20, 28–32, 46–47, 48, 74–75
Social directories, 18–24, 44, 48–49
Socialists, 11
Social Register, 18–24, 35, 38, 68, 86, 141
Southern Pacific Lines, 70
Special-interest process, 116, 129–31
Stanford Research Institute, 90
Stevenson, Adlai E., 48, 124
Stock-option plans, 75
Stock ownership, 57–59
Stone, Clarence, 181–83
Study groups, 87
Subjection, 209
Suleiman, Ezra, 207
Supreme Court appointments, 141, 142
Sweezy, Paul, 6

Taft, Robert H., 192
Taft, William, 126
Taft-Hartley Act of 1947, 146
Think tanks, 82, 84, 85, 95–98

Trade unions, 2, 11, 125, 210
Trilateral Commission, 87–88, 90, 139, 141
Truman, Harry S., 142
Tyler, Morris, 191–92, 195

Ultraconservative policy groups, 90–92
Unions, 2, 11, 125, 210
United Nations Association, 101
U.S. Housing Authority, 176
U.S. Savings and Loan League, 174
U.S. Steel Corporation, 69
Universities, 24, 27
University research institutes, 82, 84, 85, 95–98
Upper class, 1–2, 4, 9, 17–55
  debutante season, 32–34
  education, 18–20, 24–28, 44–46, 48, 75
  family continuity, 36–37
  indicators of standing, 44–49
  institutional infrastructure, 18–20
  marriage patterns, 34–36
  preoccupations of, 37–41
  social clubs, 18–20, 28–32, 46–47, 48, 74–75
  Social Register, 18–24, 35, 38, 68, 86, 141
  wealth and income, 41–44
  (see also Corporations; Policy-planning network; Politics)
Urban Institute, 95
Urban Land Institute, 175–77
Urban renewal, 173–96
Useem, Michael, 67–68, 71–73, 136–37

Vance, Cyrus, 138–39
Vogel, David, 146–49
Voluntarism, 39
Voting, 3

Wall Street Journal, 109
War-Peace Study Groups, 87
Wealth distribution, 41–42
Weber, Max, 8, 9, 214
Weinberger, Caspar, 140
Wells Fargo, 70
Westinghouse Electric Corporation, 69
Weyerhauser family, 62, 65
White, Shelby, 60
Who's Who in America, 19, 38, 48, 68, 69
Who's Who in American Women, 38
Wildavsky, Aaron B., 119
Witcover, Jules, 121
Wittman, Donald, 118
Wright, Erik, 213
Wrong, Dennis, 9

Zeitlin, Maurice, 58, 62, 215